REVOLT ON THE RIGHT

'UKIP – a quixotic project to transform UK politics or the catalyst for partisan realignment? Read Ford and Goodwin's comprehensive and expert analysis before trying to resolve the question.'

Professor Michael Thrasher
The Elections Centre, Plymouth University, UK

The UK Independence Party (UKIP) is the most significant new party in British politics for a generation. In recent years UKIP and their charismatic leader Nigel Farage have captivated British politics, media and voters. Yet both the party and the roots of its support remain poorly understood. Where has this political revolt come from? Who is supporting them, and why? How are UKIP attempting to win over voters? And how far can their insurgency against the main parties go? Drawing on a wealth of new data – from surveys of UKIP voters to extensive interviews with party insiders – in this book prominent political scientists Robert Ford and Matthew Goodwin put UKIP's revolt under the microscope and show how many conventional wisdoms about the party and the radical right are wrong. Along the way they provide unprecedented insight into this new revolt, and deliver some crucial messages for those with an interest in the state of British politics, the radical right in Europe and political behaviour more gen

Robert Ford is Lecturer in Politics in the S‹ University of Manchester, UK, and tweets (

Matthew Goodwin is Associate Professor and Interna‹
is also Assoc   inMJ.

D1344773

90710 000 414 492

Routledge Studies in Extremism and Democracy

Series Editors:

Roger Eatwell, University of Bath, and Matthew Goodwin, University of Nottingham.

Founding Series Editors:

Roger Eatwell, University of Bath, and Cas Mudde, University of Antwerp-UFSIA.

This new series encompasses academic studies within the broad fields of 'extremism' and 'democracy'. These topics have traditionally been considered largely in isolation by academics. A key focus of the series, therefore, is the (inter-)*relation* between extremism and democracy. Works will seek to answer questions such as to what extent 'extremist' groups pose a major threat to democratic parties, or how democracy can respond to extremism without undermining its own democratic credentials.

The books encompass two strands:

Routledge Studies in Extremism and Democracy includes books with an introductory and broad focus which are aimed at students and teachers. These books will be available in hardback and paperback. Titles include:

Understanding Terrorism in America
From the Klan to al Qaeda
Christopher Hewitt

Fascism and the Extreme Right
Roger Eatwell

Racist Extremism in Central and Eastern Europe
Edited by Cas Mudde

Political Parties and Terrorist Groups (2nd Edition)
Leonard Weinberg, Ami Pedahzur and Arie Perliger

The New Extremism in 21st Century Britain
Edited by Roger Eatwell and Matthew Goodwin

New British Fascism
Rise of the British National Party
Matthew Goodwin

The End of Terrorism?
Leonard Weinberg

Mapping the Extreme Right in Contemporary Europe
From local to transnational
Edited by Andrea Mammone, Emmanuel Godin and Brian Jenkins

Varieties of Right-Wing Extremism in Europe
Edited by Andrea Mammone, Emmanuel Godin and Brian Jenkins

Revolt on the Right
Explaining support for the radical right in Britain
Robert Ford and Matthew Goodwin

Right-Wing Radicalism Today
Perspectives from Europe and the US
Edited by Sabine von Mering and Timothy Wyman McCarty

Routledge Research in Extremism and Democracy offers a forum for innovative new research intended for a more specialist readership. These books will be in hardback only. Titles include:

REVOLT ON THE RIGHT

Explaining support for the radical right in Britain

Robert Ford and Matthew Goodwin

Routledge
Taylor & Francis Group

LONDON AND NEW YORK

First published 2014
by Routledge
2 Park Square, Milton Park, Abingdon, Oxon OX14 4RN

and by Routledge
711 Third Avenue, New York, NY 10017

Routledge is an imprint of the Taylor & Francis Group, an informa business

© 2014 Robert Ford and Matthew Goodwin

The right of Robert Ford and Matthew Goodwin to be identified as authors of
this work has been asserted by them in accordance with the Copyright, Designs
and Patent Act 1988.

All rights reserved. No part of this book may be reprinted or reproduced or utilized in
any form or by any electronic, mechanical, or other means, now known or hereafter
invented, including photocopying and recording, or in any information storage or
retrieval system, without permission in writing from the publishers.

Trademark notice: Product or corporate names may be trademarks or registered trademarks,
and are used only for identification and explanation without intent to infringe.

British Library Cataloguing in Publication Data
A catalogue record for this book is available from the British Library

Library of Congress Cataloguing in Publication data
Ford, Robert Anthony
    Revolt on the right : explaining support for the radical right in Britain /
    Robert Ford and Matthew J. Goodwin.
        pages   cm. – (Extremism and democracy)
    Includes bibliographical references and index.
    1. UK Independence Party.   2. Right and left (Political science)–Great
    Britain.   3. Great Britain–Politics and government–1997–2007.   4. Great
    Britain–Politics and government–2007–   I. Goodwin, Matthew J.   II. Title.
    JN1129.U45F67 2014
    324.241′093–dc23
    2013040202

ISBN: 978-0-415-69051-5 (hbk)
ISBN: 978-0-415-66150-8 (pbk)
ISBN: 978-1-315-85905-7 (ebk)

London Borough of Richmond
Upon Thames

RTWH

90710 000 414 492

Askews & Holts	
324.241 FOR	£18.99
	9780415661508

CONTENTS

FIGURES

TABLES

PREFACE

This book is about one of the most successful challenges to the established political parties in modern British history. Under their charismatic leader, Nigel Farage, the UK Independence Party (UKIP) are leading a radical revolt against the established political parties, which is guided by their Eurosceptic beliefs and wrapped heavily in the radical right-wing themes of populism and opposition to immigration. Their revolt began slowly in the early 1990s, under a long period of Conservative Party rule, gathered pace between 1997 and 2010 under three successive Labour governments and, since then, has achieved historically unprecedented gains under a Conservative-led coalition government.

This revolt has upended the political agenda, but it is not well understood.[1] In this book, we will throw light on the social changes that have created the space for a rebel party, the background and motives of the voters who have supported it, and the internal development of the party from a single-issue pressure group into a genuine political contender. In our analysis of UKIP and their supporters, we have relied on three main sources of data. First, to examine the characteristics and motives of UKIP supporters, and those of other parties in British politics, we draw on the Continuous Monitoring Survey (CMS), which forms part of the British Election Study (BES). For these data, we are grateful to Harold Clarke and the BES team, and Joe Twyman, Anthony Wells and Laurence Janta-Lipinski at YouGov. Bobby Duffy and Roger Mortimore also generously provided a vast array of opinion polling data from the Ipsos MORI archive, which helped us to develop, sharpen and check our arguments. For data on UKIP's results at local elections we also thank the BBC, and Michael

Thrasher and Colin Rallings from the Plymouth University Elections Centre. We also thank David Cutts who co-authored an earlier study of UKIP voters.[2] Throughout the book, we have made an effort to present our findings in a clear and accessible way, but we also provide some more in-depth statistical evidence for our arguments in the appendix. Readers interested in the statistical fine print will find detailed regression models elaborating our findings there.

Second, most of the chapters also draw on interviews with current and former UKIP activists. Writing in the 1950s, one of the earliest academics to study political parties, Maurice Duverger, remarked how their internal life is 'deliberately shrouded in mystery', a place where followers coexist in a 'closed and exclusive world'.[3] More than three decades later, Jean Charlot made a similar observation; political parties, he wrote, have 'two faces': a front stage that is geared towards the outside world, journalists and voters; and a back stage that is kept for the activists and the true believers.[4] When we decided to write this book, we knew that we would have to get behind the scenes, and talk and listen to those who have led and organised UKIP since the beginning. Between 2011 and 2013, we interviewed figures who have played a central role in UKIP's history, some on several occasions, and we thank them for their time and honesty. These interviews took us from the office of Dr Alan Sked at the London School of Economics, where UKIP were founded, to the house of Robert Kilroy-Silk, who has since left politics, and to the party's current headquarters near Bond Street.

Not all of our invitations were accepted, most likely because of suspicions among activists about the motives behind academic research, particularly when both co-authors have previously published work on right-wing extremism, a tradition that Ukippers vigorously reject any association with. But in the end, most activists did agree to be interviewed. Some have been kept anonymous, including current donors. We thank them, Gawain Towler, UKIP's former Press Officer, for helping this process, and prominent activists who agreed to go on record, including Dr Alan Sked, David Lott, Jeffrey Titford, Robert Kilroy-Silk, Derek Clark, Stuart Agnew, Alan Bown, Nigel Farage and Paul Nuttall.

Where possible, we have cross-checked accounts provided by activists with written memoirs, as well as a third source of information.[5] Particularly in the opening two chapters, we supplement the interviews with analysis of media reports on the party, having read virtually everything written on UKIP in the major newspapers and more recently blogs, between 1993 and 2013. During these twenty years, we have benefited from insights gathered by journalists such as Michael White, Patrick Wintour, Andrew Sparrow, Peter Oborne, Fraser Nelson and Tim Montgomerie. We are also thankful to Lord Ashcroft, whose research on UKIP we discuss at various points in the book, and to Philip Lynch, Richard Whitaker, Simon Usherwood and members of the Elections, Public Opinion and Parties (EPOP) group. Our gratitude also extends to our employers, the School of Politics and International Relations at the University of Nottingham and the Department of Politics at the University of Manchester, and to Craig Fowlie and Peter Harris at Routledge.

Writing about an earlier political insurgency in the 1980s, led by the Social Democratic Party (SDP), the academics Ivor Crewe and Anthony King noted how their book had borne a disconcerting resemblance to a biography of someone who had showed early promise but died young.[6] Despite all of the media hype and speculation about a major breakthrough, in the end the SDP fell flat, barely denting the mould of the party system that it had set out to break. It is too early to know whether UKIP will follow the same path. But what we hope will become clear to readers in the pages that follow is that there is considerable electoral potential for the radical right in Britain. Moreover, irrespective of UKIP's own path the rise of the party is also telling us much about the state of British party politics, and British society.

Our final debt of gratitude is owed to our families, who have had to listen to more conversations about UKIP over the past few years than is healthy, and despite this have remained supportive throughout this book's development. Rob is indebted to the infinite patience of his wife Maria, without which this book would never have happened, to his daughter Zofia for keeping him smiling every day and to his son Adam, who joined us in the middle of this project and has contributed joy and chaos in equal measure. Matthew would like to thank Fiona, his mother Sian, Mark Pickup and Eline de Rooij at the Department of Political Science at Simon Fraser University, who provided additional time for writing during the autumn of 2013, Chatham House, and the School of Politics and International Relations at the University of Nottingham.

Notes

1 There is a growing academic literature on UKIP. For academic accounts that wholly or partially examine the party, see Amir Abedi and Thomas Carl Lundberg (2009) 'Doomed to failure? UKIP and the organisational challenges facing right-wing populist anti-political establishment parties', *Parliamentary Affairs*, 62(1): 72–87; Sean Carey and Andrew Geddes (2010) 'Less is more: Immigration and European integration at the 2010 general election', *Parliamentary Affairs*, 63(4): 849–65; Chris Gifford (2006) 'The rise of post-imperial populism: The case of right-wing Euroscepticism in Britain', *European Journal of Political Research*, 45: 851–69; Richard Hayton (2010) 'Towards the mainstream? UKIP and the 2009 elections to the European Parliament', *Politics*, 30(1): 26–35; Peter John and Helen Margetts (2009) 'The latent support for the extreme right in British politics', *West European Politics*, 32(3): 496–513; Peter Kellner (2009) 'Britain's oddest election?', *Political Quarterly*, 80(4): 469–78; Philip Lynch, Richard Whitaker and Gemma Loomes (2012) 'The UK Independence Party: Understanding a niche party's strategy, candidates and supporters', *Parliamentary Affairs*, 65(4): 733–57; Philip Lynch and Richard Whitaker (2013) 'Rivalry on the right: The Conservatives, the UK Independence Party (UKIP) and the EU issue', *British Politics*, 8: 285–312; Simon Usherwood (2008) 'The dilemmas of a single-issue party: The UK Independence Party', *Representation*, 44(3): 255–64; Richard Whitaker and Philip Lynch (2011) 'Explaining support for the UK Independence Party at the 2009 European Parliament elections', *Journal of Elections, Public Opinion and Parties*, 21(3): 359–79.

2 Robert Ford, Matthew J. Goodwin and David Cutts (2012) 'Strategic Eurosceptics and polite xenophobes: Support for the United Kingdom Independence Party (UKIP) in the 2009 European Parliament elections', *European Journal of Political Research*, 51(2): 204–34.

3 Maurice Duverger (1954) *Political Parties*, New York: Wiley, pp. 91, 101.

4 Jean Charlot (1989) 'Political parties: Towards a new theoretical synthesis', *Political Studies*, 37(3): 352–61.

5 Including, for example, Nigel Farage (2010) *Fighting Bull*, London: Biteback; Mark Daniel (2005) *Cranks and Gadflies: The Story of UKIP*, London: Timewell Press.
6 Ivor Crewe and Anthony King (1995) *SDP: The Birth, Life and Death of the Social Democratic Party*, Oxford: Oxford University Press.

ABBREVIATIONS

AFL	Anti-Federalist League
BES	British Election Study
BNP	British National Party
BSA	British Social Attitudes
CMS	Continuous Monitoring Survey
EDL	English Defence League
EPOP	Elections, Public Opinion and Parties
EU	European Union
FN	National Front (France)
FPÖ	Freedom Party of Austria
NEC	National Executive Committee
NF	National Front (Britain)
SD	Sweden Democrats
SDP	Social Democratic Party
UKIP	UK Independence Party

INTRODUCTION

This is the story of the most significant new British political party in a generation. New parties are founded all the time, but most are tiny clusters of discontents bound together by a single, marginal issue. Most wither and die very quickly. Others, like the nationalists in Scotland and Wales, have changed the face of politics in their nations, but by its nature their appeal is geographically limited; they could not change the balance of power in Britain as a whole, nor did they aim to do so. This has left the commanding heights of British politics dominated by only three political parties – the Conservatives, the Labour Party and the Liberal Democrats – whose electoral ancestors started taking seats at Westminster a century or more ago. Their individual fortunes may have ebbed and flowed from one election to the next, but together they have reigned supreme. Only once in that time has a new force emerged with sufficient support across the whole of Britain to challenge their monopoly on political power, although even this was not a genuine grassroots insurgency.

Rising in the 1980s, the Social Democratic Party (SDP) launched one of the most serious assaults against the main parties in recent British history, attracting well over seven million voters at the general elections in 1983 and 1987. As the academic Ivor Crewe noted at the time: 'Such an eruption of third party support is unprecedented; for speed, strength and duration there has been nothing to match it since Britain's modern party system emerged in the 1920s.'[1] Yet this earlier revolt was the product of a split at the summit of British politics, not a new movement emerging from below: the SDP had been founded by Westminster insiders – four high-profile and experienced Labour politicians, who had all served in the Cabinet of the previous Labour government.[2] Generations of British voters have lived their entire lives without ever seeing the partisan status quo challenged from the grassroots. In 2013, that picture finally changed. The UK Independence Party (UKIP) established the first new movement with national reach since the emergence of the Labour Party at the end of the nineteenth century.

UKIP's emergence has been a remarkable journey. The party was founded in 1993, in the dusty office of a history lecturer at the London School of Economics, and for much of their early history they barely even registered in national politics. They were led by a small band of academics and political obsessives, who were only interested in obscure constitutional issues, and had little grasp of how to run a campaign. They fumbled around in the electoral wilderness, bickering among themselves, and focusing more on railing against the perils of European integration than on winning voters. During their first ten years, UKIP put themselves forward at 25 parliamentary by-elections; they averaged a paltry 1.7 per cent. They were barely even noticeable. On the rare occasions when the party did attract coverage in the media it was scornful: they were written off as a band of amateurs, or as a party who appeared too close for comfort to more dangerous groups on the extremist fringe. Typical of this reporting was one article that appeared before UKIP's first general election campaign in 1997; it placed them alongside the Monster Raving Loony Party, mocked the party as 'a joke' that had a 'kamikaze approach' to politics, and concluded UKIP were 'doomed to spend their lives on the fringes of politics'.[3]

The party's only moment in the sun came once every five years, at European Parliament elections, when their argument that Britain should abandon its European Union (EU) membership finally became relevant to voters. But their success was isolated and short-lived. Like a large angry bear, UKIP would stumble out of hibernation once every few years, briefly stir up popular discontent with Brussels and Westminster political elites, and then return to their slumbers. They put on a good show to entertain voters and journalists in otherwise tedious European Parliament campaigns, but once the 'real' business of British politics resumed they were quickly forgotten.

In their early years UKIP thus appeared to be a classic single-issue party; distinct enough to spark occasional interest but too narrow and inexperienced to become an enduring force with mass support. It was this inability to launch a serious and sustained challenge to Westminster politics that led several commentators to compare them with the fleeting 'Poujadist' movement in France, which in the 1950s had briefly united a coalition of anti-establishment voters against high taxes and seemingly out-of-touch elites. The Poujadists turned heads but they too had peaked quickly, before falling away just as fast.[4]

But by the time UKIP celebrated their twentieth birthday in 2013, this conventional wisdom looked way off the mark. The unwritten law that 'angry insurgents rarely prosper in British politics' had been directly challenged.[5] Since 2011, the party's revolt gathered serious momentum and was no longer confined to European elections. An unbroken series of record results in parliamentary by-elections, surging poll ratings and an unprecedented wave of victories in the 2013 local elections have propelled them into the centre of political debate. UKIP have finished second at by-elections up and down the country, winning large followings in north-eastern mining towns and southern coastal suburbs.[6] Their grassroots base has also grown rapidly, to over 30,000 members, at a time of collapsing activism in all the mainstream parties. UKIP have also regularly polled ahead of the Liberal Democrats as the third most popular party in the country, while by late 2013 pundits were speculating about a possible first place finish in the 2014 European Parliament elections. But this was not the election that occupied the minds of UKIP's high command as 2014 began. They were now more ambitious, training their sights instead on Westminster, and the ultimate goal for their grassroots insurgency: winning a seat at the high table of British politics.

This goal was in the mind of UKIP's charismatic leader, Nigel Farage, as he took to the stage in September 2013 at UKIP's twentieth anniversary conference in London to address activists once dismissed by David Cameron as 'fruitcakes, loonies and closet racists'.

When Farage had addressed his party three years earlier, at the beginning of his successful campaign for a second term as leader, just two journalists showed up. Now, there were 150, and they were hanging on his every word.[7] Farage had been in the party from the start, and was keenly aware that he was now leading a revolt with huge electoral potential. Having toured the country relentlessly, speaking in hundreds of town halls and pubs, he offered his own interpretation of what was leading a growing army of voters to join his party's revolt. 'One thing many have in common', railed Farage. 'They are fed up to the back teeth with the cardboard cut-out careerists in Westminster. The spot-the-difference politicians. Desperate to fight the middle ground, but can't even find it. Focus groupies. The triangulators. The dog whistlers. The politicians who daren't say what they really mean.' Farage also took aim at the London commentariat, who he argued had similarly lost touch with voters on the EU and immigration. UKIP, he declared, would fill the void by winning the European elections in 2014 and, in local elections on the same day, standing thousands of candidates and winning hundreds of seats. The party would then go forward, carrying the revolt to Westminster in 2015. UKIP, he declared, would change the face of British politics. At least, that was the plan.

The party had made this claim before. Ahead of the sustained rise in support for UKIP that began in 2011, over the past decade there have been two distinct surges of support for the party (see Figure I.1). The first was in 2004, and coincided with elections to the European Parliament, when they enjoyed a wave of interest following the decision by a former television presenter and national celebrity, Robert Kilroy-Silk, to stand as a candidate. The arrival of major donors allowed the party to spend serious money, while the recruitment of a seasoned American political consultant, who cut his teeth in Bill Clinton's campaigns, was another major coup. UKIP's ground offensive, focused on giving a simple message to voters on billboards, helped win over 2.6 million voters and 16.1 per cent of the national vote (see Chapter 2). They finished in third place nationwide, ahead of the Liberal Democrats. They were finally on their way, or so it seemed.

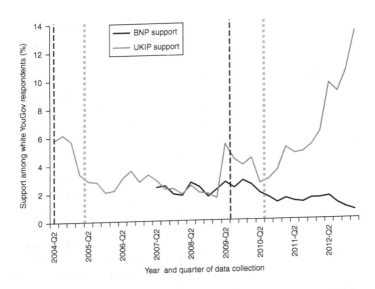

FIGURE I.1 Support for UKIP (2004–2012) and the BNP (2007–2012)
Source: BES Continuous Monitoring Survey. Thick dashes: European Parliament elections. Thin dashes: general elections.

But as many small parties have learned to their cost, sustaining such momentum at a British general election, with different issues in play and a different electoral system to negotiate, is no easy task. European elections are 'second-order' elections characterised by low rates of voter interest and participation, and a higher willingness to experiment with new parties, as voters believe the stakes are low.[8] While UKIP flourished in this benign context, seasoned political observers were not convinced that the party had what it took to succeed in the harsher Westminster climate. 'Like most small party insurgencies', reflected the journalist Michael White, 'it may all be hot air'.[9]

UKIP's performance at the 2005 general election seemed to justify this prediction. Their support slid rapidly as the European elections faded from memory, to a low point of around 2 per cent. Voters lost interest in a party still seen as a single-issue movement, a process accelerated by the eruption of a protracted bout of infighting, as Kilroy-Silk sought to take over the party he had joined less than a year earlier, which we detail in Chapter 2. UKIP were now confronted with an electoral system that required parties to accomplish were the two difficult, but essential, goals needed to win constituency battles: building geographically concentrated bastions of support and effective and well resourced local campaigns to mobilise it. The party failed on both counts and were duly punished, winning just 2.2 per cent of the vote. UKIP may have finished 2005 as the biggest of Britain's political minnows but they were still a long way from challenging the 'big three'.

Over the next three years Ukippers did not even dare to dream of elected representation in Westminster.[10] As David Cameron replaced Michael Howard as leader of the Conservative Party, and Gordon Brown replaced Tony Blair as the Labour Prime Minister, UKIP continued to tread water at between 2 and 3 per cent in the opinion polls. Then, in 2009, the advent of another European election brought a fresh burst of attention for the Eurosceptic insurgents who, once again, benefited from events that were beyond their control. This time, the European elections took place in the middle of a major political scandal over the abuse of parliamentary expenses by Members of Parliament from all the mainstream parties, and against the backdrop of the worst global economic crisis in living memory. It is hard to imagine a more favourable climate for a radical populist party railing against a corrupt and failed political establishment. Support for UKIP duly surged for a second time.

The Conservatives won the European election comfortably but the big story of the election was the return of UKIP. A party written off as in terminal decline just months earlier won almost 2.5 million votes, or 16.5 per cent of the total, a higher share than they had managed in 2004, with the assistance of Kilroy-Silk's celebrity. A party that had been battling for fourth place in the opinion polls was suddenly handed the silver medal in a national election. UKIP had bested the governing Labour Party, and secured thirteen seats in the European Parliament, an unprecedented achievement for a small and disorganised outfit. UKIP were back, again.

The 2009 European elections also saw another, although less impressive, breakthrough by a right-wing outsider. For the first time in British history, an openly racist extreme right-wing party won seats at a national election, as two candidates for the British National Party (BNP) were elected to the European Parliament.[11] Almost one million Britons voted for the BNP, despite the party's known sympathies for white supremacism, anti-Semitism and violence. Britain, unlike some other European countries, never had an electorally significant extreme right – in part due to the barrier of the electoral system, but also opposition from British voters who saw their country's defeat of Nazism as an important marker of their national identity.[12] Yet the 2009 results suggested that the BNP had, finally, found a way to overcome that reluctance and introduce a more toxic form of right-wing politics into the mainstream.

UKIP and the BNP are very different types of parties. Whereas UKIP are broadly at ease with the global free market, the BNP demand economic protectionism and the renationalisation of some industries. Whereas UKIP publicly claim to be libertarians who want to protect individuals from the state, the BNP advocate an array of authoritarian policies. Whereas the BNP subscribe to an 'ethnic' conception of nationalism, defining Britishness on the basis of race and ancestry, UKIP present themselves as a non-racist and non-sectarian party who are 'civic' nationalists, arguing that their party is 'open and inclusive to anyone who wishes to identify with Britain, regardless of ethnic or religious background. We reject the "blood and soil" ethnic nationalism of extremist parties.'[13] These two parties also build on strikingly different traditions; whereas UKIP are rooted in a politically legitimate tradition of British Euroscepticism, the BNP originates in a neo-Nazi and anti-democratic tradition, and openly argues that the British national community is closed to immigrants and ethnic minorities.

Nonetheless, the fact that in 2009 these two parties had, together, attracted one in four voters encouraged a view among some journalists and academics, that Britain was experiencing a broader right-wing revolt against the established political class, and that the two parties were drawing votes from the same groups in society, guided by the same set of concerns.[14] This view was voiced by commentators such as David Aaronovitch, who contended that 'what the BNP and UKIP have in common is the psychological suggestion that "ordinary" people are being betrayed by the political class. They are paying too much fuel tax, too much council tax, they are being pushed around by foreigners and outsiders, they are having stuff done to them and have become victims in their own countries.'[15]

Yet while both parties had cause to celebrate, their paths would soon diverge. At the next major battle with the main parties, the 2010 general election, the BNP were brought back to earth, winning just 1.9 per cent of the total vote. It was a record showing by the extreme right but a bitter disappointment for Griffin, who had promised his activists victory in the seats of Barking and Stoke Central, but could not even deliver second place in either.[16] Having failed to convince voters they were a legitimate party, the BNP suffered a dramatic and sustained collapse of support and were torn apart by debt and bitter infighting, haemorrhaging activists to new rivals like the English Defence League (EDL), who offered a more attractive and confrontational alternative to perennial failure at the ballot box. The BNP's revolt, which had attracted considerable publicity, and alarm, was now over. By the end of 2012 the party rarely polled above 1 per cent.[17]

UKIP's revolt also looked to be in terminal decline after the European Parliament elections. After the 2009 European elections the party once again started shedding support, falling steadily in the opinion polls to a nadir of around 2 per cent. UKIP recovered some ground by election day, winning 3.1 per cent of the vote, but again failed to convert a Brussels breakthrough into domestic success. The frustrated party watched as their large army of European election voters once again dwindled into a much smaller battalion of committed loyalists at a domestic general election. It was this cycle that led commentators to follow Richard Hofstadter's epigram about third parties in American politics when discussing UKIP. Challenger parties, noted the historian, are like bees: once they have stung the system, they quickly die.[18]

Yet things began to change after the 2010 general election. UKIP's support, which had ebbed away before the election, now began to rise rapidly and for the first time they found their popularity on the rebound outside of a European campaign. The general election, which gave birth to the first coalition government in Britain for over seventy years, was followed by the first sustained surge in national support for a new party in a generation. By the end of 2012, public support for UKIP in the opinion polls had increased five-fold, from barely 2 per cent to over 10 per cent.[19]

Nor was their popularity confined to poll interviews. UKIP's rebels also chalked up a series of record showings at parliamentary by-elections, increasing their record share of the vote in a local constituency from 12.2 per cent to 27.8 per cent. This continued at the 2013 local elections, where the party won over 140 county councillors, an unprecedented achievement for an insurgent in Britain. Commentators who previously dismissed UKIP as a disorganised rabble of single-issue fanatics began to give them a second look. Farage, wrote one influential blogger, should be credited for having transformed 'a rag, tag and bobtail party into an effective political campaigning force'.[20] We can quantify this growing media interest by looking at the number of times UKIP were mentioned in British newspaper articles. In 2004, the year of their first big European breakthrough, they were mentioned over 4,000 times. Five years later, interest in the party had boomed and irrespective of the election cycle: 5,300 mentions in 2009, 6,200 in 2010, 10,200 in 2012 and then almost 25,000 during all of 2013.[21] UKIP appeared more like a wasp than a bee: instead of dying after only one sting, the party kept coming back with new barbs.

Why the UKIP revolt matters

UKIP matter because they have achieved something unprecedented in modern British political history: they have taken a grassroots insurgency and grown it into a more professional political party with mass support. Our aim in this book is to explain how this remarkable revolt has happened, who has joined it, and what they want. In the chapters that follow, we draw on a mass of survey data and interviews with key insiders to chart UKIP's evolution from humble beginnings as an anti-EU pressure group, who fought elections as a hobby, to a national party with mass membership and the capacity to compete effectively in elections up and down the country. Our main source of data on UKIP supporters is the Continuous Monitoring Survey (CMS), run monthly by the prestigious British Election Study (BES), Britain's flagship political survey. We also draw on qualitative interviews with the party's leaders and activists, past and present, ranging from their founder Dr Alan Sked, to their current leader, Nigel Farage, and including many others who have played key roles in their history, such as Robert Kilroy-Silk and Paul Nuttall, experienced activists and major donors. A full discussion of the data and methodology can be found in the appendix. We show how UKIP are forging ties with clearly defined sections of British society, and are tapping into social divisions that have been evolving over the past five decades. We then turn to explain *who* is voting for the party, and *why*, before turning to consider the challenges UKIP still have to overcome if they are to take their movement into the Palace of Westminster. Before we turn to dissect this political revolt, we want to lay out some of the reasons we believe that it matters for all those who are interested in the contemporary state of British politics.

UKIP's revolt matters, firstly, because it has given a voice to groups in British society who have been written out of political debate, and turned against traditional mainstream politics. Over recent decades, deep social and economic changes have hit particular groups within British society very hard: older, less skilled and less well educated working-class voters. These are the groups we describe as the 'left behind' in modern Britain, who could once rely on the strength of their numbers to ensure a voice in each of the mainstream parties. Yet as Britain has been transformed, the relentless growth of the highly educated middle classes has changed the strategic calculus. Both Labour and the Conservatives now regard winning support from middle-class swing voters as more important than appealing to these struggling left behind voters. Before the emergence of UKIP, their response to being ignored was to turn their backs on politics, staying home en masse on election day and developing a sour, anti-establishment outlook. The political impact of this was limited – party strategists were concerned, but not threatened, by falling turnout and growing hostility to politicians. The emergence of UKIP changes the game – the left behind now have a potent voice articulating their concerns, and mainstream parties face a real and effective competitor who have mobilised sections of British society they neglected for years. As we show in Chapter 3, this revolt has been a long time coming.

The second reason UKIP's revolt matters is that these voters have a new and distinctive set of concerns, which have not been adequately reflected in mainstream political competition. As we will see in Chapter 5, UKIP's voters are not single-issue Europhobes or political protesters, they share a clear and distinct agenda, mixing deep Euroscepticism with clear ideas about immigration, national identity and the way British society is changing. The conflict between UKIP's voters and the political mainstream reflects a deep-seated difference in outlook among voters from different walks in life. Those who lead and staff the three main parties are all from the highly educated, socially liberal middle classes, who are comfortable in an ethnically and culturally diverse, outward looking society, and celebrate a cosmopolitan and globally integrated Britain. Those who lead and staff UKIP, and those who vote for them, are older, less educated, disadvantaged and economically insecure Britons, who are profoundly uncomfortable in this 'new' society, which they regard as alien and threatening. This difference in outlook is found in most modern European societies, and in many it has been mobilised into politics since the 1980s.[22] UKIP matter because they have brought this value divide into British politics for the first time, and by doing so they have raised it to the top of the political agenda.

These first two points underscore why commentators who analyse UKIP's emergence in terms of the day-to-day disputes of British party politics have profoundly misunderstood this revolt. UKIP's emergence is not primarily the result of things the mainstream parties, or their leaders, have said or done, though missteps over policy and messaging can certainly aid the rebels. This revolt, instead, is the result of their inability to articulate, and respond to, deep-seated and long-standing social and political conflicts in Britain. Their failure, in part, reflects the way in which these new divisions in the values of voters, and older social divisions, now cut across the current dividing lines of political competition. Both Labour and the Conservatives have avoided high-profile efforts to mobilise the concerns of 'left behind' voters because both parties have concluded, that electoral success or failure will depend on the support of educated middle-class voters, who hold a very different set of values and priorities. Both Labour and the Conservatives also have internal divisions over immigration, Europe, social change and national identity, which they are reluctant to expose by focusing on these issues. This is the point that many media commentators, with their natural focus on the daily ebb-and-flow of politics, tend to miss. When trying to explain UKIP's success, they point to short-term partisan factors such as EU policy and messaging, weaknesses in David Cameron's leadership, or his support for issues like gay marriage, which many argue has led disgruntled Tories to join the UKIP revolt. But this misses the longer-term, fundamental divisions which have built up over decades, and which UKIP have now organised into politics. Trying to explain UKIP's emergence in terms of mangled Tory EU soundbites is as futile, and as misleading, as trying to explain the early twentieth-century emergence of the Labour Party in terms of Liberal trade and tax policy.

Finally, UKIP's rise to national prominence matters because, as the first grassroots insurgency in modern British political history to secure double-digit national poll ratings and significant electoral success, they can teach us a great deal about how new parties develop internally and build their appeal to voters. UKIP is not (yet) a fully professional party, but they have made remarkable progress towards becoming one. For much of their history, the party repeatedly undermined their own prospects through fierce infighting, strategic miscalculations, single-issue obsessiveness and a failure to build an effective campaign organisation. That they even survived the past twenty years is, in itself, truly remarkable. Yet on these shaky foundations, and after a number of false starts, since 2010 UKIP have developed a distinct appeal, election machine and strategy that are capable of winning over a growing mass of voters. Looking to examples of more successful insurgents, the party finally embraced the fundamentals of party-building: the need to establish local bastions of electoral support; to invest in parliamentary by-elections; to establish a clear target electoral market; to fuse their Eurosceptic message with an anti-immigration appeal; and to exploit the weaknesses of the main parties and other, rival insurgents. In this way, UKIP have sought to build a cross-partisan coalition of left behind, working-class voters, and are reaching out to these Britons through a strategy that now prioritises the task of building local concentrations of rebels. Such is the strength of those divisions above that, at least for now, UKIP do not need a comprehensive ideological platform or well-oiled machine, although they are currently moving quickly to build both.

In the first two chapters we begin our study by examining the evolution of UKIP from their early formation as a single-issue, anti-EU pressure group, into their contemporary standing as a radical right party that has become a serious contender for votes and influence. How has UKIP's electoral strategy evolved since their formation in 1993? Which groups in society has the party attempted to recruit? And how have UKIP activists sought to manage competitors that have emerged at various points to challenge their position as the dominant Eurosceptic party on the radical right, such as the Referendum Party at the general election in 1997 and then, from 2001, the extreme right-wing BNP?

Chapter 3 then turns to explore how wider trends that have taken place in British society over the past fifty years, from 1964 until the present day, created room on the right for UKIP's insurgency. We will show how these wider trends left particular sections of society cut off from the values and priorities of mainstream politics, leaving them receptive to radical right appeals and open to the type of revolt that is being led by UKIP. These divisions are deep, and they are sharpening.

In Chapters 4 and 5 we turn to investigate the base of public support for UKIP's radical right revolt. Chapter 4 begins by probing the social roots of the revolt and is guided by three questions. First, does UKIP's revolt have a distinct base of support in society? To address this question we compare the rival interpretations of commentators like Tim Montgomerie and Fraser Nelson, who variously portray UKIP's voters as middle-class Tories in exile, or blue-collar workers who have been left behind by the rapid economic and social changes of the past fifty years. We ask how these rebellious voters compare to supporters of other parties in Britain and what, if anything, makes them distinct? Second, we also ask whether some, like the pollster Peter Kellner and academics like Peter John, are right to point to similarities in the bases of support for the radical right UKIP, and the extreme right-wing BNP. Third, rather than assume that UKIP's support is static, we end Chapter 4 by asking whether the character of public support for UKIP's revolt has changed over time. Has the party grown by *widening* their support among different groups in society, or have they instead gathered pace by *deepening* support among their core groups?

After exploring who the rebels are, in Chapter 5 we turn to examine their motives for joining the revolt. Putting their attitudes and beliefs under the microscope, we examine whether these voters are driven by the same motives that have fuelled radical right revolts in European democracies, namely Euroscepticism, hostility towards immigration, populist dissatisfaction with mainstream politics or a more general pessimistic outlook. To what extent, if at all, do supporters of UKIP share a clear and distinct cluster of concerns? And if they do, is it fair to describe these voters as single-issue Eurosceptics, anti-immigrant xenophobes, political protesters or citizens who are more simply just dissatisfied and pessimistic about the general direction of society? Again, we look at how these motives for supporting UKIP have evolved over time, and under the administrations of Tony Blair, Gordon Brown and David Cameron. We also push the existing research further, by examining how perceptions among voters of the performance of the mainstream parties and their leaders have played a role in mobilising support for the revolt.

Then, in Chapter 6, we consider a broader challenge facing UKIP as they move forward: Britain's formidable electoral system, which has stalled many attempted revolts in the past. We illustrate some of the weaknesses in UKIP support, and explore ways that other minor party insurgents have successfully overcome the odds to win seats in Westminster, before finally identifying constituencies that, based on our evidence, would be potentially receptive to this radical right revolt.

In our concluding chapter we not only summarise our key findings but also consider the paradoxes in UKIP's support and, drawing on some further data, ask one final question; how far can the party go? Speaking to a focus group of voters on a popular radio station in late 2013, Nigel Farage reflected: 'UKIP is not a pressure group. It is not a spin-off of the Conservative Party. It is a new political force, and it is here to stay.'[23] We believe he is right, but the new force Mr Farage leads remains poorly understood. In this book we set out to shed light on the meaning and origins of the most significant phenomenon in British party politics for a generation: the revolt on the right.

Notes

1 Ivor Crewe (1982) 'Is Britain's two-party system really about to crumble? The Social Democratic–Liberal Alliance and the prospects for realignment', *Electoral Studies*, 1: 275–313 (p. 276).

2 The Social Democratic Party (SDP) was founded by the so-called 'Gang of Four', two of whom (David Owen and Bill Rodgers) were already Labour Members of Parliament, while Roy Jenkins had left his seat and Shirley Williams had lost hers. On the SDP see Ivor Crewe and Anthony King (1995) *SDP: The Birth, Life and Death of the Social Democratic Party*, Oxford: Oxford University Press.

3 'Kamikaze parties doomed to spend their lives on the fringes of politics', *Daily Record*, 2 May 1997.

4 On comparisons between UKIP and Poujadism see David Aaronovitch, 'Talking dirty to woo the voters', *The Guardian*, 16 June 2004; Alex Massie, 'UKIP is not a libertarian party', *Spectator Blogs*, 27 November 2012. Available

online: http://blogs.spectator.co.uk/alex-massie/2012/11/dont-be-fooled-ukip-is-not-a-libertarian-party/ (accessed 28 August 2013).

5 'The UKIP insurgency', Bagehot's notebook, *The Economist*, 7 June 2012.

6 We chart these results during the book, but UKIP finished second at parliamentary by-elections in Barnsley Central, Middlesbrough, Rotherham, Eastleigh and South Shields.

7 Fraser Nelson, 'Where was the Nigel Farage fizz? UKIP speech analysis', *Spectator Coffee House Blog*, 20 September 2013. Available online: http://blogs.spectator.co.uk/coffeehouse/2013/09/wheres-the-nigel-farage-fizz-ukip-speech-analysis/ (accessed 22 September 2013).

8 Officially, the European Parliament has three places of work: Brussels, Luxembourg and Strasbourg. The main base is in Brussels, where most of the work takes place, and so we refer in this book most often to Brussels. Luxembourg is home to the administrative offices (the 'General Secretariat') while meetings of the whole Parliament take place in Strasbourg and also in Brussels.

9 Michael White, 'Collins joins Kilroy in UKIP's battle for Britain', *The Guardian*, 25 May 2004.

10 Although UKIP has gained representation in the unelected House of Lords, when Lord Willoughby de Broke defected from the Conservative Party, and Lord Pearson of Rannoch switched from being an Independent Conservative, to join UKIP in January 2007 and Lord Stevens of Ludgate switched from being an Independent Conservative to join UKIP in 2012.

11 Nick Griffin and Andrew Brons were elected respectively in the North West and Yorkshire and the Humber regions. On support for the BNP at the 2009 European Parliament elections see David Cutts, Robert Ford and Matthew J. Goodwin (2011) 'Anti-immigrant, politically disaffected or still racist after all? Examining the attitudinal drivers of extreme right support in Britain in the 2009 European elections', *European Journal of Political Research*, 50(3): 418–40. Also Matthew J. Goodwin (2011) *New British Fascism: Rise of the British National Party*, Abingdon: Routledge; Robert Ford and Matthew J. Goodwin (2010) 'Angry white men: Individual and contextual predictors of support for the British National Party', *Political Studies*, 58(1): 1–25.

12 For example, one opinion poll by YouGov and *The Daily Telegraph* in 2005 asked citizens to rank the importance of various phrases in defining 'Britishness'. The percentage who thought 'Britain's defiance of Nazi Germany in 1940' as being 'very' or 'fairly' important (87

per cent) was the second most popular phrase after 'British people's right to say what they think' (91 per cent). Available online: http://iis. yougov.co.uk/extranets/ygarchives/content/pdf/TEL050101032_1. pdf (accessed 14 August 2012).

13 UKIP General Election Manifesto 2010, p. 13. This difference has also expressed itself in the views of activists, with one in the BNP explaining the difference between the two parties as follows: 'UKIP accept f***ing anyone. At the end of the day it's a racial thing. We're the BNP, we are who we are because of race.' Originally quoted in Peter John, Helen Margetts, David Rowland and Stuart Weir (2005) *The BNP: The Roots of its Appeal*, Essex: Democratic Audit, Human Rights Centre, p. 12.

14 Peter John, Helen Margetts and Stuart Weir, '1 in 5 Britons could vote far right: UKIP and the BNP are far closer in their views and much more popular with voters than most of us realise', *New Statesman*, 24 January 2005; Peter John and Helen Margetts (2009) 'The latent support for the extreme right in British politics', *West European Politics*, 32(3): 496–513; Peter Kellner (2009) 'Britain's oddest election?' *Political Quarterly*, 80(4): 469–78 (p. 473). Others pointed to 'similar social and political attitudes among their respective supporters, which may suggest fluidity between voting for the two parties'. Richard Hayton (2010) 'Towards the mainstream: UKIP and the 2009 elections to the European Parliament', *Politics*, 30(1): 26–35 (p. 31); Robert Ford, Matthew J. Goodwin and David Cutts (2012) 'Strategic Eurosceptics and polite xenophobes: Support for the UK Independence Party (UKIP) in the 2009 European Parliament elections', *European Journal of Political Research*, 51(2): 204–34.

15 David Aaronovitch, 'Talking dirty to woo the voters', *The Guardian*, 16 June 2004. Others made similar arguments, such as Glyn Ford who described UKIP as a 'BNP-lite' party, with only barely distinguishable policies on immigration, Europe and trade unions; while right-wing commentators like Ed West similarly argue the parties 'have many things in common … and so unquestionably appeal to many of the same voters'. Glyn Ford, 'The growing threat of Europe's fascist-lite', *Morning Star*, 22 October 2004; Ed West, 'Record UKIP poll ratings – only a matter of time before they overtake the Lib Dems', *The Daily Telegraph Blog*, 27 January 2011.

16 In Barking, Nick Griffin polled 14.8 per cent and finished third. In Stoke Central the BNP candidate polled 7.7 per cent and finished fourth.

17 On the failure of the BNP see Matthew J. Goodwin (2011) *New British Fascism: Rise of the British National Party*, Abingdon: Routledge; Matthew J. Goodwin (2013) 'Forever a false dawn? Explaining the electoral collapse of the British National Party', *Parliamentary Affairs* (in print). The BNP's sudden disintegration in the shadow of a general election mirrored the fate of the earlier National Front (NF), which had similarly collapsed and fragmented after a record number of votes at the general election in 1979 had failed to get the far right into Westminster. The National Front received over 191,000 votes at the general election in 1979, or 0.6 per cent of the total vote. On support for the NF see Christopher Husbands (1983) *Racial Exclusionism and the City: The Urban Support of the National Front*, London: George Allen.

18 Richard Hofstadter (1955) *The Age of Reform: From Bryan to FDR*, New York: Random House.

19 On UKIP support in the polls see the regular series of Polling Observatory blogs, hosted by the University of Nottingham 'Ballots and Bullets' blog (http://nottspolitics.org). For example 'Polling Observatory #25: UKIP surge, but who do they hurt?' Available online: http://nottspolitics.org/2013/06/03/polling-observatory-25-ukip-surge-but-who-do-they-hurt/ (accessed 5 October 2013).

20 Iain Dale, 'Don't mock UKIP – it's the new dustbin of British politics', *The Guardian*, 8 March 2013.

21 We performed a keyword search in the Nexis database, for articles across all UK-based newspaper articles that mention "ukip". The specific figures are as follows: 573 in 2003, 4,464 in 2004, 3,371 in 2005, 1,644 in 2006, 2,080 in 2007, 2,212 in 2008, 5,279 in 2009, 6,193 in 2010, 4,135 in 2011, 10,185 in 2012 and 24,879 in 2013.

22 On the rise of the radical right see Cas Mudde (2007) *Populist Radical Right Parties in Europe*, Cambridge: Cambridge University Press. On Euroscepticism and concerns over national identity and threats to the nation see Lauren McLaren (2007) 'Explaining mass-level Euroscepticism: Identity, interests and institutional distrust', *Acta Politica*, 42: 233–51; Marcel Lubbers and Peer Scheepers (2007) 'Explanations of political Euroscepticism at the individual, regional and national levels', *European Societies*, 9(4): 643–69; Marcel Lubbers and Eva Jaspers (2011) 'A longitudinal study of Euroscepticism in the Netherlands: 2008 versus 1990', *Party Politics* 12(1): 21–40; Sara B. Hobolt, Wouter van der Brug, C. H. De Vreese, H. G. Boomgaarden and M. C. Hinrichsen (2011)

'Religious intolerance and Euroscepticism', *European Union Politics*, 12(3): 359–79.

23 Nigel Farage on London's Big Conversation (LBC) Radio, October 2013. Available online: http://www.youtube.com/watch?v=-VeCS-BFeVuE (accessed 5 October 2013).

1

A SINGLE-ISSUE PRESSURE GROUP

If only one day could lay claim as the bleakest in the history of the British Conservative Party, then 2 May 1997 would be a strong contender. As Conservatives awoke that morning to digest the results of the general election, they found they had been shunned by voters and battered by Tony Blair and New Labour. They had been thrown out of office after eighteen years and won barely 30 per cent of the national vote. It was their lowest level of support since the birth of British party politics in 1832. In the House of Commons, they now had only 165 MPs, who sat opposite the largest gathering of Labour MPs in British political history.[1] Some naïve Tories talked about a quick recovery but the reality would be quite different. They would not return to government for thirteen years, and even then they would be forced to share power with the Liberal Democrats.

Though few Conservatives would have noticed, the general election in 1997 also saw the debut of a new challenger in British politics. The UK Independence Party were a largely unknown and disorganised fringe group of Eurosceptics fighting their first parliamentary election. They had gone into the battle with high hopes. United by their defining goal of pulling Britain out of the European Union, UKIP wanted to place a 'hard' rather than 'soft' form of Euroscepticism at the heart of British politics. As hard Eurosceptics, they were opposed to the very principle of European political integration and demanded that Britain withdraw from the 'Europe project'. This stood them apart from 'soft' Eurosceptics who do not oppose the EU *tout court*: they want EU institutions and policy reformed, rather than junked; and European integration slowed or reversed, rather than ended altogether.[2] UKIP's message was total opposition to Europe: 'The UK Independence Party's policy of withdrawal is the only viable option. THE ONLY WAY IS OUT.'[3]

Beginning the revolt: the formation of a new party

The story of UKIP had begun six years earlier, in 1991, with the foundation of a small pressure group called the Anti-Federalist League. The League wanted to rally opposition to the Maastricht Treaty that had been signed earlier in the year, and which paved the way for the EU and a single European currency. The Anti-Federalists attracted little attention but when they did they talked of wanting to stop the UK 'becoming a province of a united European superstate'.[4] While some suggested the League's name had fascist connotations, their founder, Dr Alan Sked, was a former candidate for the Liberals and a historian at the London School of Economics who had chosen the name for its historical resonances: 'I thought it would be the equivalent of the anti-Corn Law League. Just as the anti-Corn Law League converted [Robert] Peel to free trade, the anti-Federalist League would convert the Tory Party to Euroscepticism and to British Independence.'[5]

Sked's Euroscepticism had developed in the 1980s, while convening the European Studies programme at the LSE: 'I just kept meeting all these bureaucrats and other Euro-fanatical academics who came to give papers, politicians from different parts of Europe, and reading endless MA theses on the EU. I just came to the conclusion that the whole thing was mad.' Influenced by Margaret Thatcher's famous 'Bruges speech' in 1988, in which the Conservative Prime Minister warned against efforts at the European level to 'suppress nationhood', 'concentrate power at the centre of a European conglomerate' and fit nations 'into some sort of identikit European personality', he joined other influential Eurosceptics in the Bruges Group, a right-wing think-tank that received financial backing from Sir James Goldsmith, who would soon play a more central role in the Eurosceptic movement.[6] But writing pamphlets was not enough for Sked, who wanted to take his message to voters. After launching the Anti-Federalist League and making clear his plans to stand against Conservatives at the 1992 general election, he was dismissed by the Bruges Group as an 'embarrassment'.[7] Sked and the Anti-Federalists were on their own.

Their early ambitions, however, were soon disappointed. At the 1992 general election the Anti-Federalists talked of making such an impact that Conservatives would be forced to adopt their harder brand of Euroscepticism. But with only seventeen candidates and no real resources they were barely visible. There was only one target seat, Bath in the South-West of England, a region that over the next twenty years would become an important source of support for Eurosceptics. But while Sked talked about inflicting serious damage on the incumbent Conservative MP, Chris Patten, who was known for his pro-Europe views, in his own words the campaign was run 'on a wing and a prayer'. Still he battled on, hoping to attract publicity by describing the Conservative Prime Minister, John Major, as the most incompetent leader in postwar Britain and declaring that after the Maastricht Treaty British sovereignty faced 'its greatest threat since Adolf Hitler'.[8] Patten did lose his seat, to a Liberal Democrat, but Sked won only 0.2 per cent of the vote in Bath while his fellow Anti-Federalists also failed to have an impact. Where they did put their heads above the parapet they averaged a paltry 0.5 per cent. Combined, they attracted fewer votes than the Monster Raving Loony Party.[9]

In the aftermath, Sked attempted to get back on track by contesting two parliamentary by-elections, one of which saw him enlist help from the famous former Conservative arch-Eurosceptic and serial rebel Enoch Powell, but at both contests he won less than 2 per cent.[10] With the League failing to capture the public imagination, the small band of activists who had coalesced around Sked now began calling for a change of direction. They wanted a political party with a new name and a serious electoral strategy, as one recalled: 'In 1846 the word "anti" may have sounded good. But it took a long, long time for a group of us to convince him that it would never work.' These discussions led to a meeting at the LSE on 3 September 1993, at which a new party would be born.

While those who gathered in Sked's office were eager to begin their revolt against the established parties, they were also aware of the need to distance their embryonic movement from a more toxic element- that had resurfaced in British politics. As most would have known, in the 1970s Britain had seen a minor insurgency by an extreme right- wing party named the National Front (NF), which was openly racist and less than keen on liberal democracy. Despite the NF's reputation for fascist ideas and violence, for a brief moment they attracted sig- nificant support, winning over 100,000 voters at the general election in October 1974, almost 200,000 at the general election in 1979, and a couple of impressive results at by-elections.[11] But the NF fell as quickly as they had risen. By the end of the 1970s the party were rapidly leaking support to Margaret Thatcher and the Conservatives, who had reached out to NF voters by openly sympathising with their concerns over immigration. The NF was also torn apart by infighting and split into several tiny, warring factions. One of these successor movements was the British National Party, who formed in 1982 and would later come to dominate the extreme right.[12]

Unlike the Anti-Federalists, some of whom had strong links to estab- lished politicians, the BNP were firmly rooted in the NF's extremist tradition of racial nationalism and were treated as a pariah by other parties and the media. Much of this reaction stemmed from the BNP's purely 'ethnic' conception of British nationalism, which defined whether somebody could become a citizen of the nation based on their race and ancestry. The BNP argued that ethnic identity is fixed from birth, and that people from other ethnic and racial groups could there- fore never be British. The party were deeply hostile towards non-whites and immigrants who were seen as a threat to the survival of the British race, and Jews whom they argued had orchestrated multiculturalism to encourage race mixing and the dilution of the purity of the British race. This worldview contrasted sharply with the mainstream 'civic' concep- tion of nationalism in Britain, which defines national identity by volun- tary affiliation and acceptance of the laws and traditions of a country. By this account, anyone who regards themselves as 'British' and respects the laws, values and institutions of the country can rightly call themselves British, regardless of their race, culture or birthplace.

But despite being ostracised, the BNP did manage to put the extreme right back on the map of British politics.

In the same month that the Anti-Federalists met to launch their new party, the BNP made national headlines after capturing their first ever local council seat, in London's East End.[13] The party's growing profile and poisonous reputation had clear implications for the Anti-Federalists, as Sked recalls: 'We didn't want British [in the party name] as that was supposed to be too racialist and associated with the British National Party. So we called it UK Independence Party. It was all done very quickly. It was obvious to all of us that if we rule out British then it had to be UK. What we stood for basically was independence.' But despite these early efforts to distance themselves from the BNP, UKIP's relationship with the extreme right would continue to generate interest for years to come.

UKIP had not even marked their first birthday when the first battle arrived. In June 1994, voters went to the polls to choose their representatives in the European Parliament, a distant institution that many knew little about.[14] Hoping for their first success, UKIP took their message to the electorate in a television broadcast but lacked the money and manpower needed for a ground campaign. 'You just didn't have the luxury of campaign strategy', noted Sked. 'We had very little in the way of money. We all paid our own deposits. Whatever funds we had were scraped together by the candidate, their family, friends and the old man and his dog who might contribute 50p. It was all done on a shoestring.' The results were uninspiring. UKIP won only 1 per cent of the vote and finished fifth, well behind the three main parties and beaten easily by the Greens. The message and the new name had failed to resonate.

Nor were these early problems confined to elections. Like most new parties that cannot afford full-time and experienced staff, UKIP relied heavily on a handful of ideological true believers and novice volunteers. Most of those who took control of high command lacked political and organisational experience, and had strong and conflicting opinions about how to run a party. The result was continual infighting. Rare moments of opportunity were frequently lost through an absence of basic party discipline and, at several points, full-blown chaos where UKIP seemed unable to unify activists around a leader or strategy. As one journalist would later remark, while the three main parties in British politics have each had their share of internal warfare, none have come close to rivalling the self-destructive tendencies of UKIP.[15]

One early point of tension was Sked, whose personality and intellectual preoccupations drew criticism from activists who had little time for theory and abstract debate. Many also disagreed with his argument that they should refuse to accept any seats they might win in the European Parliament, a move that Sked saw as 'a rebuke to Euro-federalist pretensions to represent the British people'.[16] But, from the start, deeper tensions were also inherent within the party.

One of the most important centred on UKIP's overriding goal. Were they setting out to convert their Conservative rivals to hard Euroscepticism? By extension, were they simply a single-issue pressure group, focused on poaching disaffected Tories, who would fold once their goal was accomplished? Or were UKIP destined for greater things, to lead a broader revolt against the established political class and realign British party politics, by appealing to voters across the spectrum? This unresolved tension about the nature of the party would spark regular disagreements over strategy, particularly over relations with the Conservatives. For some Ukippers the centre-right encompassed a faction of vocal Eurosceptics who were their natural allies. Aware that their efforts might draw support away from Eurosceptics who were already elected to Westminster, and in seats UKIP were unlikely to win, some thought Eurosceptic Tories who had revolted over issues like Maastricht should be given a free run. UKIP, they argued, should stand down against these candidates or run 'paper candidates' who would be named on the ballot but not backed by an active campaign. In this way, and while not elected themselves, UKIP would help to ensure that Eurosceptics had the strongest possible presence in Westminster, which kept open the possibility of a more formal alliance between the two parties in the future. But others in the party held a different view.

Seen from an alternative perspective, a UKIP–Conservative alliance at elections would merely fuel a public image of UKIP as an awkward Conservative offshoot with no real identity of their own. It would also send an awkward message to voters who would be asked to vote UKIP except if they were based in certain seats, where they would be urged to support a Eurosceptic Tory. An alliance risked undermining UKIP's credibility as an independent force, and blurred points of ideological difference that separated the two parties. Instead, went the argument, UKIP should go it alone by standing candidates across the board and appealing to all voters. This underlying tension would create constant difficulties for the party in years to come. As activists dusted themselves off after their first, bitter taste of election defeat, a far more pressing problem had arrived.

Competition on the Eurosceptic fringe

On 27 November 1994, Sir James Goldsmith announced his intention to launch a new political party dedicated to securing a referendum on Britain's relationship with Europe. 'Let me make just one promise, just one vow', proclaimed Goldsmith at a meeting of his supporters. 'We the rabble army, we in the Referendum Party, we will strive with all our strength to obtain for the people of these islands the right to decide whether or not Britain should remain a nation.'[17] Goldsmith was far from a political novice. On the contrary he posed a formidable threat. His personal wealth was estimated at around £800 million (well over £1 billion in 2013 terms), and he had already been elected to the European Parliament in France as part of a list of candidates who won 12 per cent of the national vote. Now with his eye on British politics, Goldsmith pledged to spend at least £10 million at the next general election to ensure that his party was funded to the same extent as the main parties. In the end he would spend almost three times as much as the Conservatives and five times as much as Labour on advertisements in the press.[18]

Goldsmith's was a classic single-issue party that had a simple message for voters. Unlike normal parties that address a range of issues, recruit support from particular sections of society and play a long game, the single-issue party is defined as one that galvanises support 'from different political camps on the basis of a single, all-encompassing issue, and, predictably, disappears once the issue has been articulated into the political agenda'.[19] Goldsmith's core issue was to secure a national referendum that would ask the British people whether they wanted their country to be part of a federal Europe or return to an association of sovereign nations in a common trading market. With nothing to say on other issues it was not long until some journalists described the new arrival as the 'Referendum Only Party'.[20]

The message was also backed by a serious machine. Goldsmith's resources and contacts were used to quickly register 230,000 supporters, hire sixty paid staff, rent a headquarters in London and ten regional offices, and secure celebrity endorsements, all of which generated more media interest. He also spent a princely sum to send a video to millions of homes across the country, which explained: 'We in the Referendum Party are not politicians. We don't want to be politicians. What unites us is the belief that in the true spirit of democracy we must let the people of Britain decide the future of Britain. As soon as a full and fair referendum has been held, we'll resign. That's written into our constitution.'[21]

All of this contrasted sharply with UKIP, whose campaign coffers were almost empty and lacked the experience and foot soldiers to offset Goldsmith's gathering momentum. Between UKIP's birth and the general election in 1997, the daunting task of building an organisation from the ground up had fallen to David Lott, a former squadron leader in the Royal Air Force whose sceptical views on Europe had led him out of retirement and into UKIP. Single-handedly, Lott began building UKIP a skeleton organisation. 'After a while, I'd got hold of an old horsebox, painted it all up with UKIP. I'd drive around towns, and have a contact or something. We'd meet, set up a table in a square somewhere, and hand out bits of paper. I was trying to form little groups all over the country.' Lott and his horsebox trundled across the country, from Scotland to Land's End. But while he managed to put in place an initial membership, an office in Regent Street and a newsletter, he did not have time to build serious foundations before UKIP's first general election campaign. The contrast between the two Eurosceptic parties could not have been sharper.

The 1997 general election was a watershed moment in British politics, ousting the Conservatives after eighteen years in government and ushering in New Labour for the next thirteen. But outside of major party politics the election also offered opportunities to fringe Eurosceptics. When the Anti-Federalists had campaigned in 1992 few voters told pollsters that Europe was a pressing concern. Only 14 per cent of the electorate placed Europe among the three most important issues facing Britain. This left the issue in a distant sixth place on the list of priorities for voters who were preoccupied by other concerns. But by 1997, and after the Maastricht Treaty and the prospect of a single currency had turned up the political heat over Europe, the climate had changed. The share of voters ranking Europe among the three most important issues had tripled, to 43 per cent, making it the third most important behind the National Health Service and education. British public opinion had shifted in a more Eurosceptic direction across the board. Support for European integration and a single currency had fallen, while survey evidence suggested that two-thirds of the electorate either wanted to leave the EU or reduce its powers and less than one in five thought Britain should replace the pound.[22]

UKIP were aware of these trends and pointed to opinion polls as evidence for their optimistic assertion 'that, potentially, 80% of the electorate could be converted to vote for the UKIP'.[23] But they were no longer the only Eurosceptics in town. Goldsmith was now outspending them by a crushing margin in the air-war of national advertising. The markedly different media profile of the two parties was reflected in the number of times they appeared in domestic newspaper articles during 1997: the Referendum Party were mentioned in more than 1,000 while UKIP featured in less than 200; Goldsmith was mentioned in almost 1,000 while Sked appeared in just 58.[24] Despite their common ground the two parties also failed to reach some sort of deal. While some in UKIP claim their founder was never open to the idea of a pact, Sked claims his letters to Goldsmith were never delivered. Either way, UKIP wandered into the election with only vague hopes of catching the scraps from Sir James' table.

Nor was UKIP's attempt to attract these voters helped by their narrow message. Their fanatical obsession with Europe and lack of interest in other domestic issues immediately reduced their potential to carve out a separate niche, and was obvious to those who went to some of their earliest meetings, as one recruit recalled: 'What a shambles they were. Everybody wanted to speak. Everybody went over their time. Everybody just ranted into the microphone about how terrible the EU was.' The fact that UKIP were interested in little else was reflected in their general election manifesto that contained only a few speculative ideas, built on the prospect of Britain's withdrawal from the EU. While the document hinted at issues that would become more prominent in later years, policies were woefully underdeveloped. Education would be geared towards ensuring the preservation of Britain's national cultural identity. The number of immigrants would be limited. Borders would be tightened. A tougher approach to illegal migrants would be adopted. Politically correct policies would be opposed. While advocating these hard right ideas Sked continued with efforts to distance UKIP from the extreme right. The party, he explained to voters, was 'a democratic, non-racist, non-sectarian party', which 'cannot repeat too often that it totally rejects racist views and behaviour'.[25]

UKIP were also beginning to understand the constraints imposed by British general elections. To launch a campaign the party would need candidates who would each need a deposit of £500, which would only be returned if they polled more than 5 per cent in their seat. This meant that a bad set of results could inflict large financial losses on a small party. Initial plans to fly the flag in every constituency were quashed as Sked conceded that electoral growth would not be immediately forthcoming: 'We are not a here today and gone tomorrow party', he explained, now seeking to reassure nervous Ukippers. 'We are at the beginning of an epic struggle which may take 10 years before we are out of Europe.'[26]

UKIP focused their efforts on Conservative held seats in the South of England, a strategy that reflected the activists' view that they should mainly compete with and put pressure on the centre-right, as Sked explained: 'The majority of seats were Tory and certainly in the areas where most of our local associations sprung up were Tory. We did have a lot of dissident Tories, as the aim of the party was to convert the Tory party to Euroscepticism.'Areas such as Hampshire, Sussex and the South-West were identified as particularly promising.[27] But with Goldsmith on the scene and low public awareness of UKIP, the talk of influencing the major parties was premature. As voters headed to the ballot box, Ukippers knew they could not match the targeted campaigns and electoral professionalism of the main parties.

Shortly before the 1997 general election, a journalist remarked that most new parties in British politics tend to wither and die in the face of voter indifference.[28] Confronted with the formidable barriers to entering Westminster, attracting and sustaining interest simply proves too much for them. When the results arrived, UKIP might also have concluded that most voters were not interested in what they had to say. They faced some uncomfortable facts. Overall, their 194 candidates won only 0.3 per cent of the total vote. In seats they actually contested they averaged just 1 per cent, although almost two-thirds of their candidates failed even to reach this low threshold, and more than one-third finished in last place. These were hardly the signs of a coming political insurgency. Only one candidate, a young activist named Nigel Farage, managed to save his deposit after polling 5.7 per cent in Salisbury, where he did not face a Referendum candidate: 'I was the only one who tried', he recalled. 'The rest were all intellectuals. They thought it all happens in coffee houses.'

UKIP were also thoroughly beaten by their Eurosceptic rivals. Goldsmith had led 547 candidates into the election and had been impossible to avoid: the two parties stood against each another in a staggering 165 seats. UKIP were bulldozed aside, finishing behind their competitor in all but two.[29] Sked's party also clearly suffered in seats where they were forced to compete with Goldsmith: in seats where both parties stood candidates, UKIP's average share of the vote sunk to a dismal 0.9 per cent, as compared to 1.9 per cent in seats where UKIP stood alone. The Referendum Party's performance, meanwhile, was impressive for a single-issue party competing in its first election: they took an appreciable 2.6 per cent share of the total vote, averaging 3.1 per cent in seats they contested. It might not sound like much but, as two academics noted at the time, it was the strongest performance by a minor party in recent British history, suggesting Euroscepticism could be a potent force in British politics when mobilised by a well-resourced organisation.[30]

UKIP, however, had failed to ignite popular interest and the outlook was bleak. Nonetheless, the presence of the two Eurosceptic parties on the ballot did give analysts their first chance to explore the distribution of support for politically organised Euroscepticism in Britain. The Referendum Party had been strongest in the South and East of England where they averaged almost 4 per cent of the vote. In these regions they tended to score highest in seats with large numbers of elderly voters and high levels of agricultural employment, which some traced to anxieties about the impact of EU policy on this industry and the 1996 EU ban on the export of British beef following the 'mad cow disease' crisis. Support was noticeably weaker in Northern England and London, where the average vote for Referendum candidates dropped to 2.1 per cent, and in Scotland to 1.1 per cent, suggesting Euroscepticism was an English rather than a British phenomenon.[31]

UKIP also focused on the South of England, where they stood almost three-quarters of their candidates (one-third of all candidates were fielded in the South-East). The South-East and South-West gave UKIP their strongest results: only one of their 'top ten' performances came outside these regions (the North-East seat of Hexham fought by the party's main organiser, David Lott). UKIP fought only a handful of seats in the North and less than a dozen across Scotland and Wales. This pattern of support mirrored that for the Referendum Party, again suggesting Euroscepticism was mainly a Southern English phenomenon, although some activists like Nigel Farage suggested organisation might also have been a factor: 'The early people in UKIP that were worth a light happened to live south of the M4. Had some of them lived in Nottingham then it might have looked different. But very often a lot of this is more accidental than it is by design. It was as much a function of where we had good people.'

Support for the Eurosceptic parties was also consistently higher in Conservative-controlled seats, although this does not mean their supporters were exclusively disillusioned Conservatives. Research on Referendum Party voters suggested 60 per cent of them had previously supported the Conservatives at the 1992 general election, but 20 per cent had voted Liberal Democrat, 10 per cent had voted Labour and the remainder had supported another party or stayed at home. There was a clear blue tinge, but the Eurosceptics had drawn in many former backers of other political parties as well. Moreover, while Referendum voters were united by their extreme Euroscepticism, an outlook they shared even *before* the emergence of Goldsmith's party, there was actually little evidence that they were consistently right wing: Europe was the only issue on which they placed themselves to the right of the Conservatives and they did not express strong free market beliefs. 'They were not right-wing ideologues', concluded one research team. 'Their vote does not therefore appear to have been either part of a specifically right-wing revolt against the Conservatives or a general diffuse protest vote.'[32] Analysis by John Curtice and Michael Steed also suggested support for the Eurosceptics changed as they became more popular. Where Goldsmith's party or UKIP polled up to 3 per cent, around two-thirds of their support came at the expense of the Conservatives. But when support moved above this level they began to eat into the Labour and Liberal Democrat votes.[33]

Staying in business: a breakthrough for a divided party

The Referendum Party had easily triumphed in the clash of the Eurosceptics, but within three months of the election their founder, Sir James Goldsmith, was dead, and his party soon disbanded. Goldsmith's rebels had soundly beaten UKIP in the rough and tumble of electoral politics, yet had also underscored the potential for a Eurosceptic revolt. With Goldsmith gone, the way was clear for UKIP to try and unify the fragmented Eurosceptic movement ahead of the European Parliament elections in 1999. In a cycle that would become characteristic of UKIP, however, they spurned this opportunity and instead indulged in a bout of infighting. Resentment towards their founder Alan Sked had been growing, with activists complaining about his dictatorial leadership style, intellectual persona, his failure to strike a deal with Goldsmith and rumours of infiltration by right-wing extremists, as we discuss below. With Sked now reiterating his belief that UKIP should not take up any seats they won at the 1999 European Parliament elections, tensions soon escalated into open war, as a faction led by the young Nigel Farage, seasoned organiser David Lott and a new recruit, Michael Holmes, moved to oust their founding leader.

With Sked gone, the leadership of the party passed to Holmes, a millionaire new recruit who talked about using his resources to take the party onto the next level. Farage, though only in his mid-thirties, was made Chairman and given the task of consolidating the divided Eurosceptic scene, which he had begun to do by gathering together the most successful UKIP and Referendum candidates at a meeting. 'Holmes said to me: "Your mission is to recruit the Referendum Party into UKIP." About 160 Referendum candidates joined.' The rival party, which once threatened to destroy UKIP, now became an important source of experienced new recruits, several of whom would rise quickly through the ranks, like Jeffrey Titford, a future leader, and others who would become UKIP MEPs and organise the party in London.

With the leadership crisis out of the way, UKIP began to focus on the 1999 European elections, which offered a fresh opportunity to connect with voters. Importantly for smaller parties like UKIP, these were the first ever British national elections fought using a proportional representation electoral system, allocating seats in proportion to the number of votes received. Smaller parties had a better chance of winning representation under this system than under the first-past-the-post system traditionally used in Britain (see Chapter 6). Morale was also boosted by a European by-election in Yorkshire in 1998 where even under the first-past-the-post system UKIP had won 11.6 per cent, hinting at potential further north. Encouraged, UKIP ran a full slate of candidates and campaigned hard. The overall climate was favourable – around 40 per cent of voters ranked Europe as one of the key issues facing the nation. The party hoped to mobilise these concerns with a typical single-issue campaign focused on withdrawal from the EU, though with some efforts to link Euroscepticism to other populist policy promises, such as using money saved by anti-fraud measures at the European level to build a 'fighting fund' for British people and workers who had been 'persecuted' by Brussels.[34]

Farage instantly realised the significance of proportional represen-tation, and once again dragged David Lott out of retirement to help his campaign in the South-East, as he recalled: 'I put a whole load of phone-lines in, bought a free phone number, advertised it in the odd newspaper advert that we could afford, and the phones started ringing.' During the two months before the election he claims that his cam-paign was generating at least £1,000 every day. There was, however, a new problem. UKIP now faced strong competition for Eurosceptic voters from the Conservative Party under William Hague. The new Conservative leader opposed Britain's entry into the single currency, opposed a common European immigration policy, pledged to reduce Britain's contribution to the EU budget, and promised to stamp down on corruption within European institutions. The Conservatives did not favour withdrawal, but talked of the need for Britain 'to be in Europe, but not run by Europe'. This shift was an important one, and reduced the amount of space available to UKIP. Despite this, when the results arrived, the benefits of proportional representation to small parties, including UKIP, were immediately apparent.

Only two years before the 1999 European elections, UKIP had floundered at a general election, attracting barely 100,000 voters and not even 1 per cent of the total vote. Now, under a proportional sys-tem, they had support from almost 700,000 voters, or 7 per cent of the vote in a very low turnout election. It was enough to put them in fourth place, well ahead of the other minor parties, and to give three of their candidates their first taste of elected office as Members of the European Parliament. Jeffrey Titford was elected in the East, Michael Holmes in the South-West and Farage in the South-East: 'It was a delicious double irony', noted Farage. 'For a parliament I want no part of, under a system I despise, I found myself blinking into the cameras at one in the morning saying how proud I was.'[35]

The location of the seats reflected UKIP's main areas of organisa-tional and electoral strength, who continued to draw most of their activists and votes from Southern England but remained weaker in London and the North, and weakest of all in Scotland and Wales.[36] But, once again, the party could not remain unified for long enough to capitalise on their success. By the autumn of 1999 activists were again fighting with their leader. Holmes' authoritarian style, his paranoia about potential rivals and positive statements about the EU had eroded confidence in his leadership. 'It was Holmes himself', explained one activist. 'He had this feeling that everybody was after him. He didn't like particular people and he wanted to get rid of them.' Tensions again escalated, and soon UKIP's governing body, the National Executive Committee (NEC), was split down the middle. 'Nigel was at war with Holmes', recalled Lott. 'It looked absolutely hopeless, and again as though the party was going to collapse.' Accusations about stolen databases, frozen bank accounts and legal fees were thrown back and forth, until Lott, the veteran organiser, moved to end the dispute and Holmes' leadership by gathering 900 activists together at a now famous extraordinary general meeting, in Westminster in January 2000. But as underlying tensions surfaced, the meeting quickly descended into pandemonium. The atmosphere became so heated that one activist suffered a heart attack. One of those present was Stuart Agnew, in one of his first encounters with the party who, in later years, he would represent in Brussels. 'They very nearly seemed to fall apart. This major row I realised is why my membership application hadn't been processed for five months. Someone had stolen the data. People were getting very restive. Some were leaving, saying, "Well, what is this we've joined? What a mess!"'

Watching the chaos unfold was Farage, who realised his young party had reached a watershed moment. After some delay he took the microphone, rallied the troops and restored calm: 'There were a thousand people in the room. They were walking out by the score, most never to be seen again. If I hadn't walked up to the stage, well that was it. It was over. For UKIP, it was the single most important thing I ever did.' Holmes was ordered to stand down, and again the party narrowly escaped a total implosion, or as one activist recalled: 'We had survived the crisis which most new parties often don't. The personalities tear them apart. We nearly did that. But we stayed in business.'

'Get people standing': the 2001 campaign and glimmers of hope

UKIP had managed to stay afloat but they remained extremely fragile and were soon rocked by a new crisis. From their very beginning the party had anxiously warded off accusations of being linked to the extreme right. In June 1997, at the time of the general election, they had already become familiar with the damage that these claims could cause when a popular television programme, *The Cook Report*, produced evidence that one of Alan Sked's students, Mark Deavin, had infiltrated UKIP to gather information for the extreme right-wing BNP, and their soon-to-be installed new leader, Nick Griffin. The discovery was one of several factors that had led to Sked's demise. But between the European Parliament elections in 1999 and the general election in 2001, these allegations resurfaced very publicly.

Typical of this coverage was an article in *The Times*, in 1999, which reported that UKIP were 'dangerously split over allegations of far-right infiltration'. Other reports featured pictures of Farage attending a meeting with two BNP activists, one of whom was a convicted bomber, although Farage claims this was a deliberate trap. Whatever the truth of the matter, the idea of a link between these two small, right-wing parties took hold in the minds of voters and journalists. It was reinforced by other newspapers like *The Daily Mail*, who told their readers that UKIP 'could be dismissed as the extremist fringe'.[37] Similar arguments were then made by a bitter Alan Sked, who in the national media claimed that his former party had removed an affirmation of non-racism from membership application forms, that Farage had lobbied the party to accept former members of the National Front and that many of those who had left UKIP had done so because of fears over the extent of extremist infiltration.[38] These themes would be recycled as voters headed into the 2001 general election, in articles that variously alleged UKIP members had endorsed the BNP online, made racist comments, indulged in Holocaust revisionism and that senior activists had once enrolled in an extremist party.[39] The party would always vigorously deny these charges, although senior figures like Farage conceded that they often hurt UKIP's reputation: 'There were little bits and bobs of BNP infiltration. They were never numerically very significant but politically always very damaging.'

Despite these ongoing challenges, after Holmes' departure UKIP were at least enjoying a period of relative internal peace. Their new leader was Jeffrey Titford, a former undertaker, Conservative Party supporter and Referendum candidate, who between 2000 and 2002 steered a cautious course, avoiding the bitter internal conflicts that had cost his two predecessors their jobs. Titford's term in charge was one of recovery and consolidation, and he spent much of his time resolving the grievances that had divided the activist base. 'I knew that a lot of plasters had to be stuck on the wounds', he would later recall. He toured the country, giving members an opportunity to vent their disquiet and worked closely with Farage, who had ruled out becoming leader before he was forty. 'I was doing over seventy speeches each year. I sucked up all of this hostility, this poison and everything that was being thrown. I held it together. I thought there was a future for us.' His calm and reassuring manner helped nurse the party back to health after the damage caused by a series of clashes between big egos. But Titford also sought to ready UKIP for the next battle, the general election in 2001, which for three reasons looked to be a tough campaign for the party.

First, the issue agenda was not as favourable as it had been at previous elections. For the average voter, the importance of Europe had fallen sharply. At the time of the 1999 European elections around 37 per cent of voters had ranked Europe as a core concern, but this had now fallen to 24 per cent. The single-issue UKIP had little to say on the two issues that dominated the election, the National Health Service and education. Some activists were certainly interested in widening the message but their party remained seriously hampered by EU tunnel vision. Their manifesto – *Better Off Out* – remained obsessed with the 'threat' from the EU. 'Not only is our country under threat but our entire legal system, our British nationality, our right to free speech and freedom of association, our policy, our armed forces, our own agricultural policy, our right to trade freely and the parliamentary system that underpins British liberty.' Rather than develop a broader set of policies the party doubled down on their hard Euroscepticism, offering voters a speculative 'Independence Dividend' that would arrive following withdrawal from the EU and be spent on agriculture, the NHS, raising the state pension and tax cuts.[40] As at previous elections UKIP appeared to be a narrow pressure group interested in only one issue, as even veteran activists conceded: 'I think the arguments that it was a pressure group rather than a political party held water. There was no doubt about that. It was possibly the most successful pressure group that the country had seen since the Chartists. However, it was a pressure group.'

Second, as at the European elections UKIP faced a Conservative leader who was also willing to campaign hard on Europe. William Hague framed the general election as the last chance for voters to save the pound and promised that he would veto the transfer of further power from Westminster to Brussels, oppose a European army and end EU fraud. While most Conservatives were not advocating withdrawal from the EU, to the average voter their arguments sounded very similar to UKIP's: stop giving power to the Eurocrats in Brussels; oppose the single currency; and protect the national interest. Hague also went further, wrapping his campaign in a populist cloak, demanding the country return to common sense, reduce immigration and warning that Labour was turning Britain into a 'foreign land'.[41] The strategy was not a major success, but it did reduce the amount of space available to UKIP, as Nigel Farage recalled: 'It was not an easy place to be at all. It was very difficult. Blair's political honeymoon was very long and extensive. The Conservative Party appeared to be very Eurosceptic and adopted the pound. They were very, very difficult days.'

A third problem was that UKIP's campaign in 2001 was an organisational shambles. At the beginning of the year Farage had been startled to discover that the NEC had given little consideration to the election, and now spent much of his spare time persuading supporters to stand as candidates. David Lott, who was now national organiser, painted a similar picture of a campaign that was 'a hand-to-mouth effort, with few resources but much enthusiasm'. What money was available came mainly from Paul Sykes, a new donor whose discontent with the soft Euroscepticism of the centre-right led him to finance around twenty million leaflets and advertisements for UKIP, enabling them to spend upwards of £700,000 on the campaign.[42] But little of this was devoted to the kind of campaigning that could deliver decent results at a parliamentary election, as Jeffrey Titford recalled: 'It was really just about being able to put up the badge and say, "yes we are here".'

Despite their poor prospects, however, UKIP did attract interest from some Conservatives who shared their hostility towards the EU and were anxious not to split the anti-Europe vote. Only three months before the election, it was reported that a Conservative peer in the House of Lords, Lord (Malcolm) Pearson of Rannoch, who had known Farage since the mid-1990s, had offered to raise around £2 million for UKIP in exchange for them not standing candidates against Eurosceptic Tories. Pearson's stance that the two parties should combine forces at general elections so as to ensure that the largest possible number of Eurosceptics were in Westminster was a view shared by many within UKIP. Pearson's deal, however, had not been sanctioned by Conservative central office and was quickly taken off the table. Tory ties with UKIP were severed, for now. Conservative insiders claimed such a pact would exaggerate the electoral significance of UKIP, and could damage their own party 'by being associated with an organisation viewed as extremist by many observers'.[43]

As the election neared, UKIP ignored the bleak outlook and talked enthusiastically about poaching votes not only from disaffected Tories but also blue-collar 'Old Labour' voters who were disenchanted with Tony Blair's New Labour rule, as well as protest voters who had previously backed the Liberal Democrats. Some in the party saw little point fighting Conservatives in marginal seats, because of the likely increase in their support as voters turned against the Labour incumbent. Instead, they hoped to broaden their coalition of voters by pitching across the divide. 'At the last election', declared Farage, 'we were out to kick the Tories. This time around we want to put the fear of God into Labour and the Liberal Democrats.'[44] But as one journalist would retort after the results were announced, in the cold light of day these claims looked like little more than hubris.[45]

Overall, UKIP attracted just 1.5 per cent of the total vote in 2001 and averaged 2.1 per cent in seats they contested, both figures below those achieved by the Referendum Party in 1997. UKIP won less than half as many voters as Goldsmith had attracted four years previously, with much of the former Referendum Party vote switching to Hague's Conservatives.[46] Even more worrying than the national picture was the view in some local constituencies.

The general wisdom at elections is that parties should try to increase support incrementally, by targeting key areas where they build bastions of local support over multiple elections. But in 2001, the opposite happened to UKIP – they went backwards where the Eurosceptic vote had been strongest four years previously. On average, support in seats where UKIP or the Referendum Party had stood in 1997 was 1.6 per cent *lower* in 2001, with the sharpest falls coming in seats where the anti-EU vote had been strongest in 1997. Examples included seats like Folkestone and Hythe, where support slumped from 8 per cent in 1997 to 2.6 per cent in 2001, and Suffolk West where support fell from over 7 per cent to 3 per cent. That UKIP had failed to build on Goldsmith's legacy was starkly reflected in their results in the Referendum Party's ten best seats from 1997. Goldsmith's party had finished well above the 5 per cent mark needed to retain their deposits in all ten seats, but UKIP lost their 2001 deposits in eight of them.[47] Only one candidate, Nigel Farage, received a higher share of the vote than his anti-EU predecessors had polled in 1997.

UKIP had failed to consolidate the Referendum vote and not made the local advances they needed to be taken seriously. The party had seats in the European Parliament but had again not made any waves at a Westminster election, even in seats with a track record of Eurosceptic voting. Something was clearly wrong. While smaller parties always struggle in the British system (see Chapter 6), this failure to make an appreciable dent owed much to poor strategy. UKIP were spread far too thin, fielding huge numbers of candidates but failing to build the local concentrations of support they needed to be viable as challengers in the first-past-the-post system. The party did not compete seriously for seats, instead regarding the election more as a marketing exercise, an opportunity to broadcast the UKIP message, rather than an intensive grassroots effort to win local seats, as Farage recalled: 'I viewed the '01 exercise as a very good dress rehearsal for whatever would come later. Get the party on the bloody ballot paper. Get people standing. Get stuff going through doors. Start to build, dare I say it, *the brand*.'

The lack of investment in pavement politics was reflected in the performance. While UKIP stood 428 candidates, almost three times as many as the Greens (the next largest minor party), only six of them retained their deposits. This not only cost the party over £200,000 in lost deposits but underlined how their activists were not interested in the grassroots campaigns needed to develop local strongholds, which could make the party competitive at future general elections. The lack of interest in this more labour intensive, locally focused form of campaigning owed much to the outlook of UKIP activists, who were much more interested in national and international policy debates than pounding the pavement for their candidate. This was a major strategic error, as in the British system new parties cannot hope to break through without intensive campaigns in local constituencies.

Yet there were a few glimmers of hope. For the first time in their history UKIP could now make a realistic claim to be the fourth national party in British politics. In almost two-thirds of the seats they had contested their candidates finished in fourth place, behind the three main parties, but ahead of all the other minnows. The sharp rise in their number of candidates also meant that more voters were encountering UKIP, including in regions where the party had little presence before. Though they continued to focus heavily on the South of England, they increased their presence in the North. In the North-West and Yorkshire the number of UKIP candidates increased more than six-fold on the previous election. There was also evidence the party were beginning to connect with particular sections of British society. As at earlier elections their support was concentrated in areas that tended to be more rural, had large numbers of elderly voters, low numbers of university graduates, in Southern England (excluding London) and in seats controlled by the Conservatives.[48] This suggested UKIP were mobilising a base of elderly, less well educated and Southern voters, though, as before, this may have reflected the location of their activists as much as the geography of potential support.

'It literally just took off': the 2004 campaign and a celebrity recruit

By 2002 the party were again ready for a change of leadership. Having worked hard to steady the ship and heal old divisions, a tired Jeffrey Titford made way for 58-year-old Roger Knapman, a former Conservative MP who had defected to UKIP two years earlier. Knapman was the first UKIP leader with serious mainstream political experience. He had been a Conservative MP for ten years and had served as a parliamentary private secretary and a government whip. He also held solid Eurosceptic credentials, having been among the top ten most rebellious MPs in the Conservative Party after the Maastricht Treaty, casting over forty votes against the party whip.[49] Now, he brought this wealth of experience to the still amateurish and poorly organised UKIP, a resource that was instantly recognised by senior Ukippers: 'He was not like Farage, but then you have to remember that as a party we had no political experience. Nearly all of us were people from out in the sticks, not from the political village. Knapman also didn't stir up trouble. He was a credible leader.'

The new leader wanted to move UKIP on from their general election disappointment, but he faced a tough set of challenges. The party would need to be pushed out of their English comfort zone and widen their reach by contesting elections in Scotland and Wales in 2003. They would need to prepare for the next set of European Parliament elections in 2004. And somehow they would need to replenish an activist base that had stagnated at around 10,000 for years. With a four-year term, Knapman had a lot to do. One of his first moves was to provide Farage and Lott with more of a free hand to address the party's weaknesses. Farage took control of the party's European election committee while Lott was installed as Chairman and took control of attempts to build support in local elections and outside of England. Both men were keenly aware of the need to expand the grassroots base, build a greater awareness of the party and transform UKIP into a professional and modern political force.

UKIP, however, continued to lack a voice in political debate. They may have secured three MEPs in 1999, but by the end of 2003 they were barely registering in the polls, and even struggled to beat the extremist BNP.[50] The worry inside the party was that while many voters sympathised with UKIP's Eurosceptic arguments, most were not even aware of the party and what they stood for: 'Most of the country in January '04 had never bloody heard of us!' explained Farage. 'The fact that we put a few candidates up and a few leaflets out didn't mean they knew who we were. In those days, when out campaigning the general response was "Ukip? What's that?"' This was about to change radically.

In 2003, Roger Knapman happened to meet a former adviser to Bill Clinton on a cruise. A veteran political consultant, the American Dick Morris had orchestrated Clinton's successful bid to become Governor of Arkansas in 1978 before helping craft his strategy for re-election as President in 1996. Sympathetic towards UKIP's aims, Morris agreed to help shape their European election campaign and in early 2004 he summoned the most influential activists to a meeting in Devon. Morris gave UKIP two pieces of advice. First, he urged them to focus on communicating a simple message. In the absence of a referendum on Europe, argued Morris, the phrase 'Say No' could still be enormously powerful. 'I used to think "no" was like "anti"', reflected Farage, 'a bit too negative. But it evolved into *Say No* which was a positive negative; don't just think no, get up off your arse and *say no*.' The slogan would dominate UKIP's campaign, which urged voters to say no to the euro, the EU, a European Constitution, illegal asylum seekers and economic immigrants. 'At last', declared party leaflets, 'a non-racist party with a firm line on immigration'.[51]

Morris' second piece of advice was to launch a billboard offensive, which he argued would help UKIP raise their profile among voters and compensate for the absence of well-known politicians and supporters. 'Morris said an advert in a newspaper is tomorrow's paper for the fish and chips', recalled one activist. 'But with billboards people just keep driving past.' The party took the advice and quickly went about finding sites for the new billboards. 'They were very successful', noted Lott. 'They made us look big, professional and all over the country with these great, big billboards up.' In fact, during the election UKIP would spend almost 70 per cent of their funds on advertisements, dwarfing the amounts that were spent by the three main parties who spent more of their money sending material direct to voters.[52] Dick Morris and the billboards were helping to generate interest in UKIP's campaign but the party were also about to deliver some news that would bring an unprecedented wave of media attention. One activist, who was spending much of his time putting up the billboards, recalled hearing the news as follows: 'We realised as we were putting them up none of the other parties were doing much, which was great. Then I had a call from Farage. "I want you to buy the Sunday papers tomorrow", he said. I asked him why. He said: "You'll see". So off I went to buy the papers. There was the headline: "Robert Kilroy-Silk is going to stand for UKIP".'

Robert Kilroy-Silk or simply 'Kilroy' was a former academic and Labour MP who had become a national celebrity after hosting his own daytime television chat show. 'I was very much in touch with popular opinion', he explained, 'because I had seventy people through my studio every morning. From all over the country; all classes, all colours, all races, all creeds, everything, so I had my finger on the pulse of what people were thinking and feeling.' Kilroy had long been a Eurosceptic, having never been convinced by the case for EU membership, and over the years he had also become frustrated with what he saw as a growing disconnect between the mainstream parties and public opinion. 'I used to say to my friends, Conservative cabinet ministers and Labour: "Look, you're not in touch, particularly on immigration and race".' Shortly before the 2004 European elections Kilroy had been dismissed from his job at the BBC after making derogatory remarks about Arabs in a newspaper column. The event attracted a storm of national publicity, forcing Kilroy to seek refuge at his property in Spain where he planned to plot a comeback. It was at this point that Kilroy and his wife, who in earlier years had considered becoming a Referendum Party candidate, spent time with a supporter of UKIP, Lord Richard Bradford, who encouraged the exiled television presenter to consider standing for the party. 'I got talked into it', recalled Kilroy. 'Pressure from my friends and Jan [his wife] saying it would be fun. I didn't want to get elected. I didn't expect to get elected. I didn't intend to get elected. And then all hell broke loose. It just literally took off.'

Kilroy had needed some convincing and asked the party to fund a campaign that would help publicise his arrival. As Alan Bown, a major donor who has given around £1.4 million to UKIP, recalled: 'He said he would come to us if we had a big promotion, so I financed a big campaign where we put quarter-page adverts in 32 newspapers in the Midlands. We gave him a big campaign so he would throw his hat in the ring.' Though never an official party member, Kilroy was parachuted into the top slot on UKIP's list of candidates in the East Midlands, a region where the party had struggled to connect with voters. He made an immediate impact. The billboards had begun to generate enquiries but now a national celebrity with extensive media experience and contacts brought serious attention. As one journalist observed, with Kilroy on board UKIP had 'achieved a remarkable convergence between protest politics and the celebrity culture', a dynamic that was entrenched by further celebrity endorsements from Joan Collins, Edward Fox, Patrick Moore and the motor racing champion Stirling Moss.[53] 'Mayhem creates mayhem', explained Kilroy, recalling how he was now permanently surrounded by media and witnessing the growing revolt among voters first hand:

> I walked around a market square in Northampton with a man from the local newspaper. I got mobbed. I like people. I can work a crowd. People are all coming around, crossing the street. They all said they felt sorry for me because I had been sacked, or they wanted to tell me they agreed with what I'd said about Arabs, Muslims, or whatever. Then the guy who has his

> notebook, says: 'Mr Kilroy-Silk, how would you describe your reception in Northampton?' I said: 'Well I don't need to, do I? You were there. You witnessed it. You can describe it yourself.' And he said: 'I would say it was presidential.' So I said: 'Well, I wouldn't dissent from that.' He said: 'You're going to walk it, aren't you?'

Kilroy began to dominate UKIP's media coverage and started to broaden their appeal. A natural TV performer, he pushed the party in a more populist direction, railing against the old parties for failing to listen to ordinary voters. 'They are fed up with being lied to', he declared. 'They are fed up with being patronised by the metropolitan political elite.'[54] He also fronted the party's television election broadcast where he laid out a broad, hard-hitting populist agenda: 73 million migrants from Central and Eastern Europe were about to descend into Britain; hospital waiting lists were too long; schools were overcrowded; pensioners were living in poverty; and national decisions were being made by unelected Eurocrats in Brussels. The broadcast finished with Kilroy hammering home the Dick Morris message: 'Say no to uncontrollable EU immigration. Say no to the European Union spending your money, and say no to this country being governed by Brussels.'[55]

The message was clearly resonating with voters, though with polling sparse it was hard to quantify the effect. At the end of May, one poll caused a minor sensation when it suggested UKIP were now on 18 per cent, ahead of the Liberal Democrats among those who said they were certain to vote in the European election.[56] UKIP were also rapidly winning over new members attracted by their celebrity fuelled campaign; membership almost tripled from around 8,500 in 2001 to 26,000 in 2004. But it was not all good news. Kilroy was also beginning to have a negative impact on the small party that had agreed, nervously, to host his political ambitions. His intention to stand as a UKIP candidate in the European elections was reported in the first week of May, but within ten days Kilroy was already hinting to journalists about plans to take over his new party.[57] Aside from the intense media interest, Kilroy's ambitions were being fuelled by the multi-millionaire donor Paul Sykes, who saw a Kilroy-led UKIP as a potent weapon that could, finally, force the centre-right to deliver a referendum on EU membership. With this goal in mind Sykes pledged another £100,000 to fund a further 2,000 billboards. According to Kilroy, a further injection of funds was also promised should he become leader: 'Sykes wanted to take over the party and establish a headquarters in London. He was going to spend a lot of money. He was talking *millions*. But only if I became leader.' In fact UKIP were already spending record amounts on their campaign, as Morris had urged them to do. When the election was over it would be revealed that around £10 million had been spent by all of the main parties on the European elections. Of this, UKIP spent £2.3 million, more than Labour or the Liberal Democrats and more than ten times as much as the extreme right BNP. Only the Conservative Party would spend more.[58]

By the end of May, a few days before voters went to the polls, several opinion polls suggested a surge in support for UKIP, which was creating panic in Conservative central office. This anxiety about UKIP's challenge was not calmed when four Conservative peers in the House of Lords, including Lord Pearson, had the whip removed for publicly urging voters to support UKIP.[59] The Conservatives' response was reflected in a briefing sent to their candidates, which encouraged them to frame UKIP as a party that was 'full of cranks and political gadflies' and highlight their 'links with the Far Right'. As was becoming tradition as polling day neared, Alan Sked also resurfaced in the media to attack his former party for losing their way.[60] But these efforts did nothing to dent UKIP's new popularity; indeed attacks from the mainstream may have burnished their populist appeal. Reflecting the dilemma facing the main parties, one journalist remarked: 'They could point out that the party has more than its fair share of freaks and obsessives. They could dismiss it as a single-issue movement, with no prospect of forming a government. They could portray it as kooky, inept and hopelessly divided. There would be a measure of truth in all these charges. But the voters don't seem to care.'[61]

TABLE 1.1 UKIP performance at European Parliament elections, 1999–2009

Region	1999 Vote %	Change %	2004 Vote %	Change %	2009 Vote %	Change %
Eastern	8.9	–	19.6	+10.7	19.6	0.0
East Midlands	7.6	–	26.1	+18.5	16.5	–9.6
London	5.4	–	12.2	+6.8	10.8	–1.4
North-East	8.8	–	12.2	+3.4	15.4	+3.2
North-West	6.6	–	12.1	+5.5	15.9	+3.8
South-East	9.7	–	19.5	+9.8	18.8	–0.7
South-West	10.7	–	22.6	+11.9	22.1	–0.5
West Midlands	5.9	–	17.5	+11.6	21.3	+3.8
Yorkshire	7.1	–	14.0	+6.9	17.4	+3.4
Scotland	1.3	–	6.7	+5.4	5.2	–1.5
Wales	3.2	–	10.5	+7.3	12.8	+2.3

When all votes were counted, the 2004 European elections delivered UKIP by far the best set of results in their brief history. The party attracted over 2.6 million voters and vaulted ahead of the Liberal Democrats into third place overall, only seven points behind the incumbent Labour Party. UKIP were far ahead of other fringe parties, polling more than twice as many votes as the Greens and three times as many as the BNP. Nationally, their share of the vote more than doubled to 16 per cent, enabling the party to quadruple their representation in the European Parliament from three to twelve seats. Kilroy was one of the new MEPs, having played a central role in their success, as even a wary Nigel Farage acknowledged: 'Without any shadow of a doubt, because what it [Kilroy] proved was that UKIP could pack an electoral punch.' In the East Midlands Kilroy helped increase UKIP's share of the vote by a striking 19 per cent, enabling his new party to finish second and ahead of Labour. They also finished second in their three strongest regions of the South-West, South-East and Eastern England, and although they remained weaker in Northern England, London, Scotland and Wales they advanced strongly everywhere (see Table 1.1).

An opportunity squandered: Kilroy and the attempted coup

UKIP, however, had seemingly learned nothing from their past failure to capitalise on advances. The party once again squandered a golden opportunity, as a new bout of scandal and infighting broke out. Celebrations were first cut short by the revelation that one of the party's new MEPs, Ashley Mote, was on trial for housing benefit fraud. Mote had not made the party aware of the case, and they quickly withdrew the whip, but it produced a damaging wave of negative press, weeks after UKIP's electoral triumph. The party had also overstretched itself, spending unprecedented amounts of money on ensuring success, but leaving them with few resources to capitalise on these gains. 'We've thrown the kitchen sink at these elections', remarked Farage to one journalist. 'Financially and physically, we're spent.'[62] There was little money or energy left over to invest in consolidating the growth, widening their appeal still further and preparing for a general election that was less than one year away. Some activists would later claim that the party simply 'went to sleep' over the summer of 2004.[63] But a far bigger problem was the conflict that had begun to erupt inside the party.

The European election success had further emboldened UKIP's celebrity recruit, who was now determined to take control of his new party. Kilroy had finally had a chance to spend time with his fellow UKIP MEPs in the European Parliament and was not impressed with his new colleagues: 'We went to Brussels and were appalled by the people we met. I might have moved to the Right but all my principles are still liberal socialist. I'm not homophobic. I'm not racist. I'm not xenophobic. I believe in a woman's right to choose, and in feminism. I'm against the death penalty, all those kinds of things.' Kilroy also talks of irregularities in party finances, which further convinced him of the need for new leadership: 'There were a lot of things about money, which I didn't want to know about and I didn't want to be a part of ... I thought I've got to lead it and change it, or I couldn't belong to it.' His quest to take control of UKIP would now dominate the party's agenda, and its media coverage, for months.

Few voters were as yet aware of these internal tensions, as shown by UKIP's strong showing in a parliamentary by-election in Hartlepool three months after the European elections, where the party won 10.2 per cent of the vote, finishing third and ahead of the Conservatives. It was at that time their strongest ever constituency result. Kilroy, who was already beginning to exert pressure on Knapman to stand down, was further encouraged by the result and now pushed UKIP into a protracted civil war, a period that Nigel Farage would later describe as 'just a fucking nightmare'. One week after the Hartlepool result, Kilroy addressed UKIP's annual conference and urged members to force Knapman – who still had two years left in his term – to resign as leader. He also outlined his strategy for transforming UKIP into a major force, one aspect of which would involve standing candidates against Eurosceptic Conservatives. Kilroy had little time for those in UKIP who favoured an electoral alliance with Eurosceptic Conservative MPs. 'The Conservative party is dying', he declared. 'Why would you want to give it the kiss of life? What we have to do is to kill it and replace it.'[64]

His argument touched directly on an unresolved tension within UKIP. But whereas in the past this tension had played out behind closed doors, encouraged by Kilroy some activists now wrote in to national newspapers to make their grievances public: 'Robert Kilroy-Silk represents the view that UKIP should develop into a mass movement capable of winning seats at Westminster and taking a major role at the heart of British politics', they explained. 'A small element of the Party, with disproportionate power, seem to prefer that UKIP should be just a vehicle for changing the Conservative Party's policy on the European Union.' The latter view, they continued, was contrary to UKIP's founding principles and the wishes of the majority of ordinary members.[65] In the end, Kilroy won the argument. Most delegates at the party conference voted to support his strategy, choosing to set out their own stall at British general elections regardless of the views of the local Conservative MP.

The problem for Kilroy, however, was that his speech instantly alienated more influential voices in the party, including their major funder Paul Sykes, who favoured putting pressure on the Conservatives, but certainly not 'killing' them.[66] Kilroy had also not earned his stripes inside a party that put strong emphasis on long-term commitment. While some supported his ideas, activists who had weathered past factional storms were not about to hand their party over to an untested newcomer, as Titford explained: 'I think Kilroy thought UKIP were like the other political parties. But we were a new party, and there is something quite distinct about UKIP that is not in the other parties. It is very hard to define. I always used to say we had 20,000 members but 30,000 egos.' Kilroy had simply not proved himself in the eyes of members, and lacked the activist track record that might have reassured those anxious about his volatile nature and underlying motives, as one noted:

'Kilroy joined, got elected and demanded that everybody vow to support him. Er, no. Actually you've got to do stuff before the party votes for you. He did not understand how, because he was so famous, so wonderful and so tanned, that the party would not elect him without a claim. It's an organisation, with volunteers who work hard. You don't just turn up, shine your teeth and suddenly you are the leader.'

Aware of these views among stalwarts, and also aware that Kilroy did not yet have mass support inside the party, senior activists like Farage and Lott swore allegiance to Knapman and began working to thwart the attempted coup. Their determination to oppose Kilroy only strengthened when he turned down their offers to be installed as deputy leader and then campaign manager for the 2005 general election, and became increasingly critical of UKIP in public. The conflict was now playing itself out in the newspapers and beginning to undermine the progress that had been made. Income slumped by 70 per cent and morale plummeted, as one activist recalled:

We really didn't need the battle. All we were getting was negative publicity. We had absolutely no money. Sykes had walked away. What we needed was Kilroy-Silk to help raise our profile in the northern half of the country and Farage in the South. We could all move on together, but it was so disappointing. All people could talk about was whether you were

going to side with Kilroy. We were completely self-absorbed. I
was really quite depressed for the remainder of the year thinking, are we ever going to get over this?

In October 2004, Kilroy sought to usurp the old guard by writing to local branches and attempting to call an extraordinary meeting. Knapman, however, fired back by surveying local organisers and
claiming to have support from more than 100 of them, compared to
Kilroy's 25.[67] Kilroy's refusal to take advice had also quickly lost him
any remaining sympathy from activists who might otherwise have
brokered some kind of deal, like David Lott who moved to defuse
the situation by approaching Kilroy and his wife directly, asking them
to postpone the leadership bid until the end of Knapman's term as
leader, which still had two years left to run: 'I said to them, "I don't
think either of you understand what UKIP is made of. The activists
won't have you." Kilroy couldn't accept that. She thought I was just
bullshitting. And so we all turned on him.'

Having only been involved with UKIP for barely four months, and
talking to just a handful of activists, Kilroy had misread the party and
his own level of support. As the attempted coup rapidly fell apart he
had no option but to abandon UKIP, which he did in January 2005,
less than one year after joining. Though some within the party celebrated his departure, others had mixed feelings, aware that Kilroy had
helped to attract new groups of voters to UKIP who had shunned or
ignored them before, as Titford recounts: 'We realised that many thousands of votes had come because of Kilroy, and they would have been
the Labour vote because Kilroy was a true socialist in all his ways and
thoughts and policies. These were people who had sympathised with
him and we knew we were going to have trouble holding that vote.'

The question of UKIP's appeal among Labour voters is one that
we will return to. But at the time, Kilroy's parting shot was yet another
tirade against his former party for squandering 'a golden opportunity
to reach out to those who have grown tired of the old parties with
their lies, their deceit, their broken promises, their discredited pledge
cards and their slanging matches'.[68] Though their parting was bitter,
Kilroy's brief encounter with UKIP had helped bring the small party
unparalleled levels of success and publicity, helping them reach new

groups of voters and transforming them into a household name. Few voters after the 2004 European elections and Kilroy's intervention were unaware of UKIP or what they stood for. He had also pushed some within the party to consider their wider potential among a disenchanted mass of voters who felt let down by New Labour. Ultimately, however, all of this was short-lived, fading as Kilroy, in the words of one activist, 'disappeared in a puff of vanity'.

Notes

1 The 1997 general election produced a historic total of 418 Labour MPs. Meanwhile, political commentators would also need to open the history books to find a similarly small Conservative parliamentary group, which followed the famous Liberal landslide in 1906 when the Tories were left with only 156 seats.

2 Aleks Szczerbiak and Paul Taggart (2002) *The Party Politics of Euroscepticism in EU Member and Candidate States*, Sussex European Institute Working Paper no. 51. Also Aleks Szczerbiak and Paul Taggart (2000) *Opposing Europe: Party Systems and Opposition to the Union, the Euro and Europeanisation*, Sussex European Institute Working Paper no. 1.

3 UK Independence Party Manifesto 1997 (Preface by Dr Alan Sked).

4 Peter Oborne, 'Ministers facing Euro-rebel threat', *Evening Standard*, 7 February 1992.

5 Alan Sked stood for the Liberals in the constituency of Paisley at the 1970 general election, polling 6.2 per cent of the vote.

6 Margaret Thatcher, Speech to the College of Europe ('The Bruges Speech'). Available online via the Margaret Thatcher Foundation: http://www.margaretthatcher.org/document/107332 (accessed 30 July 2013); 'The patriotic "pipsqueak" of Bruges', *The Sunday Times*, 16 June 1991; Alan Sked, 'Debate for Maastricht', *The Times*, 12 October 1991; Sheila Gunn, 'Anti-unionists to fight at election', *The Times*, 14 November 1991.

7 'Bruges bruises', *The Times*, 16 May 1992.

8 Peter Oborne, 'Ministers facing Euro-rebel threat', *Evening Standard*, 7 February 1992.

9 At the 1992 general election, Anti-Federalist candidates contested Bath (0.2 per cent), Bristol West (0.1), Chelsea (0.3), Cornwall South East (0.4), Hammersmith (0.1), Harrow East (0.1), Kensington (0.2), Kingston-upon-Thames (0.1), Leominster (1.1), Lewisham West (0.3), Oxford West and Abingdon (0.2), Pembroke (0.3), Pendle (0.5), Richmond and Barnes (0.1), Staffordshire Moorlands (3.4), Thurrock (0.2) and Westminster North (0.3).

10 Alan Sked contested a by-election in Newbury in May 1993, where he polled 1 per cent of the vote, and a by-election in Christchurch in July 1993, where he polled 1.6 per cent of the vote.

11 The National Front polled 16 per cent in West Bromwich in 1973 and 11 per cent in Newham in 1974.

12 The BNP was formed and led for seventeen years by John Tyndall who previously led the NF and had been active in neo-Nazi groups like the National Socialist Movement, in which he praised Nazi Germany, white supremacism and demanded the overthrow of liberal democracy. See Matthew J. Goodwin (2011) *New British Fascism: Rise of the British National Party*, Abingdon: Routledge.

13 The BNP candidate was elected in the Millwall ward of Tower Hamlets on 16 September 1993, after polling 34 per cent of the vote. This isolated BNP victory followed a concerted effort by some activists to experiment seriously with an electoral strategy which fused their demand for 'rights for whites' with grievances in the local working-class community over a lack of social housing, and delivered the message through face-to-face contact with voters. This marked a departure from the extreme right's traditional strategy, which saw confrontational and often violent street demonstrations – rather than votes – as the route into power, an approach that was rooted in the experiences of inter-war Europe and, in Britain, Oswald Mosley's British Union of Fascists. For some inside the BNP, like young activist Nick Griffin, these intensive local campaigns would prove highly influential in later years. See Goodwin, *New British Fascism*.

14 In June 1994 UKIP candidates also contested parliamentary by-elections in Barking (2.1 per cent), Dagenham (2.1 per cent), Eastleigh (1.7 per cent) and Newham North East (2.6 per cent).

15 Daniel Foggo, 'Chairman resigns (twice) in furious UKIP row', *The Sunday Telegraph*, 9 October 2005.

16 'Party to be re-launched', *Press Association*, 13 September 1993.

17 Sir James Goldsmith speech to Referendum Party supporters, as featured on a VHS video sent to British voters. Available on YouTube: http://www.youtube.com/watch?v=6GWkNVjvQLU (accessed 19 August 2013). See also Nicholas Wood, 'Goldsmith forms a Euro referendum party', *The Times*, 28 November 1994.

18 Overall the Referendum Party spent £7,208,000 on advertising during the campaign, although £6,768,000 of this was devoted to press advertising. David Butler and Dennis Kavanagh (1997) *The British General Election of 1997*, Basingstoke: Macmillan, pp. 72, 242.

19 Subrata Mitra (1988) 'The National Front: A single-issue movement?' *West European Politics*, 11(2): 47–64 (p. 47). See also Cas Mudde (1999) 'The single-issue party thesis: Extreme right parties and the immigration issue', *West European Politics*, 22(3): 182–97.

20 Nicholas Wood, 'Goldsmith forms a Euro referendum party', *The Times*, 28 November 1994.

21 Or, in the words of Goldsmith: 'The purpose of its existence is simply to ensure that, should the politicians refuse, the citizens of the United Kingdom will nonetheless have an opportunity to decide for themselves their future in Europe.' J. Goldsmith, 'Why we need a referendum', *The Times*, 27 January 1995. On the single-issue biodegradable party see *The Times*, 25 October 1995; on the latter quote see Referendum Party video. Available on YouTube: http://www.youtube.com/watch?v=6GWkNVjvQLU (accessed 19 August 2013).

22 Figures on the importance of issues (or their salience) taken from the Ipsos MORI Social and Political Trends archive. Available online: http://ipsos-mori.com (accessed 9 July 2013). On rising Euroscepticism see Anthony Heath, Roger Jowell, Bridget Taylor and Katarina Thomson (1998) 'Euroscepticism and the Referendum Party', in David Denver, Justin Fisher, Philip Cowley and Charles Pattie (eds.) *British Elections and Parties Review, Volume 8*, London: Frank Cass, pp. 95–110.

23 'According to opinion poll findings', explained UKIP in their 1997 manifesto, '40% of the British people want to quit the EU forthwith and another 40% want merely to trade with it. This means that, potentially, 80% of the electorate could be converted to vote for the UKIP, if its credibility continues to grow. Fortunately for Britain, it is continuing to grow.' UK Independence Party General Election Manifesto 1997.

24 Calculated through search tools on Nexis, using the terms 'Referendum Party' and 'UK Independence Party' in UK-based newspapers in 1997.

25 UK Independence Party Manifesto 1997 (Preface by Dr Alan Sked).

26 Rebecca Smithers, 'Quit Europe party claims it will save £19bn a year', *The Guardian*, 8 April 1997.

27 At the UKIP annual conference in 1996 Sked identified the following as target seats at the 1997 general election, all of which were held by the Conservatives: Salibury, Hexham, Romsey and Waterside, Hastings and Rye, Totnes and Teignmouth. The party also noted its interest in Northumbria, where David Lott stood in Hexham. David Cracknell, 'I won't defect – Gorman', *Press Association*, 12 October 1996; also Rebecca Smithers, 'Quit Europe party claims it will save £19bn a year', *The Guardian*, 8 April 1997.

28 Peter Clarke, 'Goldsmith's kamikaze raid', *The Sunday Times*, 13 August 1995.

29 UKIP candidates finished above Referendum Party candidates in Romsey and Glasgow Anniesland (in the latter by only two votes).

30 John Curtice and Michael Steed (1997) 'Appendix 2: The results analyzed', in Butler and Kavanagh, *The British General Election of 1997*, p. 305.

31 Anthony F. Heath, Roger M. Jowell and John K. Curtice (2002) *The Rise of New Labour: Party Politics and Voter Choices*, Oxford: Oxford University Press, p. 73; Curtice and Steed, 'Appendix 2: The results analyzed', p. 306.

32 Curtice and Steed calculate that, on average, Referendum Party candidates polled 3.6 per cent in seats that were being defended by Conservatives, and 2.5 per cent in seats that were being defended by Labour. Meanwhile, we calculate that over four-fifths of all seats contested by UKIP in 1997 were held by the Tories, and in these seats the party averaged 0.9 per cent, compared to 0.6 per cent in Labour held seats. Curtice and Steed, 'Appendix 2: The results analyzed'. Heath, Jowell and Curtice, *The Rise of New Labour*, p. 74.

33 Curtice and Steed, 'Appendix 2: The results analyzed'. Heath, Jowell and Curtice, *The Rise of New Labour*. See also Ian McAllister and Donald T. Studlar (2000) 'Conservative Euroscepticism and the Referendum Party in the 1997 British general election', *Party Politics*, 6(3): 359–71.

34 Michael White, 'Hague tries to pacify party', *The Guardian*, 19 May 1999. According to the Ipsos MORI Issued Index, in June 1999 37 per cent of voters ranked Europe/the Common Market/Single Currency as one of the most important issues facing the country, followed by the National Health Service (35 per cent) and Education (29 per cent). Available online: http://www.ipsos-mori.com/researchpublications/researcharchive (accessed 18 June 2013).

35 Matthew Engel, 'The outsiders', *The Guardian*, Features pages, p. 2.

36 UKIP polled 8.9 per cent in Eastern, 7.6 per cent in East Midlands, 5.4 per cent in London, 8.8 per cent in the North East, 6.6 per cent in the North West, 9.7 per cent in the South East, 10.7 per cent in South West, 5.9 per cent in West Midlands, 7.1 per cent in Yorkshire, 1.3 per cent in Scotland and 3.2 per cent in Wales. Figures obtained from the UK Office of the European Parliament.

37 On 'dangerously split' see Andrew Pierce, 'BNP link allegation hits Euro party', *The Times*, 5 June 1999; on right-wing newspapers see Edward Amory, 'Your chance to save the pound', *The Daily Mail*, 8 June 1999.

38 Alan Sked, 'I would advise people on Thursday to help the Tory revival', *The Times*, 8 June 1999.

39 Roland Watson, 'Far right fear splits UKIP as 200 leave party', *The Times*, 29 April 2000; Jay Rayner, 'Far right invades anti-Europe party', *The Observer*, 21 May 2000; David Hencke, 'UKIP hit by new row over Holocaust denial', *The Guardian*, 27 February 2001.

40 UK Independence Party Manifesto 2001.

41 Sarah Womack, 'Hague in retreat over talk of "foreign land"', *The Daily Telegraph*, 10 March 2001; see also Conservative Party (2001) *2001 Conservative Party General Election Manifesto: Time for Common Sense.*

42 According to data collected by the Electoral Commission, UKIP spent a total of £743,904 on the campaign across the UK. Electoral Commission (2002) *Election 2001: Campaign Spending.* Nicholas Watt and David Hencke, '£10 million Sykes gift boosts UKIP', *The Guardian*, 18 May 2001; Ben Russell, 'Europe Independence Party claims it will have 400 candidates', *The Independent*, 15 May 2001; Patrick Wintour, 'Football club owner funds anti-EU party', *The Guardian*, 30 April 2001; UKIP Statement of Accounts 2002, obtained from the Electoral Commission.

43 On the proposed pact see Patrick Wintour and Michael White, '£2 million pound deal to shield Tory marginals', *The Guardian*, 3 March 2001; Andrew Pierce, 'Tory peer offered anti-EU party £2 million to drop candidates', *The Times*, 2 March 2001; Marie Woolf, 'Tories deny talks with anti-EU party', *The Independent*, 2 March 2001; Andrew Sparrow, 'Tory peer offered £2 million election deal', *The Daily Telegraph*, 2 March 2001. On the views of Conservative insiders see Andrew Pierce 'How Euro-plot was born among the heather', *The Times*, 2 March 2001.

44 UKIP strategists pointed to seats like the Liberal Democrat-controlled Devon North, and Devon West and Torridge, alongside the Labour-controlled seats of Falmouth and Camborne, and Stafford. Andrew Sparrow, 'Anti-EU party targets Labour and Lib Dems', *The Daily Telegraph*, 8 December 2000; on UKIP strategy in 2001 see also David Lott, 'UKIP strategy to effect change', *The Times*, 19 March 2001.

45 Lucy Ward and Paul Kelso, 'UKIP: anti-euro campaign falls flat in "disappointing night"', *The Guardian*, 8 June 2001.

46 John Curtice and Michael Steed (2002) 'Appendix 2: An analysis of the results', in David Butler and Dennis Kavanagh *The British General Election of 2001*, Basingstoke: Palgrave Macmillan.

47 These ten seats were Harwich (9.2 per cent in 1997 to 5.1 per cent in 2001), Folkestone and Hythe (8 per cent to 2.6 per cent), Suffolk West (7.6 to 3.1 per cent), Reigate (7 to 2.7 per cent), St Ives (6.7 to 3.9 per cent), Cotswold (6.6. to 2.9 per cent), Yeovil (6.6 to 2.3 per cent), Falmouth and Camborne (6.6 to 2.8 per cent) and Truro and St Austell (6.5 to 3.3 per cent. In Bexhill and Battle Nigel Farage polled 7.8 per

cent, compared to the Referendum Party's 6.7 per cent in 1997. See also Curtice and Steed, 'Appendix 2: An analysis of the results', p. 325.

48 As in 1997 only one of UKIP's ten strongest results came outside Southern England, which was Stafford in the West Midlands. In numerical order the top ten seats were Bexhill and Battle (7.8 per cent), Totnes (6.1 per cent), Devon East (5.6 per cent), Stafford (5.2 per cent), Harwich (5.1 per cent), Devon North (5 per cent), Esher and Walton (4.9 per cent), Chichester (4.8 per cent), Devon West and Torridge (4.8 per cent) and Arundel and South Downs (4.7 per cent). As before, UKIP fielded the largest number of candidates in the South East while their share of the vote was highest in the South East, South West and Eastern regions but lowest in London, Scotland and Wales. In 2001 over half of all seats contested by UKIP had Labour incumbents, while the Conservatives controlled one-third and the remainder were split between the Liberal Democrats, Plaid Cymru and the Scottish National Party (SNP). But UKIP continued to poll strongest in seats that were in Conservative hands: they averaged 2.7 per cent in Conservative seats, but 1.8 per cent in Labour seats.

49 Philip Cowley (1999) 'The parliamentary party', in P. Dorey (ed.) *The Major Premiership*, Basingstoke: Macmillan, pp. 1–25.

50 Less than 1 per cent of respondents in eight Ipsos MORI polls at the end of 2003 declared an intention to support UKIP. Support for the BNP was about the same level.

51 UKIP 2004 European Election leaflet for London. Available online via the British Election Ephemera Archive: http://www.by-elections. co.uk/ (accessed 2 August 2013).

52 Based on estimates gathered from the Electoral Commission UKIP spent 67 per cent of their campaign expenditure on advertising, as compared, for example, to 18 per cent for the Conservatives and Labour, and 10 per cent for the Liberal Democrats. In contrast, whereas the Conservatives spent 55 per cent on sending material to voters, Labour spent 42 per cent and the Liberal Democrats spent 71 per cent, UKIP spent only 13 per cent. See Electoral Commission (2005) *The 2004 European Parliamentary Elections in the United Kingdom: Campaign Spending*, p. 25.

53 Andrew Sparrow, 'Kilroy-Silk turns on the charm for voters', *The Daily Telegraph*, 27 May 2004.

54 Andrew Sparrow, '"Voters fed up with lying elites", says Kilroy-Silk', *The Daily Telegraph*, 13 May 2004.

55 UKIP European Parliament Election Broadcast, 2004. Similar messages were delivered to voters on leaflets from UKIP, which featured pictures

of Kilroy while stating: 'We have to fight to get our country back from Brussels, from the politically correct brigade, and from the patronising political class in Westminster.' UKIP 2004 European Election leaflet for the East Midlands. Available online via the British Election Ephemera Archive: http://www.by-elections.co.uk/ (accessed 2 August 2013).

56 Andrew Sparrow, 'Surge by UKIP hits big parties', *The Daily Telegraph*, 24 May 2004.

57 Jasper Gerard, 'Stand up and be counted for Little England', *The Sunday Times*, 16 May 2004.

58 Based on data compiled by the Electoral Commission UKIP spent a total of £2,361,754 on the campaign, as compared to the Conservative Party's £3,130,266, Labour's £1,707,224, the Liberal Democrats' £1,188,861 and the BNP's £228,813. It is also worth noting that UKIP focused the vast majority of this money on England, spending £2,124,733 as compared to only £148,577 in Scotland and £88,444 in Wales. Electoral Commission (2005) *The 2004 European Parliamentary Elections in the United Kingdom: Campaign Spending.*

59 The letter was signed by five Tory peers – Pearson, Baroness Cox of Queensbury, Lord Laing of Dunphall, Lord Stevens of Ludgate and Lord Willoughby de Broke, as well as seven crossbenchers. Andy McSmith, 'Howard sacks peers for endorsing UKIP', *Independent on Sunday*, 30 May 2004.

60 Toby Helm, 'Howard rages at UKIP "gadflies"', *The Daily Telegraph*, 31 May 2004; Alan Sked, 'As founder of the UKIP I will vote Tory', 30 May 2004.

61 'UKIP scoring on the anti-Brussels card', *The Daily Telegraph*, 24 May 2004.

62 Sarah Hall and Ian Black, 'UKIP starts to plan its wrecking tactics', *The Guardian*, 15 June 2004.

63 Paul Nuttall speech to UKIP conference, Southport, 2009.

64 Andrew Porter and Dipesh Gadher, 'Howard is warned heads must roll', *The Sunday Times*, 3 October 2004.

65 See, for example, a letter written by Gerard Batten MEP, Damian Hockney (Leader of the UKIP group on the London Assembly), the National Vice Chairman, NEC member and party chairman. 'Letter: Debate within UKIP', *The Independent*, 21 October 2004.

66 'Kilroy-Silk: We will still fight every seat', *Evening Standard*, 5 October 2004.

67 On income see Brendan Carlin, 'Kilroy threatens another tilt at UKIP leadership', *The Daily Telegraph*, 30 November 2004. Some media accounts put the figures at 147 for Knapman, 29 for Kilroy-Silk and 32 undecided. See Brendan Carlin, 'UKIP snub for Kilroy-Silk', *The*

Daily Telegraph, 20 October 2004; Michael White, 'UKIP branches reject Kilroy-Silk', *The Guardian*, 20 October 2004; Brendan Carlin, 'Kilroy-Silk faces moves to force him out of UKIP', *The Daily Telegraph*, 21 October 2004; Melissa Kite, 'The "orange" Kilroy-Silk would be a useless leader for UKIP', *The Sunday Telegraph*, 24 October 2004.

68 Matthew Tempest, 'Kilroy quit UKIP "charade"', *The Guardian*, 20 January 2005.

2
BECOMING A SERIOUS CONTENDER

Infighting, like a dismal election result, can have a devastating impact on a party's morale. In the aftermath of the 2004 European elections, UKIP went from elation to despair in just a few months. Wrenching internal disputes had once again threatened to undo their historic electoral achievement. While activists should have been enjoying their new success, the fallout from Robert Kilroy-Silk's departure left them weakened and demoralised. Instead of charging into the next battle with the main parties, the general election in 2005, they could only limp. Watching from the sidelines, one journalist spoke for many when he wondered whether UKIP's 'bubble may have burst'.[1]

As the 2005 general election approached, the party's deteriorating prospects were clear to all, including the handful of journalists who had gathered at the launch of the UKIP manifesto. They were met by a beleaguered Roger Knapman, who asked whether they had questions. 'What happened to the UKIP?' asked one. 'Where is the breakthrough in domestic politics so confidently predicted after your triumph at the European elections last June?' While apologising for sounding unsympathetic, the journalist continued to explain how she was now only one of a few in Westminster assigned to report on UKIP. 'I share your fate', she continued. 'If you are, as you say, the gadflies of British politics, I am the flea on the gadfly, and pickings have been thin.'[2]

Dusting off and moving on: the 2005 campaign

The problem was now a familiar one to UKIP. Their European election campaign had been a triumph, but as soon as they were back at a general election two key political ingredients – unity and momentum – suddenly vanished. It was not a new sensation for senior activists, who remembered the infighting that had undermined the campaigns in 1997 and 2001, which failed to produce anything close to the level of support seen at European elections. By now, UKIP should have been maturing into a serious domestic challenger. Instead, they appeared as a political phenomenon that could only thrive once every five years, when the issue agenda and the electoral rules were tilted in their favour.

The divisions in 2004 left a depressing legacy. National party income fell back from around £2 million to less than £700,000 as major donors fled the infighting, forcing the closure of a call centre and the downsizing of operations. Membership also fell off a cliff, down nearly a third from 26,000 in 2004 to around 17,500 by the end of 2005, and would fall further. This slump owed much to a failure to sustain the loyalty of new recruits who had joined during the excitement of the 2004 campaign. The period of division and decline now ensured that UKIP had little energy, money or activists for a general election, and would cast a longer shadow. 'After Kilroy', recalled an exasperated Farage, 'we had a couple of years of real misery, real doldrums. Banging our heads against a brick wall.'

The dire state of affairs was immediately evident to David Lott who, once again, postponed his retirement to coordinate the 2005 campaign, recalling: 'We'd had the Kilroy-Silk affair and the membership started crashing. I think that the whole business, in the end, set the party back five years. I think we lost any credibility that we'd gained at the European elections, and it was bleak. I knew that we weren't going to do very well.' Whereas UKIP had thrown at least £2 million into the 2004 campaign, the national budget for the general election was less than 10 per cent of this figure, just £198,000.[3] With this paltry war chest, Lott was forced to run a radically different campaign to that which had propelled UKIP to the forefront of British politics only a few months earlier:

> It was a money-less campaign. It made it a nightmare to run it. Nearly all candidates paid their own deposits. Alan [Bown – a major donor] was paying for three people to help me. That

was all I had: a five-man campaign. That was it. It was a mess. Then they all went down with flu. We were in the midst of getting all of the leaflets organised and there was literally me, on my own. This was as the postal deliveries were going out, about two weeks before the election. It bloody nearly killed me. It was nightmarish. The candidates never really knew how desperate it was.

Nor did the wider political climate offer encouragement. By 2005 the issue agenda of British politics had moved decidedly against a party that continued to focus heavily on attacking the EU. Europe could always be relied upon to excite UKIP activists, but the issue was only a remote concern for the electorate. On the eve of the 2005 election, less than 10 per cent of voters considered Europe one of the most important issues facing Britain, leading one journalist to remark: 'The European dog has not just failed to bark. It hasn't even stirred from its slumbers.'[4] Now that the European elections had passed, most voters lost interest in the issue and focused on domestic priorities, including the NHS, education, crime, defence, the economy and pensions, on which UKIP had little to say. While the party talked of the need to develop a wider appeal, they remained fanatically obsessed with the EU, and still had little in the way of credible domestic policies, as Lott recalled: 'Although we had other policies, they were pretty primitive to be quite honest. It was something that wasn't looked at until after that campaign; the whole question of policy and to take it a bit more seriously.'[5] The party's continuing single-issue focus was also instantly apparent to new recruits, like Paul Nuttall, who joined after the 2004 success and would rise quickly through the ranks, becoming UKIP's Chairman and deputy leader: 'The party was a bit patchy on domestic policies back then. It was just bullet points', he recalled.

With the issue of Europe not exciting voters, some might have pointed to other opportunities for a group of radical anti-establishment rebels. One issue that was arousing stronger public concern, and by 2005 was the third most important issue for voters, was immigration. The issue had generated little interest in UKIP's early years, as migration remained low and was tightly controlled by the Conservative Major government, who were still trusted by voters on the issue.[6] But from 2000, immigration gradually moved up the agenda, with the percentage of voters ranking the issue as one of the most important facing the country rising from 11.5 per cent in 2000; to 21 per cent in 2002; and 31 per cent in 2005.[7] This growing concern was being driven by historically unprecedented levels of migration into Britain, which in turn were fuelled by a booming economy and liberalising reform of the migration system by the post-1997 New Labour government. From an average of around 300,000 migrants each year in the 1990s, migration inflows increased by more than 60 per cent to an average of over 550,000 in the mid-2000s. Net migration – inflows to Britain minus emigration from the country, which later became the government's preferred statistical target – rose from around zero in the early 1990s, when inflows were balanced by outflows, to over 200,000 in the peak years of the mid-2000s.[8]

Yet in 2005 UKIP were not in a position to capitalise on these growing public anxieties. The party remained dominated by hardcore Eurosceptics, most of who saw immigration as a distraction from the main goal of withdrawing Britain from the EU. There was also a strong concern within the party that an outspoken campaign on immigration would encourage voters and journalists to link UKIP with the extreme right BNP. Furthermore, at this time the party lacked the media profile and resources that would be needed to communicate a new policy initiative to the electorate, making it hard to challenge the EU-obsessed UKIP stereotype. Also, under the leadership of Michael Howard, the Conservatives had begun placing immigration at the centre of their general election platform. Hoping to find some way of preventing a historic third successive election victory for Labour, the Conservatives promised to withdraw Britain from the 1951 United Nations Convention on refugees, limit the number of asylum seekers and assured voters it was 'not racist to talk about immigration'. This platform left little room for an anti-immigration campaign by the UKIP insurgents, and there was another factor. The immigration issue was also already the focus of the resurgent BNP, who offered a radical policy package for voters angry about high immigration: an immediate halt to all immigration; the 'voluntary' removal of settled migrants; and the redeployment of troops from Afghanistan and Iraq to patrol national borders. UKIP were wedged between a Conservative Party that had ventured onto radical right territory and far-right extremists who offered hardcore policies couched in unapologetic racism.

Given their internal problems and the wider environment, UKIP's mediocre results in 2005 were not surprising. Lott had somehow managed to convince a record 496 candidates to stand, but aware that most would not save their deposits, and that prospects were bleak, the party had once again treated the election as a marketing exercise, hoping to build on their 2004 success by raising their national profile, as Farage recalls: 'I think the share of the national vote is terribly important. I also think we have to make people aware of our existence. Even a leaflet through the door is better than nothing.' Yet these efforts saw little reward, and a meagre improvement on their results at the previous general election in 2001.

UKIP's share of the total vote increased only marginally, from 1.5 to 2.2 per cent, while their average vote share in seats fought increased from 2.1 to 2.8 per cent. Only 40 candidates polled at least 5 per cent and saved their deposits; only one polled over 10 per cent of the vote (in South Staffordshire, which held its vote a month late due to the death of a candidate); only one Ukipper managed to break into the top three; and over two-fifths failed even to finish among the top four.[9] Lott and his small team had won over 600,000 voters, an impressive achievement in the circumstances, but the overall message was clear: in their third domestic general election, UKIP had once again fallen a long way short.

There were some consolations. The party's support had followed the same geographical pattern as at previous elections, suggesting there were some areas of strength to build on. The top tier regions remained the South-West, Eastern and South-East, where they averaged over 3 per cent. The second tier was the North-East, North-West and Yorkshire, where they averaged between 2 and 3 per cent, leaving the bottom tier of Scotland, Wales and London, where the party averaged less than 2 per cent.[10] For the first time, UKIP also averaged over 3 per cent in the Midlands, which reflected a lingering 'Kilroy effect' and a pocket of support in Staffordshire.[11] While they failed to seriously impress the electorate, they were at least beginning to move away from their exclusively Southern origins (see Table 2.3).

Further comfort also came from the fact that UKIP had thoroughly beaten a new splinter party, Veritas (meaning 'truth'), founded by their celebrity candidate turned rival, Robert Kilroy-Silk. While Kilroy's new venture had won over two UKIP members of the London Assembly, his party flopped on polling day.[12] UKIP and Veritas competed in 48 constituencies, and Kilroy's party finished behind UKIP in all but four of these – in one of which, Erewash, Kilroy stood and won just 5.8 per cent. The result was a bitter disappointment for a man who had briefly captivated British politics and then almost destroyed UKIP. Finally, he was forced to abandon his political ambitions. But as one challenger was defeated, another more resilient opponent was rising.

Competing with extremists: UKIP and the BNP

It was once noted by a journalist that parties which move away from the centre of political gravity often contain a weakness in their DNA: they attract fanatics.[13] Ever since their foundation UKIP had been all too aware of this weakness, having frequently faced allegations from journalists, politicians and even former leaders that they had been infiltrated by extremists, who wanted to steer UKIP onto extreme right territory or prevent them from blocking the BNP's rise. As the journalist continued: 'UKIP is well aware of this. It hasn't become "the BNP in blazers" – but only thanks to constant vigilance. The party has the same problem that breakaway Catholic traditionalists do: keeping racists away is hard work.'

UKIP had always strenuously denied these charges, but by 2005 the idea that they were attracting similar voters as the BNP had gained widespread currency. In January of that year, the *New Statesman* ran a front cover, which read: 'One in five Britons could vote for the far right', and included UKIP under the umbrella term 'far right'. The article was based on research by a team of academics whose analysis of exit polls after the elections in 2004 revealed significant overlaps in support for the two parties. Around half of those who had voted BNP at the local elections voted for UKIP at the European elections, and around half who had voted BNP in the London mayoral race gave UKIP their second preference vote. The votes also flowed the other way; one-quarter of UKIP voters in the London mayoral elections gave their their second preference vote to the BNP. While stressing that the parties were bitter rivals and rooted in different traditions, the academics concluded that both 'draw from the same reservoir of support, and opinion polls and focus groups suggest they are linked in voters' minds'.[14] The implication was that UKIP and the BNP were competing for a common pool of voters, and, if they combined, could win support from up to 20 per cent of voters, a formidable figure. Even this estimate looked conservative as the combined vote shares of UKIP and the BNP at the 2004 European elections was almost 23 per cent.

Unsurprisingly, the research sparked a fierce debate and the assumed associations were rejected by UKIP and others, including the think-tank researcher Catherine Fieschi who described it as 'mainly nonsense', reliant on an unjustified conflation of two parties with very different outlooks. Whereas UKIP belonged to the populist right and appeared more like the French Poujadists of the 1950s, argued Fieschi, the BNP belonged to the race-obsessed hard right of Jean-Marie Le Pen.[15] We will throw new light on these questions in Chapters 4 and 5, which put UKIP's support under the microscope, but what was clear in 2005 was that both parties were encountering each other far more frequently at elections. This intensifying competition on the fringe would have a clear impact on UKIP's development.

The BNP's rise had followed a very different path to UKIP's. Lacking resources and allies in the media, the party had avoided expensive national elections and, until 2005, had been hardly visible in national politics, fighting fewer than 60 seats at the 1997 general election, abstaining from the 1999 European elections and contesting just 33 seats at the 2001 general election. Instead, the cash-strapped and ostracised party invested in local elections, hoping to use intensive, community-focused campaigning to overcome their negative image and the first-past-the-post system. Inside the BNP this was known as the 'ladder strategy'; they would climb the ladder of British politics by forging ties with voters and building local bastions of support, while downplaying the crude racism and street violence that had turned voters off in the past. The party focused on a small number of areas where they campaigned intensively, targeted community grievances and, in some cases, wore high visibility jackets to draw attention to their 'days of action', when they would descend on neighbourhoods to remove graffiti or tidy gardens. Griffin adopted the idea from the Liberal Democrats who pioneered pavement politics methods after their predecessor in the 1980s, the SDP, failed to win major power in Westminster because concentrations of support (we return to this point in Chapter 6). He had also taken lessons from the rise of Jean-Marie Le Pen's Front National (FN) in France, who in the mid-1980s had used intensive campaigns in the poor and ethnically divided suburbs around Paris to break into national politics.

The impact of the BNP's campaigns was soon highlighted in one report, which observed how in some areas in North-West England voters had more face-to-face contact with the BNP than with any of the three mainstream parties.[16] While UKIP avoided labour-intensive local campaigns, the BNP saw them as their route into power. By the time of the local elections in 2004 the different paths that were being followed by the two parties were clear to all; the BNP fought more seats, won more votes, gained more councillors and scored a higher average share of the vote per candidate. Farage might have told journalists that 'the BNP doesn't exist', but in private he knew the extreme right was beginning to move ahead of his own party in domestic politics, a realisation that was underscored by the outcome of the 2005 general election.[17]

The two fringe parties had first met at a general election in 1997, when they competed in sixteen seats with mixed results; UKIP finished ahead in seven seats, the BNP in nine.[18] At the next election

TABLE 2.1 The BNP and UKIP general elections, 1997–2010

	No. of seats with UKIP and BNP candidates	No. of seats where UKIP ahead of BNP	No. of seats where UKIP behind BNP	UKIP average % vote share in seats with BNP	UKIP average % vote share in seats with no BNP
1997	16	7	9	0.9	1.1
2001	17	5	12	1.5	2.2
2005	92	19	72	2.6	2.9
2010	303	127	176	3.4	3.8

in 2001 they again only met rarely, reflecting their different geographical focus. UKIP concentrated on areas in Southern England that were outside of London, while the BNP focused on the eastern half of the capital city (their historic birthplace) and declining and ethnically divided towns in the North-West and Yorkshire. This time the parties met in seventeen seats and the BNP had the better of the contests, finishing ahead in twelve seats and behind UKIP in five. There was also evidence that the competition, which was about to reach new heights, was having an electoral impact. As shown in Table 2.1, where UKIP competed with the BNP they received a lower average vote share, suggesting they were losing some support to their extremist and more locally active rival.

By the time of the 2005 general election both parties had widened their ground offensives, fielding record numbers of candidates. Hoping to build on their local advances the BNP stood 120 candidates, more than three times their 2001 total, while Lott had mobilised almost 500 for UKIP. One by-product of this was that the number of seats fought by both parties rocketed, to over ninety. The BNP's message was now more similar to UKIP's: they opened their manifesto with a promise to withdraw Britain from the EU, while both parties were now demanding a halt on immigration, tougher sentences for criminals, more bobbies on the beat, protection of the NHS, help for rural areas and the restoration of traditional teaching methods.[19] UKIP hoped the extremists would fall flat, and that their success in 2004 would be enough to carry the day, but they miscalculated.

Despite being shunned, it was the BNP who delivered the stronger performance, as their strategy of cultivating local concentrations of support paid off. Though neither party came close to winning a seat, the BNP finished ahead of UKIP in over seventy seats, and behind in only nineteen. The competition also had a clear geographical pattern; over 80 per cent of seats where the BNP polled higher than UKIP were in the North-West, Yorkshire, Midlands and London, all regions the Eurosceptics had long avoided and where the BNP, and before them the National Front, had been active. As Griffin's activists had been knocking on doors, UKIP had hardly bothered to engage with voters.[20]

In the aftermath of the 2005 contest UKIP's prospects looked bleak. They had attracted a meagre set of results and been trounced by an openly extremist party. They were fragile, demoralised and had been reminded about the harsh reality of British general elections. There were few glimmers of hope. The next set of elections to the European Parliament were still four years away and, until then, it seemed as though a poisonous party on the extremist fringe had a better chance of breaking into Westminster. As Ukippers surveyed the landscape, they knew something would have to change.

Enter Farage and the deal that never was: 2005–2010

UKIP's immediate response was to refocus on broadening their domestic appeal. If they were to attract loyal supporters then they had to have more to say on issues like education, trade, identity cards, immigration and taxation. Towards the end of 2005, this shift became more attractive as it became clear that not all Conservatives favoured the centrist approach of their new leader, David Cameron. Unlike his predecessors, who often targeted the core Conservative vote, Cameron publicly warned his party against such a rightward drift and advocated a more socially liberal agenda, emphasising a more compassionate and inclusive form of Conservatism that would address issues such as climate change and gay marriage, and increase the number of women and ethnic minorities in his party. His election provided a new opening for the flagging UKIP, who quickly began exploring ways of appealing to discontented, socially conservative voters

In the first instance, a new Chairman, David Campbell Bannerman, was tasked with leading a policy review, designed to rebrand UKIP as campaigning for independence from the established political class, whether in Brussels or Westminster. Activists talked of presenting the disgruntled electorate with a 'radical libertarian alternative' to the 'social democratic consensus' in Westminster politics.[21] But UKIP still had little media profile and the policy review process was slow, complicated and opaque, so few voters noticed. What did catch many voters' attention, however, as Britain headed into the 2006 local elections, was an attempt by Cameron to cover his radical right flank, by describing UKIP in a widely covered interview as 'fruitcakes, loonies and closet racists'. Elaborating, the Conservative leader pointed to Alan Sked's earlier decision to leave UKIP because of his fears over infiltration by extremists.[22] Once again, Ukippers had been lumped in with the extremist fringe, although this time by a contender for the highest office in Britain.

The party's revolt had stalled, and internal changes over the summer of 2006 provided a further distraction. Roger Knapman's term had come to an end. His experience and steady hand had served the party well, helping to earn a record result in 2004 and keeping the party together as it fended off the Kilroy challenge, even if he had failed to broaden out UKIP's agenda and recruit new voters at domestic elections. There was only one obvious successor. Looking at a party that was tired and pessimistic, Farage was now convinced that the time was right to stand, as he recalls: 'It made the choice for me very easy. I was then over forty. I'd done every other job in UKIP. Becoming leader of UKIP when it was less than one per cent in the opinion polls and off the radar, well it was a good time to buy stock. Taking over at that time, I simply couldn't lose.' Following a ballot of party members, that saw Farage win 45 per cent and finish well ahead of three rivals, he was finally and comfortably elected leader of UKIP.[23]

Looking at the challenge ahead, Farage was keenly aware his party had not managed to transition from a single-issue pressure group into a professional electoral force. One of his first announcements was a plan to turn UKIP into 'a fully-fledged political party' that welcomed traditional Conservatives who felt alienated by Cameron's 'liberal Conservatism'.[24] To win them over he knew his party would need to widen their offer. Alongside withdrawal from the EU, activists now began making a series of new policy proposals designed to appeal to the Conservatives' right flank: sharp reductions in immigration; tax cuts; the restoration of grammar schools; and opposition to Cameron's new climate change agenda.

These attempts to broaden UKIP's base, however, were again constrained by internal problems. Farage's activists remained demoralised and, since 2004, membership had slid to around 15,000. There was also little administrative support for the new leader, so Farage often found himself managing several roles and was soon exhausted: 'I was utterly hacked off with the job', he would later recall. 'I felt completely under-appreciated by my own party. I felt I was being asked to be not just political leader but head cook and bottle washer as well, to be in charge of virtually everything.' There was also a more serious and growing tension inside UKIP, which one way or another he would need to resolve.

Though UKIP seldom mentioned it publicly, the continued rise of the BNP was generating alarm. Since 2005, Griffin's party had grown further in confidence, increasing their presence in elected office by capturing more local council seats and making progress in areas where UKIP were weak, such as Wales, where in 2007 the BNP won a higher number of votes in the Assembly election regional list.[25] The next year, they won a seat in the Greater London Assembly and were easily out-performing UKIP in local elections, and often by large margins. At three consecutive sets of local elections between 2006 and 2008 the BNP attracted over 200,000 voters; three times as many as UKIP in 2006 and 2007, and almost twice as many in 2008 (see Table 2.2).

TABLE 2.2 Support for UKIP and the BNP at local elections, 2000–2013

	Candidates		Total votes		Average % vote		Local seats won	
	BNP	UKIP	BNP	UKIP	BNP	UKIP	BNP	UKIP
2000	13	39	2,364	4,981	8.3	7.4	0	1
2001	4	40	867	12,716	3.7	5.7	0	0
2002	66	150	29,071	19,065	16.3	5.5	3	0
2003	217	0	101,066	0	17.3	0	13	0
2004	317	278	190,495	110,119	16.5	14.8	14	2
2005	47	277	22,776	111,668	8.0	7.1	0	0
2006	364	323	22,9485	72,167	19.4	9.1	33	1
2007	747	442	293,063	102,119	14.9	11.0	10	1
2008	612	454	234,527	96,933	14.2	9.3	15	4
2009	442	550	170,865	314,148	11.2	16.0	3	7
2010	716	620	346,540	226,569	9.1	7.9	2	1
2011	264	1112	60,143	297,662	9.0	11.6	2	7
2012	132	694	26,513	218,671	8.4	13.6	0	5
2013	100	1,742	13,143	1,141,487	5.6	24.3	0	147

Source: Plymouth University Elections Centre.

As the two parties geared up for the 2009 European elections, it was the BNP that featured heavily in discussions about insurgent electoral breakthroughs, a situation which was generating anxiety within UKIP. Farage, as he recalls, was now beginning to face growing pressure from inside his party to reach some form of accommodation with the extreme right:

> There were a lot of people saying to me at that time, 'You've got to do a deal with them.' I even had Tory MEPs saying to me, 'Nigel you've got to do a deal with these people.' We were being beaten by them regularly, in local elections. So there was huge pressure on me. 'We should do a deal.' I always said it was completely unthinkable, unconscionable, and I'm not doing it. They're authoritarian, we're libertarian. I believe in free trade and globalism and they believe … you know a list

> as long as your arm. [Nick] Griffin and I were fucking poles
> apart really on virtually all aspects of policy.

In fact, Farage had already taken steps to root out potential BNP
sympathisers by instructing his new Chairman, Paul Nuttall, to draw
a line at their conference in September 2008, as Nuttall explained:

> Nigel wanted me to come in with a big stick really and sort
> the whole thing out. The party had quite blatantly been
> infiltrated by the BNP; we knew that. So I came in, and the
> speech that I gave went down well with one half of the audi-
> ence and poorly with the other half. I said, either get on board
> or get out. The party had just broken into all sorts of factions
> and was quite frankly out of control.

Those who appeared open to an electoral pact with the BNP
included members of the party's National Executive Committee,
who at a meeting in November 2008 moved to out-flank Farage by
tabling the idea of a possible agreement between the two parties.[26]
Their chosen messenger was Buster Mottram, a former professional
tennis player who had been introduced to UKIP by a member of
the aristocracy and, in earlier years, had been a vocal supporter of the
1970s National Front. Though not a member of the NEC, Mottram
appeared to have support from some of those who were present
at the meeting and demanded to speak. While some urged him to
leave, Farage, who was keen to identify supporters of a pact, allowed
him to make the pitch, which Mottram did with the claimed bless-
ing of BNP Chairman, Nick Griffin. 'He was waving a bit of paper
around like Neville Chamberlain', recalled Nuttall, who was chair-
ing his first ever NEC meeting. "I have this paper, it's a deal, and Mr
Griffin has ok'd it."' Mottram was offering an agreement that would
transform the 2009 European elections. 'The nature of the deal',
explained Farage, 'was the BNP would stand in some regions in
the European elections in the North, and UKIP would stand in the
South and that would be the electoral pact and we wouldn't oppose
each other.' Once Mottram had finished, Farage turned to the table

and canvassed opinion from the seventeen or so NEC members who had listened to the offer. Only two expressed some form of support. 'They were the angry old men of *old* UKIP who thought UKIP were doomed', claimed Farage. After calling the police to come and remove Mottram, who had refused to leave, Farage turned back to the table: 'I said to them, "Well, we can have a vote around the table to expel you or you can just leave." They left. That was it. It was a very important moment for us, a very, *very* important moment.'

Farage had rebuffed Mottram and rooted out pockets of sympathy for a pact among the highest echelons of UKIP, drawing a line under the debate and firmly distancing his party from the BNP as they headed into a crucial set of European elections. 'I played a good hand of cards that day', recalled Farage, 'because I knew I could smoke out those from within who felt that way. That was a big moment. We had faced them down.' Nuttall concurred: 'That was one of the pivotal moments in UKIP's history actually, because we then had an NEC for the first time in many, many years where we were all a cohesive group, and could start to get the party ready for the 2009 European elections.'

Success at the election, however, seemed far from certain. As UKIP began preparing for the contest, there was little evidence that their revolt was regaining the momentum it had built in 2004. Though many commentators expected the Eurozone crisis to benefit radical right parties that called for their countries to withdraw from the EU, and saw migrants as a strain on scarce resources, UKIP did not appear to be gaining. As the campaign got underway in May 2009 the party were averaging 7 per cent in the polls, less than half the share they won in 2004.[27] But as is often the case in politics, a single event can transform a party's fortunes.

Less than one month before polling day, *The Daily Telegraph* published details of parliamentary expenses claimed by members of the Labour Cabinet and, in the following days, further revelations linking MPs from all three main parties to widespread abuse of the expenses system. The long drawn-out scandal, which fixated the press and revolted the nation, turned the European elections into an immediate outlet for public anger at the behaviour of their elected representatives. One snapshot of public opinion, taken only days before polling day, suggested 84 per cent of voters wanted MPs involved in the scandal expelled from Parliament. In another, almost one in two voters agreed that most MPs were 'personally corrupt'.[28] UKIP provided the obvious outlet for this surge in populist rage at a corrupted establishment, and they were quick to exploit the crisis, as reflected in one leaflet that combined references to expenses claims and the popular television show, *The Apprentice*: 'You've cleaned the moat. You've furnished a second home. You've paid the housekeeper. You've ripped off taxpayers. YOU'RE FIRED!'[29] In the week after the scandal broke, three different companies published four opinion polls, and all of them pointed to a surge in support for UKIP. The party's average support now stood at 16 per cent, more than double that registered before the scandal. As the leading poll observer Anthony Wells summarised: 'It appears that UKIP – despite their MEPs' own problems with fraud and expenses, have been the overwhelming victors from the expenses row.'[30]

Now hopeful of a major breakthrough, UKIP's campaign offered a potent mix of Eurosceptic, populist and anti-immigration messages: EU membership was costing Britain £40 million every day, and each British family £2,000 each year; corruption in the European Parliament was endemic; Britain had lost control of its borders; immigration was out of control; the country was losing its national identity; and, recycling the message proposed by Dick Morris in 2004, voters should 'say no' to the EU and corrupt politicians in Westminster. The elections, which before the expenses scandal had looked to be a disaster for UKIP, now turned into another triumph.

Although the party added only 0.4 points to their 16.1 per cent share of the vote in 2004, they finished in second place, behind the Conservatives, but above the incumbent Labour Party and the Liberal Democrats. The result delivered thirteen seats in the European Parliament and a much needed injection of morale. It also shed further light on UKIP's evolving base of support, which remained strongest in areas in Southern England (but not London), and weakest of all in Scotland. But unlike in 2004, their support had also increased most sharply in the West Midlands, where UKIP finished second with 21 per cent of the vote. Only the South-West provided a higher vote share, underscoring how the geographic base of support for UKIP's revolt was widening. In fact, while their support had remained comparatively strong in the South it had also stagnated, while the North-West, Yorkshire and North-East, all traditionally weaker regions for the Eurosceptics, registered increases in UKIP's share of the vote. By contrast, support fell back by almost ten points in the East Midlands, where the campaign was no longer driven by Kilroy-Silk, and smaller falls in support were recorded in London and Scotland.[31] The social base of UKIP support also shifted noticeably – the party saw the sharpest increase in its average share of the vote in local authorities with higher than average numbers of working-class voters, residents with low education and in poor health (an indicator of deprivation). In contrast, support for UKIP fell back in areas with higher than average concentrations of professionals and university graduates.[32] The finer grained results thus suggested a discernible shift towards an electorate that was more blue-collar and less well educated.

Once again UKIP were the comeback kids, having recovered from a dismal general election to win a record share of the vote at a European Parliament election. While the party continued to draw much of their strength from the South, they were now attracting rising support in the North, particularly in economically struggling, working-class areas. UKIP topped the bill in a number of poorer, Northern, working-class local authorities, including Hartlepool, Dudley, Newcastle-under-Lyme, Stoke-on-Trent and Kingston-upon-Hull.[33] They also trounced the BNP, who had similarly targeted public concerns over the economy and the palpable anti-establishment mood by anchoring their campaign in two slogans: 'British jobs for British workers', and 'Punish the pigs'. UKIP attracted more than twice as many voters as their extremist rivals, who still managed to enter the European Parliament for the first time with two seats in the North-West and Yorkshire. Yet it soon became clear that the BNP were not cut out for top-flight politics. Shortly after the election, Farage sat down to watch Nick Griffin's much publicised debut on the flagship BBC politics programme *Question Time*: 'There was one moment when I just roared with laughter, when he said: "And the Ku Klux Klan are now almost entirely a non-violent organization." I said to my wife:"I'm not sure the dockers down in Bermondsey and their families are buying into this." He was awful.'

The 2009 European elections were a watershed in other ways. UKIP had now, finally, recognised they could not afford to repeat the mistakes of 1999 and 2004 by squandering their European election windfall. Some figures who had risen quickly through the ranks, like Paul Nuttall, urged the party to begin focusing immediately on the next general election and exploring ways to widen their domestic appeal. Encouraged by private polling that suggested UKIP voters were not driven simply by concerns over the EU but also immigration and crime, Nuttall used his annual conference speech in September 2009 to tell the party they should stop talking only about Europe and start taking domestic politics more seriously.[34] This change of strategy, however, would need strong leadership, and Farage was about to give his party some surprising news.

The 2010 general election, and finding a radical right formula

Having steered UKIP away from turmoil and back on the road to success, Farage might have been expected to push on to the 2010 general election. But, only three months after leading his party back to glory and being re-elected himself to the European Parliament, he shocked the party faithful by announcing his decision to stand down as leader.'I'd bought this stock at a tuppence, and like Poseidon shares it had gone to one hundred and twenty eight quid. I thought for the first time in my life I'm going to get out on top.' Publicly, Farage attributed the decision to his goal of entering Westminster at the 2010 general election, which he planned to do by breaking with historic convention and standing against the Speaker of the House in Buckingham. Privately, however, he had felt under-appreciated and overworked by his party, and was also aware that his chances of a win under the first-past-the-post system were slim. Following the example of Alec Salmond, who almost ten years previously had resigned as leader of the Scottish National Party after leading them to success, Farage followed suit. 'Buckingham was *a* reason. I was free! I was out!'

UKIP remained fragile, but Farage was leaving them in much ruder health. He had helped stabilise the membership, which at the end of 2009 stood at over 16,000, up from 14,600 in 2008. Total income had passed £1.2 million in 2009, much of it driven by donations, and they had kept a significant faction in the European Parliament, which would ensure further funding and profile.[35] The party had also clearly beaten the extremist BNP, and expunged their influence from within UKIP. But most importantly, they were now more united than ever before, with few signs of the infighting that had almost ruined UKIP following earlier campaigns.

The succession contest centred on two front-runners, both of whom wanted to broaden UKIP's appeal by focusing more heavily on the radical right themes of opposition to immigration and Islamic fundamentalism.[36] Concerns about the faltering economy now dominated British politics but immigration had continued to generate anxiety among working-class, older and more disadvantaged voters, as we chart in Chapter 3. As the 2010 general election approached, immigration had become the second most important issue for voters, behind the economy and above unemployment, and UKIP were clearly aware of the trend. Pointing to the growing polling evidence, internal party documents in 2010 reveal how UKIP decided to shift gear, launching a campaign against 'the effects of continuing unlimited mass immigration'.[37]

Nor had the sudden emergence of the English Defence League (EDL) gone unnoticed. Since their arrival in June 2009, the EDL had attracted national publicity after organising confrontational and often violent demonstrations against radical Islam and British Muslims, attracting a growing base of mainly young, working-class and poorly educated men. While the EDL would later enter into a short-lived alliance with a minor party led by a former UKIP candidate, the British Freedom Party, for a brief moment they also attracted interest from some Ukippers, although this soon evaporated after closer inspection, as one activist recalled: 'When the EDL were first set-up ... they got in touch with one of our MEPs ... I looked at what I'd seen so far, and at that point they seemed perfectly ok. A bit extreme, but nothing wrong with them. This was before the riots. So I said, "Yeah go down and meet, see what they are like, and sound them out." He [the MEP] came back and said: "No they're not. They're fucking nutters."'

Nonetheless, the arrival of the EDL highlighted anxieties held by many voters about an issue that none of the main parties were addressing. This was reflected in the findings of the respected British Social Attitudes (BSA) survey, which suggested British public attitudes about Islam were uniquely negative. At the time of the 2010 general election, less than 25 per cent of respondents held positive views about Islam, by far the lowest figure of the religions surveyed.[38] Around the same time, the growing prominence of Islam in British politics was reflected in the national media, with one newspaper pointing to the popularity of Marine Le Pen in France who had detoxified her party while remaining opposed to Islam. 'Britain', noted *The Daily Telegraph*, 'is beginning to experience French-style anxiety about Islamisation', as the paper called on the government to 'start dismantling an Islamisation that threatens the freedoms of ordinary Britons'.[39] Whereas in the past UKIP's concerns about steering too close to the extreme right led them to avoid these issues, this was about to change.

In November 2009, and with support from almost half of the 9,900 members who had cast a vote, Lord Pearson of Rannoch was elected as the seventh leader of UKIP in sixteen years.[40] To the irritation of four other contenders, Farage publicly endorsed Pearson as the 'only serious, credible' candidate to replace him, although the choice remained odd for a band of anti-establishment rebels.[41] While some supporters of the party in the media hailed Pearson's election as 'the worst nightmare of the political class', the former Conservative peer appeared the very embodiment of the British establishment.[42] After making his millions in insurance, Pearson had been appointed to the House of Lords in 1990 by Margaret

Thatcher. But despite his elite political connections the new leader lacked first-hand experience of party politics and elected office. He had only been a member of UKIP for two years, was the only leadership candidate to not hold elected office and, as one journalist noted, had only stood for election on one other occasion, to become a prefect at Eton.[43] UKIP's claims to be an anti-establishment force also sat uneasily with Pearson's declaration that, if elected, he would not stop stalking on his Scottish estate or dining at White's, an exclusive members-only club in London. Some activists might have cheered, but few voters who were angry at the establishment and concerned about their own economic prospects would have found such announcements appealing.

It was not long before questions about Pearson's leadership surfaced. Trouble began within days of his election following a media revelation that, through an intermediary, Pearson had made an offer to David Cameron: at the 2010 general election he would stand down UKIP candidates in return for a referendum on EU membership.[44] The offer stemmed from Pearson's strong belief that UKIP should actively support Eurosceptic MPs in mainstream parties, and that 'it would be mad' to stand against them.[45] His view on the issue was well known, having been expressed nine years earlier when Pearson described voters who risked unseating Eurosceptic Conservative MPs by voting for UKIP as 'shooting their cause in the knee, and their country in the heart'.[46] Cameron never replied but the revelation angered UKIP activists who opposed the idea of a pact with mainstream MPs and complained they had not been consulted. Such a strategy, they argued, would undermine UKIP's credibility as well as their attempt to reach out beyond disgruntled Tories and connect with disenchanted Old Labour voters, as one explained: 'Having a Lord as leader of the party who is trying to do deals with the Tories is going to make it that much harder to win the disenchanted working-class votes.'[47] Pearson's image was further damaged by new revelations that the leader of UKIP, who had led the charge against the abuse of expenses, had himself avoided a £275,000 tax bill on the sale of a £3.7 million estate.[48] This was not a promising start.

Over the next few months Pearson battled on, talking ambitiously of forcing a hung parliament in 2010, mobilising support on a wide range of issues and expressing his view that UKIP had 'concentrated too much on the business of leaving the European Union'.[49] Although the party had traditionally lacked the media exposure required to communicate new policies to voters, the second place finish at the 2009 European elections was beginning to open new doors, as Farage, who had agreed to stay on as media spokesperson, explained: 'After the [2009] European elections … we had the opportunity. Before that you could say it to the party faithful but how's that going to get out through the window? Before then we did try but we didn't really reach anybody to be honest.' With Pearson at the helm, these efforts to draw in new voters led UKIP in a particular direction.

While some of the party's ideas, such as opposition to immigration, a return to grammar schools and a flat tax, had been circulating for some time, others, such as implementing Swiss-style referenda, opposing the 'new religion' of global warming and taking a firm stance against Islamism were shaped more strongly by Pearson's own beliefs.[50] His views about Islam attracted the most media, though they were known long before his election. In the House of Lords in 2009, and alongside Norman Tebbit who had compared Sharia law to the organised criminal fraternity run by the Kray brothers, Pearson asked the British government to ensure 'resident Muslim men are no longer allowed to commit bigamy by being allowed to bring in their second, third and fourth wives and their children to enjoy the benefit of our welfare state'.[51] Four months before that he had tried to bring the radical right Dutch politician, Geert Wilders, to the House of Lords to show his anti-Islam documentary *Fitna*, which features footage of terrorist attacks alongside verses from the Koran, which Wilders claims promoted terrorism. On that occasion, the Home Office banned Wilders from entering Britain on public safety grounds, prompting Pearson to accuse the Labour government of 'appeasing militant Islam'. After successfully appealing the ban, Wilders entered the House of Lords in March 2010 when Pearson, now UKIP leader, described Islam as a 'world domination movement'.[52] He would continue to express similar views: that the British Muslim population is 'rocketing'; that Sharia law is 'gender apartheid'; and that a 'large and growing sector of our society is set against our way of life and laws, our treatment of women and our religion'. Pressed on the effects of wider social change in Britain, Pearson expressed deeper concerns about ethnic change: 'It does worry you sometimes when you drive through parts of the country and you don't really see a white face very much.'[53]

These views were not endorsed by all Ukippers. Anxious about their electoral impact, one of Pearson's leadership rivals had pledged to abandon UKIP after thirteen years of membership if the Lord were elected, arguing that his anti-Islam views would undermine their carefully guarded reputation as a non-racist and non-extremist party distinct from the extreme right. In fact, Pearson's positioning had already attracted the attention of Nick Griffin's party, who claimed he was taking UKIP into 'BNP territory by adopting policies which nominally opposed the Islamic colonisation of Britain'.[54] Activists in UKIP were also aware that they were being taken in a more hard right direction, as one recalled: 'I think he took the party, at least as a headline, into a position that was more concerned with the threat of political Islam than the party had been previously, or since. For Nigel, it just was not an issue.'

These attempts to win over new voters who were concerned about immigration and Islamic fundamentalism continued with UKIP's 2010 general election campaign. The party had opened the year with an announcement that they were now demanding a ban on the burka and niqab in public and some private buildings. Such religious dress, they argued, was 'incompatible with Britain's values of freedom and democracy'.[55] UKIP would also call for the deportation of radical Islamic preachers, the reintroduction of a Treason Act to prosecute citizens who attacked Britons or the armed forces, and for Parliament to ensure Sharia courts do not override UK law. Opposition to Islam was also joined by a more detailed set of policies on immigration, which UKIP were now targeting as a key, vote-winning issue.

Aware that Cameron was downplaying issues that might reinforce his party's reputation as an anti-immigrant 'nasty party', and that the BNP were beginning to buckle under the strain of factionalism and the unpopularity of Nick Griffin, UKIP saw an opportunity to offer voters a more coherent radical right message, fusing hard Euroscepticism with anti-immigration and populist attacks against the established political class. Setting out the party's stall before the election, Farage represented UKIP as 'the party that can talk about immigration – we don't want that to be an extremist party'.[56] The issue was now placed at the centre of their campaign, with UKIP demanding an immediate, five-year freeze on the permanent settlement of immigrants, an end to uncontrolled immigration from the EU, an annual limit of 50,000 migrants, a three-fold increase in the number of staff patrolling national borders, the expulsion of illegal immigrants, an end to benefits for settled migrants, the repeal of the Human Rights Act, withdrawal from the European Convention on Human Rights, and an end to 'the active promotion of the doctrine of multiculturalism by local and national government and all publicly funded bodies'.[57] Such messages were reinforced on leaflets and billboards, many of which read simply: '5,000 immigrants arrive here every week: Stop mass immigration'.[58] As we will show in the next chapter, such policies resonated strongly with disadvantaged, elderly and working-class sections of the British electorate.

UKIP offered other policies that were designed to enhance their domestic appeal and burnish their image as a 'potential party of government'.[59] For the first time they went into a general election with relatively detailed proposals on domestic and foreign policy and a costed economic programme, all of which were organised around four central principles: personal freedom; democracy at the national and local level; small government; and tax reduction. UKIP were pushing ahead with a clear attempt to rally a coalition of socially conservative and financially insecure working-class voters, offering them tough opposition to the EU and immigration, but threatening also a range of measures designed to appeal to their economic needs and right wing ideological preferences: a flat-tax to help the lowest paid workers, investment in the manufacturing sector, new jobs for manual workers, more police on the streets, stronger prison sentences for criminals, grammar schools, an end to political correctness, Swiss-style referenda, a more proportional election system and the restoration of British values. UKIP were no longer the single-issue, anti-EU pressure group: they had become a fully-fledged radical right party.

Pearson also employed a new strategy. Though his offer to the Conservatives had been ignored, he remained committed to ensuring that the maximum number of Eurosceptics were elected to Westminster. Building a strong Eurosceptic cohort in the legislature took priority over the unlikely prospect of winning seats for UKIP. But as we have seen, the strategy also touched on a tension inside his party that had still not been resolved. The party's leadership and senior activists remained generally open to the idea of working with mainstream Eurosceptics, so as to ensure they had a strong voice in Parliament. But the grassroots were even more firmly opposed than before to such pacts, as UKIP's independence from, and hostility to, the established political class had been a core part of their appeal to these foot soldiers. When Pearson advocated collaboration with Conservative Eurosceptics, he misread the balance of opinion in his party.

At the 2010 election Pearson led UKIP into battle with a campaign strategy that most grassroots activists disliked and a message that confused many voters. Nationally, UKIP urged voters to reject the political establishment by supporting them, but in some marginal seats they openly endorsed mainstream Eurosceptic MPs, including the Conservative MPs Philip Davies, Douglas Carswell and Philip Hollobone. This meant that in some local seats voters would have seen the leader of UKIP – who nationally had launched billboards across the country that featured pictures of the three main party leaders and urged voters to 'Sod the Lot' – campaign alongside mainstream Conservative politicians such as Hollobone, who was praised for his Euroscepticism and 'brave' views on Islam, the burqa and Sharia law.[60] Publicly, Pearson claimed to be putting the country above party politics, but inside his own party the strategy was creating turmoil.

Some rank-and-file activists were dismayed at the prospect of allowing Eurosceptic Conservatives a free run, saying they had betrayed Britain by consistently reneging on promises to hold a referendum. Others pointed to the fact that the Conservatives were supporting the accession of Turkey to the EU, which was at odds with UKIP's new interest in stemming the spread of Islam. Still others complained (publicly) that Pearson was damaging their credibility by 'confirming suspicions some may hold that UKIP is a single-issue party concerned only with getting Britain out of the EU'.[61] Such concerns were also quietly held by members of the high command, such as Nuttall who later recalled his view that Pearson's strategy was preventing UKIP from fully abandoning their roots as a pressure group out to convert the Tories to hard Euroscepticism:

> The tactical campaign was fundamentally wrong. What I wanted to do was pick a series of seats where we were performing well in local elections and go for it. What Malcolm wanted to do was to affect the outcome of the result, to plough all of the money into marginal constituencies where you could stop a Conservative getting elected. It was almost as if the party regressed into being a pressure group.

Once again, UKIP's lack of a coherent campaign strategy was undermining their efforts at a general election.

By polling day these tensions had escalated into open rebellion. Some UKIP candidates simply ignored their leader's orders to stand down. In the South-West, UKIP's traditional activist heartland, Pearson faced angry candidates who were outraged he had appeared in local newspapers encouraging voters not to support UKIP in three local seats. 'I am absolutely fuming about what Lord Pearson is asking', explained one. 'I think he is doing great damage to our party. I was never a Conservative voter so to ask my constituents to do so now would be wrong.' One of these seats was Wells, where with full support from local branches the UKIP candidate refused to stand down (and would go on to poll 3.1 per cent while the Conservative MP lost the seat by 1.5 per cent).[62] Reflecting the general mood in the grassroots the candidate also demanded Pearson's resignation, claiming his strategy undermined UKIP candidates across the country.[63] Nor were these sour relations

TABLE 2.3 UKIP's general election performance by region and country, 1997–2010

Regions or country	General election			
	1997	2001	2005	2010
Eastern	0.8	**2.3**	**3.3**	**4.4**
South-East	0.9	**2.5**	3.2	**4.3**
South-West	**1.1**	**2.5**	**3.8**	**4.5**
Greater London	0.6	1.5	1.9	2.1
East Midlands	**1.1**	2.1	3.2	3.5
West Midlands	0.7	2.2	**3.3**	4.2
Yorkshire & Humber	1.0	2.2	2.9	3.8
North-West	0.7	1.9	2.4	3.4
North-East	**1.4**	2.1	2.5	3.2
Wales	0.7	1.4	1.85	2.4
Scotland	0.4	0.9	1.05	1.5
Average % vote in seats contested	1.0	2.1	2.8	3.5
Total number of candidates	194	428	496	558
Deposits saved	1	6	40	99

Note: Average % share of the vote. Bold = strongest three regions at election.

helped when a secret recording, reported in the media, appeared to reveal Pearson describing UKIP members as 'neanderthals'. Pearson compounded these private gaffes with public ones in a series of weak and incoherent media performances, including one national TV interview in which he did not appear to know what was in his party's manifesto.[64]

Polling day opened with a bad omen for UKIP when Farage, who had taken to the air in a small plane to drag a banner encouraging people to vote for UKIP, crashed in a field. He survived but early news reports from the day were dominated by images of UKIP's bloodied figurehead staggering from a plane wreck, hardly the image UKIP wanted voters to take with them into the polling booth. The party's results were disappointing, though not disastrous. They fought a record 558 seats, putting UKIP on the ballot in nearly 90 per cent of mainland British seats. The average share of the vote in seats contested rose again despite the larger number of candidacies, up 0.7 points to 3.5 per cent; and with 99 deposits returned, they had passed the 5 per cent barrier in more than twice as many seats as in 2005. The party had also increased their presence in regions where they had been weakest; their number of candidates either declined or held steady in the core Southern regions, while sharp increases were recorded in Yorkshire, the North-East and Wales. The geographic pattern of UKIP's strength remained stable, however. In descending order of strength and as shown in Table 2.3, UKIP averaged over 4 per cent in the South-West, Eastern, South-East and West Midlands; over 3 per cent in Yorkshire, the East Midlands, North-West and North-East; over 2 per cent in Wales and London; and 1.5 per cent in Scotland. The picture was one of slow but steady progress, though actual seats remained a distant dream.

As at previous general elections UKIP continued to score highest in seats controlled by Conservatives, where they averaged 4.3 per cent, compared to 3.2 per cent in Liberal Democrat seats and 3.1 per cent in Labour seats. But now more of UKIP's strongest results were coming outside of the South. As shown in Table 2.4 at the end of this chapter, at their first general election in 1997 all but one of the party's 'top ten' results had come in the South-East or South-West, but in 2010 these two regions provided less than half of their top showings. Yet despite these positive signs, there remained some fundamental problems.

At the 2010 general election, the party, which had finished second at the European elections with 16 per cent of the vote now polled only 3.1 per cent, and came nowhere near to winning an MP. Overall, there was scant evidence that UKIP could break the mould of domestic party politics: only four of their candidates broke into the top three places, and none of them came close to the first placed winner. The closest was in Buckingham, where even though Farage was free from mainstream party candidates and won 17 per cent of the vote, he still finished a staggering 30 percentage points behind the Speaker, a long way short of his promise to cause a political earthquake.[65] Similarly, in other seats where the party broke into the top three they remained at least 40 percentage points behind the winners. The outcome, therefore, confirmed the established rule in British electoral politics: that smaller parties will struggle to overcome the first-past-the-post system, a barrier we dissect in greater detail in Chapter 6.

Gunning for Westminster: 2010–2013

In August 2010 Pearson resigned as leader, aware of his unpopularity and conceding he was 'not much good at party politics'.[66] Despite feeling anxious about stepping back into a role he had walked away from only one year earlier, Nigel Farage now also recognised the unique opportunities presented by the new political context. The 2010 general election had produced the first coalition government in Britain for seventy years, one that combined a Conservative leader who was unpopular among his traditional right-wing base and the Liberal Democrats, who had long absorbed support from voters who were disaffected with 'politics as usual'. Alongside a protracted financial crisis, the BNP had also suffered a sudden and dramatic collapse of support, after failing to break through in their target seat of Barking and because of Griffin's divisive leadership. UKIP now looked out at the space that lay before them: an unpopular centre-right leader in government; an outsider protest party - the Liberal Democrats - who had become an insider member of the Coalition Government; a centre-left party that was exhausted after three terms in office; and an extreme right party in disarray. Farage was easily re-elected, winning 60 per cent in the ballot, and a victory strong enough to ensure unity over a new four-year term.[67] Coincidentally, the day of his re-election was 5 November, the annual commemoration of Guy Fawkes' failed revolt against the seventeenth-century British establishment.

Four months later, Farage addressed his party's spring conference in confident mood. Pointing to an opinion poll that had put UKIP ahead of the Liberal Democrats, he declared that the new goal for his party was to become the third force in British politics by the time of the 2015 general election. 'The party is on the up', he declared. 'No longer is UKIP on the fringes of any national debate. We are right on the centre ground of public opinion in this country.'[68] While such talk might have been dismissed as the blind optimism that often afflicts minor parties, Farage had good reasons to be confident. Internally, he had enacted changes that were designed to overcome the problems that had plagued his first term as leader. 'The priority was to try and make sure that I could *lead* the bloody thing. I said I would do the three M's: media, messaging and money', he recalled. Other administrative burdens were passed over to a team that included three new appointments: the former Conservative donor and millionaire Stuart Wheeler was brought in as treasurer; a full-time Chairman was installed, a role that was previously filled by activists with other duties; and a full-time party Director was employed, all of whom would provide Farage and the party 'with permanent professional senior management'.[69]

Also, building on the 2010 campaign Farage continued with efforts to 'broaden the attack', which involved talking less about who governs Britain and more about how Britain should be governed. 'When we started the only way we could establish ourselves was by pointing out negatives', he told activists. 'Our job now is to outline how we think an independent Britain should be run.'[70] This would see Farage and the party focus far more heavily on establishing a clear domestic agenda, and was accompanied by a more aggressive media strategy, to communicate these changes to voters: 'That was very conscious', explained Farage. 'We had domestic manifestos before but nobody really knew, unless you were really involved in the minutiae of politics and read *The Times* letter columns every day. The great British public thought we just stood for one thing.' Yet rather than simply talk about domestic policies, aware of the shifting terrain in British politics, Farage now concentrated on cultivating a message for the electorate that merged two particular issues: hard Euroscepticism and firm opposition to immigration, with both proposals wrapped up in a broader appeal to traditional ideas of national identity, as Farage explained during one interview:

> There is a rebirth of identity politics in this country and it is fascinating. We've seen it in Scotland and it's happening in

England but no one has noticed. It's little things. It's the turn-out at Remembrance Day parades. They go up every year! A younger generation, an under-45 generation is hungry to know about their history and what their grandparents did and where they come from. It's very interesting. It's actually bloody happening! So there is identification with us because they see us as a patriotic party, but I always emphasise that's with a small 'p' and not a big 'p' as I think that's important. It's tough to define but a sense that we're speaking for them. That the rest of the political class don't even speak the same language. And I think that the impact that mass immigration, particularly mass EU immigration, into this country has had on that particular community has been *huge*. They've made the connection. It took me bloody years to get immigration and Europe together but I knew at the local elections this year [in 2013] that it was now the same thing. For years I tried. I think that has been a very big factor.

Farage's widened attack was not a 'catch-all' strategy, but was clearly targeted toward groups in British society that were the most hostile towards the EU and immigration: disadvantaged and working-class voters, who saw these social changes as a threat and shared a deep sense of anger towards the established political class for failing to listen or respond to their concerns. The shift was encouraged by activists around Farage who had experience of campaigning in working-class towns, and who pointed to UKIP's success in Labour-run areas in 2009 as evidence that the party was very attractive to struggling voters alienated from mainstream politics.[71] Some saw disenchanted working-class voters as offering UKIP an opportunity to expand beyond their traditional base of Eurosceptic Tories in the South, bringing in working-class Conservatives who felt Cameron had abandoned their core ideals, and blue-collar Labour voters who felt marginalised by the two main parties' shift to the centre and their acceptance of mass immigration.

This strategy of supplementing Euroscepticism with appeals on immigration and attacks against the established political class became increasingly evident in campaigns between 2011 and 2013. During this period the British political context became as favourable as UKIP had ever known, and their support in the opinion polls more than tripled from 3 per cent in 2010 to over 10 per cent at the end of 2013. There were now numerous opportunities to present a socially conservative, Eurosceptic, anti-immigrant message: an ongoing Eurozone crisis; an ailing national economy; in early 2012, the delayed deportation of a radical Muslim cleric, Abu Qatada, from Britain following a ruling by the European Court of Human Rights; in early 2013, frequent revolts by Conservative backbenchers against their leadership over gay marriage and plans for an EU referendum; and, through much of this period, growing public concern about migration from Bulgaria and Romania in 2014, unstoppable under EU rules.[72] UKIP had never had it so good.

Farage and his unified party met the opportunities with a clear strategy focused on building their revolt through parliamentary by-elections and local elections. The days of UKIP focusing their ambitions only on European Parliament elections, and talking only about one issue, were over. Between 2011 and 2013 the party contested fourteen parliamentary by-elections, eleven of which were in Labour-controlled seats.[73] Though UKIP did not prosper at all, some of these contests brought record results, national headlines and speculation that the party had finally developed the campaign skills needed to win seats under a challenging electoral system. Their results were impressive for a young and outsider party: in March 2011, UKIP polled 12.2 per cent in Barnsley Central; eight months later, they won 14.3 per cent in Corby, 11.8 per cent in Middlesbrough and 21.7 per cent in Rotherham; in February 2013, they reached a new peak of 27.8 per cent in Eastleigh; and, in May 2013, the party seemingly came from nowhere to take 24.2 per cent in the North-East seat of South Shields. We cover these campaigns in detail in Chapter 6, but suffice to say they put the revolt firmly back on course and demonstrated unprecedented support for UKIP in domestic British politics. This electoral growth was also mirrored internally, as UKIP's membership swelled from 15,535 in 2010, to

17,184 in 2011, and then to a new record of over 32,000 by the close of 2013.[74]

Some of these by-elections took UKIP into previously uncharted territory, enabling them to refine their core Eurosceptic, anti-immigration appeal. One of the most important of these campaigns, though it received less press attention than others like Eastleigh, was in the Labour-controlled and North-West seat of Oldham East and Saddleworth, in January 2011. The by-election was called only weeks after Farage had returned as leader, and marked the first serious attempt by UKIP to win over a financially disadvantaged and working-class electorate, including voters who had previously backed the BNP. UKIP recognised the potential for electoral growth and moved quickly to win over a base of disgruntled, working-class and poorly educated voters, some of whom had shifted behind Nick Griffin, as their Oldham candidate and new deputy leader, Paul Nuttall, reflected: 'The BNP were once polling 7 per cent. I think a residual 2 per cent of those people are downright racist and would never vote UKIP, but 15 per cent were people who just felt completely ostracised from society and were going in and voting BNP while holding their nose. They didn't really want to vote BNP, but they just felt there was nobody out there for them. And they're the kind of people I want to see come over and vote for UKIP.' Farage, who trudged around Oldham's working-class estates and pubs with Nuttall, similarly recalled the significance of the campaign:

> We [said] on the doorstep: 'If you're a BNP voter cause you're a skilled/semi-skilled worker who thinks his job has been seriously impinged upon, his income's gone down, his local community's changed and he's not happy with the make-up of the local primary school, whatever it may be. If you are a BNP voter for those reasons *but* you don't support the BNP's racist manifesto and you are effectively holding your nose at voting BNP, don't vote for them, vote for us. We are a non-racist, non-sectarian alternative to the British National Party.' It was the first time that we ever said to BNP voters: 'Come and vote for us.'

The Oldham campaign, which saw Nuttall finish ahead of the BNP and save his deposit, fuelled Farage's interest in the power of local activism and by-elections. Since their foundation, UKIP's Achilles' heel had been a reluctance to engage in the locally focused pavement politics that are essential to building success in a first-past-the-post system, as one insider noted: 'UKIP had neglected this branch of British democracy because its leaders had felt that the European question was altogether too large for such parochial contests, which were concerned rather with matters such as traffic regulations, dog wardens and the like.'[75] By 2011, however, Farage had become keenly aware of the need to build local roots for UKIP's revolt if it was to succeed at domestic elections, a lesson he learned from studying how the Liberal Democrats had navigated Britain's difficult electoral system by knocking on doors and building local bastions of support. 'The Ashdown strategy was brilliant, brilliant', Farage explained. 'No one noticed what Paddy was doing until he succeeded. They built an electoral machine, they targeted district and county council by-elections where appropriate, they built up a local base.'[76] But he was also influenced by his own activists who, in May 2011, had managed to win control of Ramsey Town Council; 'I could see these people knew what it was about. They understood that the postal vote thing mattered. They understood canvassing mattered. They understood knocking up on the day can increase your vote by 15 per cent. They understood it all.'

By the spring of 2012 money had started to flow into the party coffers and UKIP poll numbers were on the rise. UKIP were now regularly polling ahead of the Liberal Democrats, and investing more heavily at the local level. When Farage first became leader in 2006, UKIP had fought 323 seats in the local elections and averaged 9 per cent. But since then, the party had continually increased their presence: over 400 candidates in 2007 and 2008; over 500 in 2009; over 600 in 2010; over 1,000 in 2011; and, in 2013, over 1,700, 73 per cent of the available seats. Compared to the last time the county council elections in 2013 were fought, in 2009, UKIP saw their average share of the vote jump from 16 to 24 per cent, and their total number of votes increase more than three-fold, to over

1.1 million. Many UKIP candidates won high shares in areas where the party had never stood before. Research on UKIP's performance in 2013 revealed that the party's percentage change in the share of their vote had increased by at least 20 points in no less than 66 authorities, which the researchers noted 'must be regarded as spectacular by any yardstick'.[77]

UKIP's results in 2013 also further highlighted the growing class dimension to their support. This support was significantly higher in areas with large numbers of blue-collar voters, voters with no educational qualifications and voters with poor general health, while UKIP did significantly worse in areas with large numbers of university graduates or ethnic minorities.[78] There was thus clear evidence that the strategy of targeting white, working-class voters was paying dividends. Analysis by the academic Stephen Fisher suggested that, in 2013, UKIP were taking more votes from Labour than the Conservatives, and that the correlation between UKIP support and the proportion of working-class people was stronger in 2013 than in both 2009 and 2012.[79]

What also made these strong results remarkable was the large number of UKIP candidates standing for the first time, with no previous experience of electoral battles. Almost 30 per cent of those who stood for UKIP had not even been a party member for one year, compared to 3 per cent of those who stood for the Conservatives, 2 per cent for Labour and 4 per cent for the Liberal Democrats. This underscored how UKIP were throwing inexperienced new recruits into the battlefield yet were still achieving impressive results.[80]

Shortly after the 2013 local elections the party continued their efforts to win over working-class voters, including specific appeals to disenchanted Labour voters. During the elections UKIP had placed billboards in deprived areas, taking their Eurosceptic, anti-immigrant message to blue-collar voters in red territory, while Farage took to the media to declare he was mounting a drive for support from 'white, working class Labour voters who feel abandoned by Ed Miliband's party'.[81] Some commentators had derided the adverts in urban working-class areas that were largely unaffected by the county council elections but the move had been deliberate, intended to bring disgruntled Old Labour voters into the revolt. As we elaborate in the next chapter, this owed much to a view among some activists that the 'Old Labour' base, comprising elderly, working-class, insecure and pessimistic voters, might be especially receptive to UKIP's message, as one explained: 'The low hanging fruit for us are not former Tories, but people who have traditionally, and culturally, always been Labour.' Bolstered by the string of record results, activists talked of exploiting the failings of a liberal metro-politan intelligentsia who are uncomfortable among working-class voters and find their concerns over issues like immigration distaste-ful. One activist elaborated on the party's strategy as follows: 'Who suffers from poor crime? Who suffers from villains who get seven-teen cautions? Who suffers when the local comprehensive is not effective? Who lost their job in the pub because of a nice-looking girl from Slovakia? It ain't nice middle-class Tories. It's people in council estates.'

Conclusions: from pressure group to party

In August 2013, British politics was temporarily gripped by news that the country might launch military strikes against the Syrian regime in response to its alleged use of chemical weapons. As the mainstream parties furiously debated military action, a van began driving around the streets of London, carrying a simple message: 'UKIP says NO to war in Syria'. In the days that followed, Nigel Farage popped up repeatedly in television and radio studios, elaborating on UKIP's opposition to war, and attacking the Westminster elite for failing to listen to public opinion, which was firmly against intervention. The episode underscored just how far UKIP had travelled in British politics; from their origins in the 1990s as a single-issue, anti-EU pressure group who were typically ignored, dismissed or ridiculed, to a serious contender for votes whose leader's views on a brewing international crisis were taken seriously by the national media.

Over the past two decades, UKIP's transformation has taken them from the amateur margins to the professional mainstream. In 1997, a handful of fanatics had set out on their first general election campaign, naïvely hoping to convert Conservatives to hard Euroscepticism, but they failed to register on the electoral radar and were then regularly torn apart, not by other parties but by themselves. That UKIP have even survived in the brutal British political habitat is truly remarkable. Having overcome a series of false starts and vicious civil wars, it was only in 2010 when the party began to emerge as a cohesive and serious political organisation. UKIP were now on the verge of becoming a professional political party, with a clear strategy for attracting voters, and a clear sense of where their electoral potential lay. Far from a catch-all party, or one focused solely on winning over disgruntled Conservatives, they have tailored a Eurosceptic, anti-immigrant appeal for disadvantaged, working-class voters who feel under threat from the changes that surround them, and alienated from a seemingly unresponsive and disengaged established political class. By 2014 they could look ahead to a set of European elections they were widely expected to win and, in 2015, a general election, where for the first time in their history they had a genuine chance to win seats. All of this, however, tells us much about the party but little about the political context in which they are operating, and the voters they are trying to win. These are the issues we turn to next.

TABLE 2.4 Top ten UKIP constituency results at general elections, 1997–2010

	Seat	2010 General election			
		Region	% Vote	Place	Incumbent
1	Buckingham	SE	17.3	3rd	Speaker
2	Boston & Skegness	EM	9.4	4th	Con
3	Christchurch	SW	8.5	4th	Con
4	Spelthorne	SE	8.4	4th	Con
5	Dudley North	WM	8.4	4th	Lab
6	Walsall South	WM	8.4	4th	Lab
7	Cambridgeshire North West	E	8.2	4th	Con
8	Dudley South	WM	8.2	4th	Lab
9	Devon East	SW	8.1	4th	Con
10	Staffordshire Moorlands	WM	8.1	4th	Con

TABLE 2.4 (*cont.*)

	Seat	2005 General election			
		Region	% Vote	Place	Incumbent
1	Staffordshire South	WM	10.4	4th	Con
2	Boston & Skegness	EM	9.6	3rd	Con
3	Bognor Regis & Littlehampton	SE	8.0	4th	Con
4	Plymouth Devonport	SW	7.9	4th	Lab
5	Staffordshire Moorlands	WM	7.9	4th	Lab
6	Torbay	SW	7.9	4th	Lib Dem
7	Louth & Horncastle	EM	7.7	4th	Con
8	Totnes	SW	7.7	4th	Con
9	Castle Point	E	7.5	4th	Con
10	Devon South West	SW	7.5	4th	Con

	Seat	2001 General election			
		Region	% Vote	Place	Incumbent
1	Bexhill & Battle	SE	7.8	4th	Con
2	Totnes	SW	6.1	4th	Con
3	Devon East	SW	5.6	4th	Con
4	Stafford	WM	5.2	4th	Lab
5	Harwich	E	5.1	4th	Lab
6	Devon North	SW	5.0	4th	Lib Dem
7	Esher & Walton	SE	4.9	4th	Con
8	Chichester	SE	4.8	4th	Con
9	Devon West & Torridge	SW	4.8	4th	Lib Dem
10	Arundel & South Downs	SE	4.7	4th	Con

	Seat	1997 General election			
		Region	% Vote	Place	Incumbent
1	Salisbury	SW	5.7	4th	Con
2	Torbay	SW	3.6	4th	Con
3	Romsey	SE	3.5	4th	Con
4	Bognor Regis & Littlehampton	SE	3.3	4th	Con
5	Devon West & Torridge	SW	3.1	5th	Con
6	New Forest West	SE	3.1	5th	Con
7	Dorset West	SW	2.9	4th	Con

TABLE 2.4 (*cont.*)

| | | 1997 General election | | | |
	Seat	Region	% Vote	Place	Incumbent
8	Arundel & South Downs	SE	2.9	4th	Con
9	Hexham	NE	2.5	5th	Con
10	Teignbridge	SW	2.5	4th	Con

Note: Regional breakdown: SW = South-West; SE = South-East; E = Eastern; WM = West Midlands; EM = East Midlands; NE = North-East.

Notes

1 Nigel Morris, 'UKIP's bubble may have burst but Kilroy-Silk's party also fails to take off', *The Independent*, 7 May 2005.

2 Helen Rumbelow, 'Withdraw from UK should be UKIP's cry', *The Times*, 5 May 2005.

3 UKIP Statement of Accounts for 2005. Obtained from the Electoral Commission.

4 Toby Helm, 'Strange case of the European dog that didn't manage one bark', *The Daily Telegraph*, 4 May 2005; Ipsos MORI Issues Index. Available online: http://www.ipsos-mori.com (accessed 10 July 2013). Figures reported are for May 2005.

5 Indeed the UKIP manifesto for the 2005 general election opened by explaining to voters why the UK must leave the EU and subsumed immigration under a section on home affairs. See UK Independence Party (2005) *UK Independence Party Manifesto 2005: We Want Our Country Back*, UKIP.

6 With the exception of a short and slight increase in the early 1990s, a response to conflict in Yugoslavia, immigration and asylum did not feature very regularly as one of the most important problems named by voters until towards the end of 1998. Shortly before the general election in 1997, for example, only around 3 per cent ranked the issue (unprompted) as one of the most important facing Britain.

7 These figures have been calculated from the monthly Ipsos MORI Issues Index.

8 For more detail on migration statistics, see the Oxford Migration Observatory, for example Carlo Vargas-Silva (2013) 'Briefing: long term international migration flows to and from the UK'. Available online: http://www.migrationobservatory.ox.ac.uk/sites/files/migobs/Briefing%20-%20Long%20Term%20Migration%20Flows%20to%20and%20from%20the%20UK_0.pdf (accessed 3 October 2013).

9 The Staffordshire South poll was, however, delayed by a month due to the death of a candidate. It was therefore more like a by-election, with low turnout and a strong showing for anti-government candidates. UKIP polled 10.4 per cent in Staffordshire South (where they finished fourth) and almost reached 10 per cent in Boston and Skegness, where they polled 9.6 per cent (and finished third).

10 At the 2005 general election, 70 per cent of all seats where UKIP polled at least 5 per cent of the vote were based in the three 'stronghold' regions of the South-west, South-east and East. For averages of UKIP support across the different regions see Table 2.3.

11 At the 2001 general election UKIP polled 5.2 per cent in Stafford, which was one of only six seats where they managed to save their deposit.

12 In early 2005 Damian Hockney and Peter Hulme-Cross, who were elected to the London Assembly in 2004, defected to Veritas. 'UKIP could sue Veritas defectors', *BBC News*, 24 February 2005.

13 Damian Thompson, 'UKIP doesn't have a grassroots and has to fight to keep the loonies out', *The Daily Telegraph*, 20 April 2012.

14 Peter John, Helen Margetts and Stuart Weir, '1 in 5 Britons could vote far right; UKIP and the BNP are far closer in their views and much more popular with voters than most of us realise', *New Statesman*, 24 January 2005. On the academic research see also Peter John and Helen Margetts (2009) 'The latent support for the extreme right in British politics', *West European Politics*, 32(3): 496–513.

15 Catherine Fieschi, 'Far right alarmism', *Prospect*, 17 February 2005.

16 JRCT (2004) *539 Voters' Views: A Voting Behaviour Study in Three Northern Towns*, York: Joseph Rowntree Charitable Trust. See also Stuart Wilks-Heeg (2009) 'The canary in the coalmine? Explaining the emergence of the British National Party in English local politics', *Parliamentary Affairs*, 62(3): 377–98. On BNP strategy see Matthew J. Goodwin (2011) *New British Fascism: Rise of the British National Party*, Abingdon: Routledge.

17 Michael White, 'Collins joins Kilroy in UKIP's battle for Britain', *The Guardian*, 25 May 2004.

18 In 1997 UKIP also competed with non-BNP extreme right-wing candidates in a further four seats, finishing above National Front in Bromley and Chislehurst and Beckenham, and above the National Democrats, a splinter group from the BNP, in Plymouth Devonport and Devon East.

19 BNP (2005) *Rebuilding British Democracy: British National Party General Election 2005 Manifesto*, Powys: British National Party; UKIP (2005) *UK Independence Party Manifesto 2005: We Want Our Country Back*, UK Independence Party.

20 In sharp contrast, only two seats where the BNP finished ahead were in the South-East and none were in the South-West. At the 2005 general election UKIP also competed with the extreme right-wing National Front in a further eight seats, finishing behind the NF in three seats and above the NF in five seats. UKIP faced both the BNP and NF in two seats: Uxbridge and Birmingham Erdington. UKIP finished joint last with the BNP in the constituency of Stockton North. BNP candidates finished ahead of UKIP in 15 seats in the North-West, 15 in Yorkshire, 18 in the West Midlands, 4 in the East Midlands, 2 in the South-East, 9 in Greater London, 5 in Eastern, 3 in the North-East and 1 in Wales. On the northward shift of the BNP see Robert Ford and Matthew J. Goodwin (2010) 'Angry white men: Individual and contextual predictors of support for the British National Party', *Political Studies*, 58(1): 1–25; also Goodwin, *New British Fascism*.

21 Fraser Nelson, 'UKIP seeks out Conservative voters with domestic agenda', *Sunday Business*, 15 January 2006; 'UKIP targets "abandoned" Tory voters', *The Guardian*, 21 February 2006.

22 Pippa Crerar, 'UKIP loony racists, by Cameron', *The Evening Standard*, 4 April 2006.

23 Nigel Farage beat Richard Suchorzewski, by 3,329 votes to 1,782. The Chairman, David Campbell Bannerman, finished third with 1,443, and David Noakes finished last with 851 votes.

24 'Farage wins UKIP leadership battle', *Yorkshire Post*, 13 September 2006; 'Farage elected UKIP leader', *The Independent*, 13 September 2006.

25 Overall the BNP polled 42,197 votes compared to UKIP's 38,490 votes. The BNP had finished ahead of UKIP in South Wales Central, South Wales West, North Wales and South Wales East. UKIP finished ahead in Mid and West Wales.

26 Interview 2 with Nigel Farage, 6 August 2013.

27 ICM/Tax Payers' Alliance, 1–4 May 2009, UKIP 9%, available online: http://www.icmresearch.com/pdfs/2009_may_taxpayers_poll.pdf (accessed 18 August 2013); YouGov/Sunday Times, 7–8 May 2009, UKIP 7%, available online: http://yougov.co.uk (accessed 18 August 2013); Populus, 8–10 May 2009, UKIP 6%, available online: http://populuslimited.com/uploads/download_pdf-080509-The-Times-Times-Poll---May-2009.pdf (accessed 18 August 2013).

28 In the poll, 46 per cent of respondents agreed with the statement that 'Most MPs are personally corrupt', while 35 per cent disagreed and 19 per cent said they did not know. YouGov/Daily Telegraph, 27–29 May 2009. Available online: http://yougov.co.uk (accessed 13 July 2013).

29 Norwich North by-election leaflet. Available online: http://by-elections.co.uk/norwich09/nnukip03a.jpg (accessed 12 August 2013).

30 Anthony Wells, 'UKIP surge in the wake of expenses expose', May 14 2009. Available online: http://ukpollingreport.co.uk (accessed 16 July 2013). On UKIP support see YouGov/The Sun, 13–14 May 2009. Available online: http://yougov.co.uk (accessed 13 July 2013).

31 Overall, and in order from highest to lowest, UKIP polled 22 per cent in the South-West, 21.3 per cent in the West Midlands, 19.6 per cent in Eastern, 18.8 per cent in the South-East, 17.4 per cent in Yorkshire and the Humber, 16.5 per cent in the East Midlands, 15.9 per cent in the North-West, 15.4 per cent in the North-East, 12.8 per cent in Wales, 10.8 per cent in London and 5.2 per cent in Scotland. Compared to the European elections in 2004, support grew by 3.8 per cent in the West Midlands, 3.7 per cent in the North-West, 3.4 per cent in Yorkshire and the Humber, 3.2 per cent in the North-East and 2.3 per cent in Wales. But support fell by 0.03 percent in Eastern, 0.5 per cent in the South-West, 0.7 per cent in the South-East, 1.5 per cent in London and Scotland and 9.6 per cent in the East Midlands.

32 Stephen Fisher, Robert Ford, Will Jennings and John Curtice, 'BBC 2009 European Election results database' (unpublished).

33 Ibid.

34 Paul Nuttall speech to UKIP conference, Southport, September 2009. Available online: http://www.youtube.com/watch?v=wS-lgQQjTQw (accessed 15 September 2013).

35 In 2009 the party claimed to have received cash donations and bequests totalling £780,816 compared to £257,840 in 2008, of which £508,651 was reportable to the Electoral Commission. UKIP Statement of Accounts 2009. Available online via Electoral Commission: http://www.electoralcommission.org.uk/ (accessed 15 July 2013).

36 David Charter, 'UKIP front-runners target Islamic fundamentalism', *The Times*, 27 November 2009.

37 As the party reflected in their 2010 Annual Statement of Accounts: 'During the year, several polls and surveys showed that the majority of British people now favour withdrawal from the European Union. In addition, immigration emerged as the second most important issue for voters, after the economy.' UKIP Statement of Accounts 2010. Available from the Electoral Commission.

38 David Voas and Rodney Ling (2010) 'Religion in Britain and the United States', in A. Park *et al.* (eds.) *British Social Attitudes: The 26th Report*, London: Sage.

39 'Cameron must face the challenge of Islamisation', *The Daily Telegraph*, 28 December 2010.

40 In the leadership election Lord Pearson polled 4,743 votes (48 per cent), Gerard Batten 2,571 votes (26 per cent), Nikki Sinclaire 1,214 votes (12 per cent), Mike Nattrass 1,092 votes (11 per cent) and Alan Wood 315 votes (3 per cent).

41 'Farage backs peer for UKIP leader', *BBC News*, 11 November 2009.

42 Patrick O'Flynn, 'UKIP should back Lord Pearson', *The Express*, 7 November 2009.

43 Andy McSmith, 'Lord of misrule: The new UKIP leader's honeymoon ended as soon as it had begun', *The Independent*, 3 December 2009.

44 Andrew Hough, 'UKIP offered Tories a deal to disband', *The Daily Telegraph*, 28 November 2009.

45 Lord Pearson of Rannoch, Leader of the UK Independence Party, Straight Talk with Andrew Neil, *BBC News*, 18 April 2010.

46 'UKIP and the Eurosceptic cause', *The Times*, 1 June 2001.

47 David Charter, 'UKIP faces resignations over offer to disband if Tories held EU referendum', *The Times*, 30 November 2009.

48 Jon Swaine, 'UKIP leader avoided £275,000 in capital gains payment on £3.7 million home sale', *The Daily Telegraph*, 1 December 2009.

49 Lord Pearson of Rannoch, Leader of the UK Independence Party, Straight Talk with Andrew Neil, *BBC News*, 18 April 2010.

50 Patrick O'Flynn, 'UKIP should back Lord Pearson', *The Express*, 7 November 2009.

51 Nicholas Randall, 'Tebbit compares Sharia law to Krays' rule', *Press Association*, 4 June 2009.

52 Christopher Hope, John Bingham and Bruno Waterfield, 'Dutch MP Geert Wilders deported after flying to Britain to show anti-Islamic film', *The Daily Telegraph*, 12 February 2009; Craig Woodhouse, 'UKIP leader condemns radical Islam ahead of Wilders visit', *Press Association*, 5 March 2010.

53 Rachel Sylvester and Alice Thomson, 'UKIP's hunter-in-chief is going for the Tory jugular', *The Times*, 28 November 2009.

54 'UKIP's Lord Pearson legacy: betrayal and a failed attempt to steal BNP policy'. Available online: http://www.bnp.org.uk/news/ukip%E2%80%99s-lord-pearson-legacy-betrayal-and-failed-attempt-steal-bnp-policy (accessed 15 August 2013).

55 Suzy Jagger, 'UKIP woos white working class with call for total ban on burkas', *The Times*, 16 January 2010.

56 Chris Smyth, 'Freeze on immigration at centre of UKIP manifesto', *The Times*, 20 March 2010.

57 UKIP (2010) *UKIP Manifesto: Empowering the People*, Devon: UK Independence Party.

58 An extensive range of UKIP and other party literature is available via the website Election Leaflets. Available online: http://www.election-leaflets.org/ (accessed 11 August 2013).

59 UKIP Statement of Accounts, p. 5. Available from the Electoral Commission.

60 David Trayner, 'UKIP boss says: "Vote for Phil"', *Northants Evening Telegraph*, 29 April 2010.The Eurosceptics identified by Pearson included Conservatives Philip Davies (Shipley), Douglas Carswell (Clacton), Philip Hollobone (Kettering) and Richard Shepherd (Aldridge-Brownhills), Labour's David Drew (Stroud) and the Independent and former UKIP member, Bob Spink (Castle Point), who were all seeking re-election, and Conservatives Janice Small (Batley and Spen), Alex Story (Wakefield) and Mark Reckless (Rochester and Strood) who were fighting key marginals.

61 Michael Heaver, 'I respect Lord Pearson's strategy, but disagree fundamentally with it'. Available online: http://michaelheaversblog.blogspot.co.uk/2010/04/i-respect-lord-pearsons-strategy-but.html (accessed 12 July 2013).

62 The three seats were Wells, Somerton and Frome and Taunton Deane. 'Vote Conservative, says UKIP leader', *Wells Journal*, 29 April 2010;Tom Palmer,'UKIP supporters angry at tactics', *Yorkshire Post*, 30 April 2010; 'Party at war as UKIP leader asks public to vote Conservative', *The Herald*, 29 April 2010;'UKIP candidate will not stand down', *Fosse Way Magazine*, 30 April 2010.

63 'Candidate calls for a resignation', *Wells Journal*, 13 May 2010.

64 Solvej Krause, Daniel Foggo and Claire Newell, 'There's more than one way to hide a donor', *The Sunday Times*, 4 April 2010. Similar observations were made at the local level where at one event Pearson did not appear to know his party's stance towards a controversial airport scheme. See 'UKIP concern over immigration', *East Kent Mercury*, 22 April 2010.

65 At the 2010 general election UKIP finished in third place in Buckingham, Devon North, Devon West and Torridge and Cornwall North, and in each of these seats finished a long way behind the winner (30 percentage points behind in Buckingham, 40 points behind in Devon North, 40 points behind in Devon West and Torridge and 43 points behind in Cornwall North). On earthquake: Lauren Turner, 'Farage urges voters: Cause a political earthquake', *Press Association*, 13 April 2010.

66 Adam Gabbatt, 'Lord Pearson stands down as UKIP leader because he is "not much good"', *The Guardian*, 17 August 2010.

67 Farage won 60.5 per cent of the vote, after a postal ballot of 10,073 members (a turnout rate of 65 per cent). The economist Tim Congdon took 20.2 per cent, MEP David Campbell Bannerman took 14 per cent and former boxer Winston McKenzie took 5.3 per cent, turnout 65.1 per cent. 'Farage re-elected as UKIP leader', *Press Association*, 5 November 2010.

68 Nigel Farage Spring Conference 2011 Speech.

69 UKIP Statement of Accounts 2010. Available from the Electoral Commission.

70 Robert Chalmers, 'They govern through fear??? I want to tear them all down', *The Independent on Sunday*, 5 February 2012.

71 Some of UKIP's highest vote shares in 2009 came in poorer, working-class local authorities including South Staffordshire (29.1%); Dudley (27.5%); Hartlepool (25.3%); Boston (25.1%); Walsall (24.6%); and North-East Lincolnshire (Grimsby) (24.4%).

72 'Up to 70,000 Romanian and Bulgarian migrants a year "will come to Britain", when controls on EU migrants expire', *Daily Mail*, 17 January 2013. Available online: http://www.dailymail.co.uk/news/art-icle-2263661/Up-70-000-Romanian-Bulgarian-migrants-year-come-Britain-controls-EU-migrants-expire.html (accessed 2 October 2013).

73 UKIP candidates contested Oldham East and Saddleworth in January 2011, Barnsley Central in March 2011, Leicester South in May 2011, Inverclyde in June 2011, Feltham and Heston in December 2011, Bradford West in March 2012, Cardiff South and Penarth, Corby, Manchester Central, Croydon North, Middlesbrough and Rotherham in November 2012, Eastleigh in February 2013 and South Shields in May 2013. Only Corby (Conservative) and Eastleigh (Liberal Democrat) were not controlled by Labour.

74 Figures taken from UKIP's annual statements of accounts submitted to the Electoral Commission, except the 2013 figure which was obtained from correspondence with the party.

75 Mark Daniel (2005) *Cranks and Gadflies: The Story of UKIP*, London: Timewell Press, p. 104.

76 James Forsyth, 'UKIP's new deal', *The Spectator*, 26 May 2012.

77 Michael Thrasher, Galina Borisyuk, Colin Rallings, Mary Shears and Michael Turner, 'UKIP candidates and policy positions in the 2013 local elections'. Paper presented to the Elections, Public Opinion and Parties Annual Conference, University of Lancaster, 13–15 September 2013.

78 Stephen Fisher, Robert Ford, Jonathan Mellon and John Curtice, 'BBC local elections keywords database 2013', unpublished.

79 Stephen Fisher, 'UKIP hurt Labour at least as much as the Tories'. Elections Etc blog. Available online: http://electionsetc.blogspot. ca/2013/05/local-elections-2013-why-did-ukip-do-so.html (accessed 2 October 2013).

80 More generally, these candidates were also more likely than those from the main parties to be men, aged over 65 years old and to have no university degree, and were less likely than candidates from the other parties to be in a professional occupation. We will examine the backgrounds and attitudes of UKIP voters in Chapters 4 and 5, but this provides some evidence that the party recruited older, more disadvantaged and less well-educated men. Thrasher *et al.*, 'UKIP candidates and policy positions in the 2013 local elections'.

81 'Now UKIP leader Nigel Farage sets his sights on working-class Labour voters', *Mail on Sunday*, 25 May 2013.

3
ORIGINS

A long time coming

The rise of a new political party is exciting. Their initial breakthrough, new ideas and challenge to the status quo capture the attention of voters, other parties and journalists looking for the next story. In newspaper columns and tweets, commentators compete to explain the new challenger's appeal, while party strategists head to retreats to debate how to neutralise the electoral threat. But the significance of new parties like UKIP, which is one of the youngest parties in British politics, also extends beyond the day-to-day buzz of journalistic reaction, political strategising and Twitter arguments. Rather than being driven by short-term factors, a new party's emergence often highlights deeper, long-term changes within society, and the opening up of new conflicts and divisions within the electorate. The decision of millions of voters to shift to a new and untested alternative, in a political system that makes it difficult for outsiders to break through, also suggests a failure on the part of the established parties to recognise or respond to these new divisions. In short, to fully explain the arrival and success of a party like UKIP, we need to trace its roots all the way back.

In this chapter, we look at how long-term social and political trends in Britain over the past fifty years created demand for UKIP's radical right revolt. We will answer two questions. First, how has British society changed over recent decades to create room for a party like UKIP? Is this a story about a population that has become increasingly Eurosceptic over the years, or which has steadily lost faith in established politics? Or is the story more nuanced, and about how wider trends have impacted on specific groups in society, only rendering some of them receptive to the appeals of the radical right? Second, how have the two main parties that dominate British politics contributed to this process? Has room for UKIP been created simply by David Cameron's more socially liberal brand of Conservatism, as many claim, or have deeper changes in party competition played a role?

So far, we have charted the evolution of UKIP from their origins as an anti-EU pressure group into a radical right party that is determined to become a major political force. A key element driving this strategy has been UKIP's own analysis of how changes in British society have impacted on particular social groups. In their early years, this led the party to focus on appealing to middle-class, Southern and Eurosceptic Conservatives, who were angry after the Maastricht Treaty and felt disconnected from their natural political home. UKIP saw themselves as a pressure group, who existed to convert the Conservative Party to hard Euroscepticism. This strategy changed after 2009, when the party began appealing to disadvantaged voters, including those from traditionally Labour voting groups; white, working-class people whose traditional loyalty to the centre left had eroded, and who stayed at home on election days or flirted with the extreme right BNP. To attract these voters, UKIP began fusing their hard Eurosceptic message with stronger nationalist, anti-elite and anti-immigration elements in the hope of taking votes from both Labour and working-class Tories, who once backed the assertive nationalism and traditional values of Margaret Thatcher, but who since 2005 have been less receptive to Cameron's compassionate Conservatism.

While UKIP's interest in the potential value of a working-class appeal was sparked by their brief affair with Robert Kilroy-Silk, who polled strongly in Labour areas, it was not until 2007 that activists such as Paul Nuttall began to cultivate these ideas more seriously. Nuttall was a rising star who had campaigned for UKIP in the North-West seat of Bootle, held by Labour for seventy years. Now, he felt confident enough to share his argument to the party in an article titled, 'How and why UKIP can attract the Old Labour vote?' Departing from longstanding conventional wisdom, he argued the party were well placed to appeal to disenchanted Old Labour voters in the North.[1] 'I have concluded from my experience that much of what UKIP is saying is not too dissimilar to what the Old Labour voters are looking for – we just need to get the message across.'

The Labour voters Nuttall was urging his party to target were very different to the middle-class, socially liberal and Southern voters who had turned to Blair's rebranded 'New Labour' in the late 1990s. They were, he argued, less likely to vote, more hard-line on crime and punishment ('the hang 'em and flog 'em types'), less concerned about 'new left' issues like multiculturalism, human rights or climate change and instinctively opposed to the EU ('they don't like foreigners telling them what to do', explained Nuttall). But he also highlighted a powerful new issue, where New Labour's action in government had enraged their traditional supporters to such an extent that many were now questioning their political loyalties: immigration. Consistent with UKIP's platform, argued Nuttall, the Old Labour electorate were strongly opposed to mass migration, and angry they had not been consulted about it. These voters, he argued, saw the influx of 'foreigners' as threatening their jobs, wages, identity, the cohesion of their local communities, and the nation at large. The implication was clear: 'If UKIP can impress upon the Old Labour voters that it has solid policies in this area and is committed to cutting immigration drastically, then the Old Labour vote will follow.'

Nuttall's argument, and UKIP's broader assessment of their appeal to the working class, is at odds with many contemporary commentaries, which often claim UKIP voters come mainly from the Conservative Party, and therefore resemble stereotypical Conservative voters: middle-class, Southern, Eurosceptic and right-wing across the board. But the thrust of Nuttall's argument was supported by a comprehensive analysis of UKIP support conducted by Conservative peer Lord Ashcroft, who polled over 20,000 people and held fourteen focus groups with UKIP voters in 2012. Ashcroft rejected much of the conventional wisdom, including the claim that UKIP's rise is primarily the result of public dissatisfaction with the EU. The UKIP voters he talked to showed little interest in EU policy or public policy in general. Instead, they were drawn to UKIP by the party's critical messages about the state of British politics and society, which chimed with their own pessimistic views, something we return to in Chapter 5. But Ashcroft's research highlighted another important finding, which received little attention at the time: UKIP's support was heavily concentrated in more disadvantaged and insecure groups in British society.[2]

The picture emerging from Ashcroft's polling was confirmed in the focus groups, which he found were dominated by expressions of doom and gloom. UKIP, he argued, appealed to Britons who were struggling, deeply worried about the rising cost of living, job security and working long hours for stagnant wages. Some complained about having to take a calculator to the supermarket. In fact, alongside Labour voters it was those who backed UKIP who were the most likely to tell Ashcroft that things in Britain, and for their families, had got worse over the past decade, and to expect things to get even worse over the next ten years. 'These voters', he concluded, 'think Britain is changing for the worse. They are pessimistic, even fearful, and they want someone and something to blame. They do not think mainstream politicians are willing or able to keep their promises or change things for the better.'[3]

It is impossible to make sense of UKIP's appeal without reference to the social and economic changes that have transformed British society over recent decades. Both Nuttall's account and Ashcroft's research suggest that UKIP appeal most strongly to the most disadvantaged in British society. At the same time, however, these accounts tell us little about *why* these groups might find a radical right alternative attractive. Important questions remain unanswered. Where exactly in British society is UKIP support coming from? Is there, as Nuttall argues, latent sympathy for UKIP's ideas among Old Labour's working class base? Is Ashcroft right to assert that public concerns over Britain's EU membership are only secondary to other motives? Has the nature of UKIP support changed as the party has professionalised and expanded its support?

These are the questions that we will answer over the next three chapters, through a detailed, three-stage examination of UKIP's electorate. First, in this chapter we explore how wider social change in Britain over the past fifty years has created room for a radical right revolt. This will shed light on the *potential* support for radical right policies in Britain among members of different social groups, including those identified by Nuttall and Ashcroft. We will show how economic, social and political changes have cut off a large section of the electorate from the values and priorities of mainstream politics, and generated demand for a new and radical alternative. Second, in Chapter 4 we turn to examine whether UKIP are *actually* drawing their votes from this reservoir of potential supporters, by probing the backgrounds of people who openly support the party, and examining how this support base has evolved over time. Then, in Chapter 5 we complete the story by investigating the attitudes and beliefs that unite these voters and which, together, furnish the motives for joining Farage's political revolt.

We begin by examining the social changes which have shaped the British electorate over the past fifty years, the period for which we have reliable data. We make use of two long-running and well respected academic surveys: the British Election Studies, which were started by David Butler and Donald Stokes in 1964 and have surveyed the public immediately after every subsequent general election; and the British Social Attitudes surveys, which have run almost every year since 1983.[4] These long-running surveys provide us with an invaluable record of the changing circumstances, attitudes and priorities of the British public. In what follows, we use these data to chart the long-term changes in British society, the values and attitudes of different social groups towards key issues, and the positioning of the two main parties, all of which – as we will explain – have created 'room on the right' for UKIP's revolt.

A blue-collar revolt: why Europe's working class defected to the radical right

Britain's radical right revolt is a late-starter. Writing in 1993, the year UKIP were founded, the academic Hans-Georg Betz noted how radical right parties in Europe were already becoming serious national competitors. In fact, since the 1980s insurgent parties like the Freedom Party of Austria, National Front in France, Flemish

Blok in Belgium and the Progress Parties in Denmark and Norway had rallied large numbers of voters by fusing nationalist and anti-establishment appeals with strong opposition to immigration and, increasingly, the EU. For Betz, one of the most striking aspects of their support was its concentration among poorer, working-class voters who had once been loyal social democrats. The modern radical right, he noted, was not drawing in voters from across society but poaching support from the bottom rungs.

After two decades of steady growth for Europe's radical right, in 2013 Betz returned to examine these parties again.[5] He found even stronger support among poorer, blue-collar workers than before. In fact, working-class voters had proven so receptive to the radical right that Betz described these parties as 'today's new working-class parties'. Their success, he argued, owed much to their ability to seduce what the French describe as the *couches populaires*: blue-collar workers and lower-level employees who in earlier years had formed the traditional left's base. There were numerous examples. In France, opinion polls in 2012 revealed Marine Le Pen as the preferred Presidential candidate of the French working class. In Austria, the Freedom Party recruited one in four working-class voters. In Italy, the Northern League made advances among trade union members and in 'red territory' held by the left, and in Denmark the People's Party emerged as the most clearly defined working-class party.[6]

Attempting to explain the shift, Betz pointed to wider social changes, but also to changes in the strategies of the established political parties. The onset of a post-industrial economy that prioritised white-collar skills, training and professional qualifications had given blue-collar workers few opportunities to progress and left them feeling isolated, insecure, pessimistic about the future and resentful towards the established political class. The decline of heavy industries that were once at the centre of local communities compounded these effects. Then, the onset of mass immigration and rising ethnic diversity further enhanced feelings of insecurity and the belief that a once-secure way of life was now under threat. These changes intensified the economic concerns of working-class voters, and coincided with the rise of a new politically and socially dominant middle class who were university-educated, skilled, financially secure and able to adapt and prosper in the new social climate.

The rise of the middle class and marginalisation of blue-collar workers presented a dilemma to the centre-left, one that was summarised by Adam Przeworski in his classic study, *Capitalism and Social Democracy*.[7] Przeworski noted that manual workers, the group centre-left parties were founded to represent, were shrinking as a group across Europe, meaning social democrats could no longer win elections by appealing to these workers alone. The dilemma facing the traditional left was clear: either they maintain their pure appeal to workers and risk becoming politically marginal, or they appeal to the rising middle classes but risk alienating their traditional working-class base. Most (but not all) European centre-left parties opted for the latter.

As the financially more secure and socially more liberal middle classes in Europe continued to grow, so their influence on electoral competition and centre-left politics became ever stronger. These new groups brought a distinct set of values and priorities to the left-wing parties they joined. Their 'post-material' agenda prioritised issues like the environment, civil liberties, global social justice and human rights, prompting centre-left parties to overhaul their strategy to win them over. Socialist economic ideas of a planned economy and strong state intervention were downplayed, and replaced by an acceptance of a strong role for free markets and a globally integrated economy. Redistribution and workers' rights were also given less emphasis, with a greater focus on improving public services, a cause which united both 'new' and 'old' left, and on efforts to boost opportunities rather than equalise access to resources. Across Europe, the centre-left also shifted more firmly in favour of European integration. Whereas previously some social democrats had been openly hostile towards the Europe project, viewing it as a capitalist club that opposed socialism, from the 1980s they became more supportive, viewing the EU instead as a valuable mechanism through which they could tame capitalism and entrench social democratic principles at the supranational level.[8]

But as Przeworski predicted, these changes came with a cost: the new middle-class agenda marginalised the left's traditional voters. Their old working-class electorates became dissatisfied with a political system where their traditional voice appeared to have been lost, and showed a growing willingness to back more radical parties that articulated their sense of abandonment from the mainstream and responded to their concerns about issues that aroused little interest among new left elites: immigration; national identity; the perceived threat from the EU; and rapid social change more generally.

This was all happening in Europe, however, but not in Britain. Unlike countries such as Austria or France that were grappling with the rise of the radical right, Britain was traditionally thought of as an exception to this general trend, a view driven by the historic failure of radical and extreme right parties to make an electoral breakthrough, and an electoral system that throws up a high barrier to entry for smaller and radical parties, as we examine in Chapter 6.[9] Britons, it appeared, were either not interested in what the radical right had to offer, or unwilling to back radical challengers who appeared doomed to fail. However, as we will now see, the same long-term social and political changes that had fuelled popular radical right revolts on mainland Europe were happening in Britain as well.

Left behind: economic change and the decline of Britain's white working class

Over the past few decades Britain has experienced dramatic changes in its social structure. White working-class groups who were once large enough to decide elections have shrunk relentlessly, a trend that we chart in Figure 3.1, and which is well documented in studies of British politics.[10] At the time of Labour's 1964 general election victory under Harold Wilson, almost half of the workforce did blue-collar work, over 70 per cent of voters had no formal educational qualifications, 40 per cent of the workforce belonged to a trade union, and 30 per cent lived in council houses. It was impossible for leaders of the two main parties to ignore such large groups of voters.

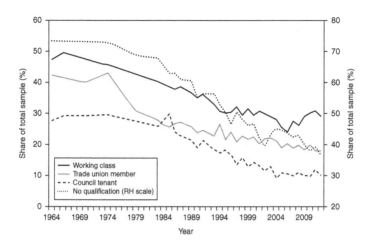

FIGURE 3.1 Decline of the working class

Source: British Election Studies 1964–1983; British Social Attitudes 1984–2012. Social class measured using the Goldthorpe–Heath 5-category class schema. Figures are percentage share of total sample, except for class which excludes those who have never worked.

When 'New' Labour and Tony Blair were elected thirty-three years later, however, their landslide win came from a very different electorate. Less than one in three workers toiled in working-class jobs, down nearly twenty percentage points from Wilson's time. The proportion holding trade union members' cards had dwindled to just over 20 per cent, down ten percentage points from 1964, though this understates the true level of change, as the unions of Blair's era were dominated by white-collar, public sector workers such as teachers and nurses. The mighty industrial unions of Wilson's time – armies of miners, steelworkers and machinists, whose fiery leaders could bring down governments – were no more. Nor were the voters of Blair's era dependent on the state for a roof over their heads: the share of the electorate renting their homes from the council in 1997 was 14 per cent, half the level seen in 1964. The voters of Blair's Britain were also more educated than those who had gone to the

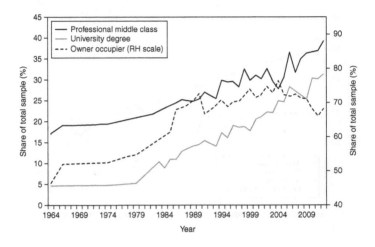

FIGURE 3.2 Rise of the middle class

Source: British Election Studies 1964–1983; British Social Attitudes 1984–2012. Social Class measured using the Goldthorpe-Heath 5 category class schema. Figures are percentage share of the total sample, except social class which excludes those who have never worked.

polls to elect Wilson; only about half of those who were interviewed in 1997 had left school without any qualifications, compared to seven in ten in 1964. In the years since New Labour swept to power, all of these trends have continued. The working class and low education groups of voters have continued to shrink, and their electoral significance has faded with their numbers. By 2012, when UKIP were surging in the polls, the share of the labour force doing blue-collar work was down to 29 per cent; only 18 per cent of workers belonged to a trade union; only one voter in ten rented their home from the local council; and just 36 per cent of voters had no formal educational qualifications, half the level in Wilson's time.

The long-term decline of the working classes is mirrored by the steady rise of the middle classes to dominance. Figure 3.2 tracks the growth in three more privileged groups in society: the professional middle classes, university degree holders and homeowners. When Wilson was elected, less than half of the electorate owned the home they occupied, less than one in five of the workforce did a professional middle-class job, and less than one in twenty had a university degree. By the time Blair came to power in 1997, 70 per cent of voters owned their own homes, almost one-third were in professional middle-class jobs, and one in five had university degrees. A couple more numbers help to throw the political implications of these trends into sharp relief. In 1964, working-class voters outnumbered professional middle-class voters two to one; but by 2010 the professional middle classes had a four to three advantage. In 1964, for every voter who attended university there were fourteen who left school with no qualifications; but by 2010 the two groups were almost equal in size. If we split the electorate into cohorts, this educational change is even more dramatic. Among those born before 1931, the unqualified outnumber university graduates twelve to one; but among the cohort born after 1975, graduates outnumber the unqualified by more than three to one. In fifty years, therefore, Britain has been transformed from a society where poorly skilled and blue-collar voters decided elections, to one where such voters have become spectators in electoral battles for the educated middle-class vote.

Not our country any more: the impact of changing social values

The rise of the university-educated middle class has done more than just transform Britain's economic structure. It has changed the values that dominate in British society. As sociologists such as Ronald Inglehart have shown, growing prosperity and rising education levels have changed the social goals that voters prioritise. The voters of the 1950s and 1960s, most of whom grew up amidst economic depression and war, prized 'material' values, like basic economic security and social stability. In sharp contrast, their children and grandchildren take such things for granted and, instead, focus on 'postmaterial' values, like liberty, human rights and environmental protection. The same underlying social dynamics have also sparked other shifts in values. Younger voters, who have grown up and prospered in a more mobile and interconnected world, tend to have weaker attachments to their nation of birth, a thinner and more instrumental sense of what national identity means, a greater openness to immigration, and a greater acceptance of ethnic diversity. In politics, they also tend to be more supportive of transnational institutions, including the EU. These shifts are related to class as well as age – it is the middle-class professionals who benefit most from Britain's integration into a global economy, and who embrace the cosmopolitan and postmaterial values associated with it. The groups who have been left behind economically over the past thirty years tend to have very different views to the rising middle classes on all of the core elements of the radical right's ideological appeal – Euroscepticism, nationalism, opposition to immigration and populism – and these differences have grown over time.

Figure 3.3 begins to shed light on these differences, by showing a large division between the educated middle classes and unskilled workers over Europe: from the mid-1990s, around 20–25 per cent of working-class voters and those with no qualifications have supported withdrawing Britain from the EU altogether, two to three times the level of support for this position among university graduates and middle-class professionals. This sharp social divide has widened since the onset of the post-2008 financial crisis: by 2012, nearly half of British voters with no formal qualifications, and 40 per cent of blue-collar workers, wanted to leave the EU, while less than a fifth of professionals or graduates favoured this option. If we were to add in the option of reducing the EU's powers, the chart would show that majorities of working-class Britons have wanted 'less Europe' since at least the time of the Maastricht Treaty, while majorities of professionals and graduates have favoured the status quo, or even called for 'more Europe'. Unskilled workers have never been sold on the idea of European integration, and the financial crisis has greatly intensified their opposition. By contrast, the professional middle classes who set the political agenda tend to have a positive view of the EU, and a majority of these voters have continued to back the status quo after 2008, despite the economic crisis in the Eurozone.

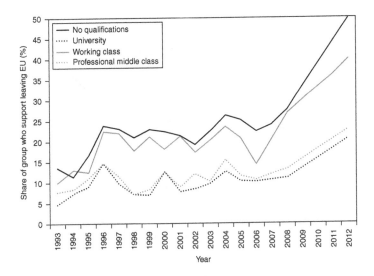

FIGURE 3.3 Support for leaving the EU, by social class and education level

Source: British Social Attitudes 1993–2012.

The differences do not stop there. There is also a clear generational divide in British public attitudes towards the EU. Older cohorts, who grew up before Britain joined the EU, are consistently more likely to support leaving it, as we show in Figure 3.4. More than 20 per cent of voters who were born before 1945 backed British withdrawal in the 1990s, a figure that has doubled since the onset of the financial crisis. This figure, however, is substantially lower for younger cohorts, and the gap between the generations has not closed even as the overall levels of Euroscepticism in Britain have risen. Younger Britons, who were born after 1975, and so have no memory at all of Britain outside the EU, nor of the repeated debates over membership in the 1970s, are the least willing to support calls for withdrawal. For these younger voters, this is a leap into the unknown, pulling out of a political arrangement that has been part of Britain's social fabric for their whole lives. In 2007, fewer

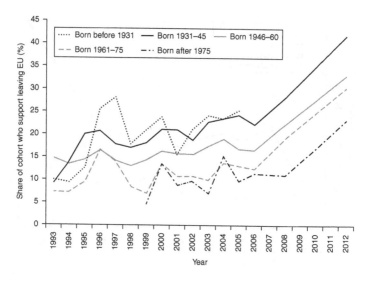

FIGURE 3.4 Support for leaving the EU, by birth cohort

Source: British Social Attitudes 1993–2012.

than one in ten of these young people supported the idea of with-drawal, a figure which rose substantially during the crisis, but which in 2012 still remained below one in four.

These social and generational gaps are driven by differences in both economic circumstances and social values. Disadvantaged, blue-collar workers stand to lose most from the greater economic integration that flows from the EU, as they are the most likely to be undercut by workers from other member states, who have more skills or are willing to work for lower wages. These disadvantaged groups also tend to hold a stronger and more assertive sense of nationalism, as Table 3.1 illustrates.[11] Here we show the propor-tion of voters in different social groups who hold 'ethnic' ideas about British national identity – that is, they think Britishness is something acquired through ancestry, birth and cultural tradition, and therefore not open to migrants and ethnic minorities. This ethnic conception of citizenship differs from 'civic' ideas, which

TABLE 3.1 Ethnic national identity beliefs among different social groups

	Working class	Middle class	No quals	University graduate	Born before 1946	Born after 1965
Born in Britain important for being British						
1995	55.4	41.1	63.5	35.7	60.8	38.5
2003	55.6	34.8	60.9	25.7	61.5	34.6
Change	*+0.2*	*−6.3*	*−2.6*	*−10.0*	*+0.7*	*−3.9*
Those who don't share British customs aren't British						
1995	52.9	50.6	58.7	34.0	60.3	44.2
2003	55.0	41.3	63.3	31.4	64.0	42.5
Change	*+2.1*	*−8.0*	*+4.6*	*−2.6*	*+3.7*	*−1.7*
British ancestors important to being British						
(2003)	39.9	17.2	46.4	12.9	51.2	9.4

Source: British Social Attitudes 1995, 2003.

maintain Britishness is a legal and political idea – anyone can be British if they choose to adopt the identity, and express loyalty to the legal and political institutions of Britain.

As with Euroscepticism, we see a similar pattern of large and widening social divides in beliefs about British national identity. Working-class voters, those with no educational qualifications and those who were born before 1946 are all much more likely to believe that British identity is defined by birth, culture and ancestry than middle-class professionals, graduates, and those who were born after 1965. We have two measures which were asked in 1995 and again in 2003, and the social divides in attitudes widened on both of these measures, as the middle classes, graduates and young people further abandoned ethnic nationalist ideas, while the working class, least educated and the old continued to emphasize them. While they are also more Eurosceptic, the social groups who have lost out over recent decades thus hold very different views on a fundamental social issue – the nature of British identity – to the groups who have risen to dominance. This difference helps explain the sharp divergence in views of the EU, and also provides an opening which radical right parties can exploit: it is no accident that UKIP place great emphasis on 'traditional' ideas of Britishness in their campaign material.

Britain's 'left behind' social groups also have very different views to the more highly educated and socially mobile middle classes on a contentious issue which has been at the heart of radical right revolts across Europe: immigration. Although public scepticism about immigration is widespread, the strength of feeling on the issue varies a great deal. Left behind voters are more likely to think immigration should be reduced 'a lot', and that it has negative economic and social effects. What is more, the gap between advantaged and disadvantaged groups on all three of these attitudes has widened over time. The proportion of working-class, low education and older voters holding negative views on immigration has risen by 10–15 per cent on all three items between our first and last survey dates; the rises for middle-class, university graduate and younger respondents are, with one exception, always below 10 per cent (Table 3.2).

The large and growing social divides over immigration reveal why the issue has proved such a potent one for radical right parties – the 'left behind' groups who are struggling most with economic and social change see immigration as a serious economic and social threat, and want it reduced drastically. The educated middle classes who dominate politics, however, do not share their urgency – they see the problems caused by immigration as mild, and are also more likely to believe that migration and minorities bring significant benefits.[12]

British attitudes about immigration have changed in other subtle and important ways. Since the 1980s and 1990s, there has been

TABLE 3.2 Negative attitudes about immigration, by social group

	Working class	Middle class	No quals	University graduate	Born pre-1946	Born post-1965
Immigration needs to be reduced 'a lot'						
1995	45.6	37.4	51.9	18.9	49.5	29.8
2003	58.2	36.5	63.9	21.8	54.7	44.2
2011	60.6	41.6	68.6	28.6	64.6	42.4
Change	*+15.0*	*+4.2*	*+16.7*	*+8.7*	*+15.1*	*+12.6*
Immigration has negative economic impact						
2002	50.8	36.1	51.3	25.9	48.7	44.2
2011	62.2	40.3	65.7	30.4	57.9	46.3
Change	*+11.4*	*+4.2*	*+14.4*	*+4.5*	*+9.2*	*+2.1*
Immigration has negative cultural impact						
2002	39.8	26.0	41.6	16.7	42.1	26.9
2011	55.9	37.2	62.4	24.2	55.6	41.8
Change	+16.1	+11.2	+20.8	+7.5	+13.5	+14.9

Source: British Social Attitudes 1995, 2003, 2011; European Social Survey 2002 (British data only).

a 'quiet revolution' in public attitudes about race and identity, and one that has affected how members of different generations of citizens see this issue. Similar to the differences that we saw in British attitudes towards European integration, old and young Britons differ sharply in how they think about the immigration issue. Unlike their parents and grandparents who grew up before the larger waves of immigration into Britain in the 1970s, and can remember an almost exclusively white Britain, younger Britons who have grown up since the onset of mass migration are more accepting of immigration, and more strongly opposed to racism and discrimination.[13] As with other views, this quiet revolution in attitudes about immigration and diversity has proceeded furthest among the educated middle classes, and most slowly among the left behind groups. The result is a steady divergence in attitudes, between an educated middle class which is outward looking and accepting of diversity, and the less privileged left behind, who still feel that these fairly rapid social changes threaten their economic security and sense of identity.

The degree to which Britain's social groups diverge in the emphasis they place on immigration can be seen in Figure 3.5. This charts the proportion of voters from each social group who spontaneously named immigration as one of the most important problems facing Britain since 2004, which we calculate using data from the Continuous Monitoring Survey, run by the BES. This question provides an unusual window into the minds of voters, as they are provided with a blank text box and invited to fill it in, detailing the issues that they think matter, without any prompting or guidance from the survey.

Throughout the decade covered by the surveys, immigration looms far larger in the minds of the 'left behind' groups. Between 20 and 30 per cent of them mention the issue spontaneously every year, around double the level of mentions from more privileged and secure groups. Secondly, attitudes have diverged sharply since 2010, as the economic crisis has faded a little from the political agenda. In 2008–2009, immigration dropped down the agenda for all social groups in Britain, as the financial crisis gripped the nation and pushed all other issues to one side. The left behind groups, however, continued to worry about the issue far more than the privileged middle classes, with 15–20 per cent naming immigration even in the depths of the recession. As the economic crisis faded, immigration has returned to the top of the agenda for these groups. By 2013, concern about immigration among left behind voters was as intense as it had been before the crisis. The story is very different for the middle classes, whose levels of concern about immigration dropped sharply in 2007–2009 and have not rebounded since. At the time of writing, therefore, immigration is once again a top priority for the

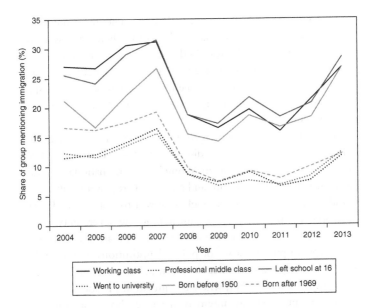

FIGURE 3.5 Spontaneous mentions of immigration as one of the most important problems facing Britain, 2004–2013, by social group

Source: British Election Study Continuous Monitoring Survey.

economically and socially disadvantaged, but is well down the list for the educated middle classes.

Anxieties about immigration and its effects, demands for reductions in the number of migrants, and the belief that immigration poses a serious problem to the nation are all expressed most strongly by the left behind coalition of older, less skilled and white workers. Already disillusioned by the economic shifts that left them lagging behind other groups in society, these voters now feel their concerns about immigration and threats to national identity have been ignored or stigmatised as expressions of prejudice by an established political class that appears more sensitive to protecting migrant newcomers and ethnic minorities than listening to the concerns of economically struggling, white Britons. The resentment this has generated was well summarised by Lord Ashcroft in his analysis of focus groups held with UKIP supporters: 'Struggling on low incomes despite long hours made many more acutely aware, and more resentful, of others who seemed to get more help despite being apparently less deserving. Immigrants usually bore the brunt of this resentment.'[14]

The picture that has emerged, therefore, is clear: Britain's left behind social groups share a distinct set of social attitudes. They place greater emphasis on an 'ethnic' sense of national identity, passed down through culture and ancestry. Partly as a result of this worldview, they are more strongly opposed to political and social developments that they see as threatening the sovereignty, continuity and identity of the British nation. They are more strongly Eurosceptic, opposing a set of political institutions they regard as alien and foreign, and demand a return to the status quo ante that many of them remember, when Britain stood proudly apart from the continent. They are intensely negative about the impact of immigration, which threatens their economic security and more ethnic sense of British national identity. In all of these respects, the left behind are different to the younger, university educated and more secure middle-class professionals who set much of the political and social agenda in modern Britain. Unlike these groups who have generally embraced these wider changes, it is the left behind who see a cosmopolitan, multicultural and globalised Britain as an alien and threatening place. These are the voters who, in Chapters 4 and 5, we expect to find are fuelling UKIP's revolt on the right, and backing Nigel Farage's pledge to 'get their country back'.

No voice: how the established parties have marginalised the left behind voters

When voters find themselves falling behind economically, and without a mainstream political voice for their concerns, one plausible reaction is that they will lose faith in the political system which they feel has failed them. As Figure 3.6 shows, this

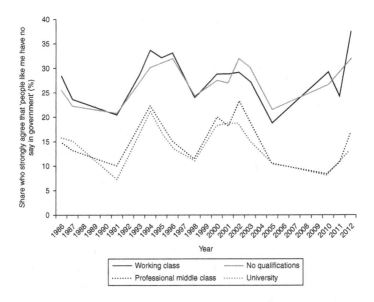

FIGURE 3.6 Share of respondents strongly agreeing 'people like me have no say in government', 1986–2012, by social group

Source: British Social Attitudes.

is precisely what has happened with the left behind voters. The working class and those with no formal educational qualifications are twice as likely as middle-class professionals and graduates to strongly agree that people like them have no say in government, a ratio which has held steady for most of the past twenty-five years. The attitudes of all groups tend to move together, with peaks in political disaffection in the later years of the John Major government, and in the early 2000s, around the time of the record low turnout at the 2001 general election. A third peak in the last few years is different, however: working class and less well educated voters feel more alienated from the political system than ever before, while disaffection levels among the middle classes and graduates have risen much less. Nearly 40 per cent of working-class Britons now strongly agree they have no say in government, well over twice the proportion (16 per cent) of middle-class voters who feel this way. The social changes that have cut these voters adrift from the British mainstream have contributed to these feelings of alienation, but so have the strategic decisions made by the political parties.

The profound changes we have explored so far have impacted strongly on citizens, shaping their concerns about particular issues and how they see the world around them. These are the underlying 'bottom-up' social changes that have gradually altered the balance of politics. But just as important as bottom-up trends are the 'top-down' changes in how Britain's political elites have crafted their strategies and messages, which changed the political choices available to voters.[15] As we will now show, the choices made first by Labour under Tony Blair and then by the Conservatives under David Cameron further marginalised the left behind voters in each of the main parties. Both of these strategic shifts made sense in terms of building election winning coalitions in a middle-class society, and are mirrored in the choices of parties elsewhere, but their cumulative effect has been to leave the less well educated and working class voters without a mainstream political champion, who *is* willing to respond to their concerns.[16]

In Britain, it was the 1983 general election that demonstrated to Labour that unadulterated socialism was a recipe for electoral disaster. Running on a hard left platform, dubbed by one moderate 'the longest suicide note in history', the party slumped to their lowest share of the national vote since the introduction of the universal franchise.[17] Accepting Labour could not win from the radical left, Neil Kinnock and John Smith, the party's leaders after 1983, spent a decade trying to convince their party of the need to return to the political centre, while retaining the loyalties of their shrinking working-class base. This did not, however, deliver success at the 1987 or 1992 general elections and, following Smith's death in 1994, Labour elected a new leadership team who proposed a more radical approach.

Tony Blair and Gordon Brown had little interest in socialist orthodoxy, and were determined to find a winning formula that could return Labour to power after a decade and a half in the wilderness. They undertook a root-and-branch reform of their party, abandoning electorally unpopular socialist shibboleths, and regularly expressed their enthusiasm for capitalism and market enterprise.[18] 'New' Labour's goal was not a wholesale reorganisation of society, but better quality provision of the public services – health care, education and welfare protection – that all voters valued. There would be no punitive taxation for the rich, no dramatic redistribution of wealth and no sweeping nationalisation of private industry. In electoral terms, this pitch proved tremendously successful, helping to deliver a landslide victory for Labour at the 1997 general election, followed by a historically unprecedented three terms of Labour majority government. But as Przeworski predicted, the strategy also came with costs.

The heavy focus on more socially mobile, aspirational and ideologically moderate voters steered Labour away from the left behind groups, who were once the party's core electorate. The reformers' goal was to escape from the 'Old Labour' associations with 'tax and spend' profligacy and a 'levelling down' focus on the poor, which they believed would alienate electorally crucial middle-class voters. Symbolic and substantive commitments to helping poor and economically insecure workers were downplayed in favour of commitments to tough spending discipline and free market reform of 'inefficient' state services. The needs of traditional Labour voters – for affordable housing, secure work, higher incomes and access to training – were marginalised in rhetoric, and often in policy too. Before all this took place, Przeworski had predicted that when socialist parties 'attempt to increase their electoral support beyond the working class they reduce their capacity to mobilize workers'.[19] This is precisely what happened to Labour after 1997.

Labour's first term was characterised by such strong commitment to the policies of the previous administration that, during the 2001 election campaign, *The Economist* captured the public mood by portraying Tony Blair with a Margaret Thatcher hairdo when endorsing Labour for a second term.[20] New Labour economic policy was Thatcherism-lite: low taxation, low regulation and strict spending limits. Although unemployment fell steadily and incomes rose, the yawning inequalities between classes and regions which had opened up during the previous Thatcher and Major governments did not narrow and large numbers of working-class families remained in poverty, untouched by the economic recovery that was benefiting the middle classes. There was no large-scale policy effort directed at the millions of former manufacturing workers living in economically depressed northern towns and cities, which had never recovered from de-industrialisation under the previous administration, and lacked the skills and experience necessary to prosper in the new services economy. Many of the former industrial workers in these regions now eked out a living on long-term disability benefits, whose claimant numbers rose remorselessly even as unemployment fell, a displaced army of unwanted workers who had withdrawn altogether from the labour market.[21]

While this cautious, incremental approach helped Labour retain their new middle-class electorate and win a second landslide victory in 2001, the costs of centrism became clear when they returned to the polls.[22] At 59 per cent, turnout had slumped to the lowest level ever in a universal suffrage election. This fall was largest in Labour's heartlands, where millions of 'Old Labour' working-class loyalists stayed home.[23] Unwilling to consider voting for one of the alternatives, many of these traditional Labour voters withdrew from politics altogether. This growing detachment from the political mainstream was reflected in the 2001 British Election Study, which found that 26 per cent of voters thought there was 'not much' difference between Labour and the Conservatives, the highest figure since the question was first asked in 1979, and 29 per cent said they didn't care who won the election, the highest figure since 1974. Labour's economic centrism delivered an unprecedented second landslide for the party, but millions of their traditional voters now saw little benefit from having a centre-left party in power, and little point in participating in politics.

Another source of working-class discontent came to the fore in Labour's second term: immigration. The issue had already featured in the first term, as liberalising reforms to the immigration system and a surge in asylum applications led to a sharp increase in migration, attracting a lot of hostile media attention. The proportion of voters naming immigration as one of the most important problems facing the country rose from 2 to 16 per cent in Blair's first term.[24] This trend then accelerated when, in 2004, Labour decided to allow migrants from Central and Eastern European countries joining the EU unrestricted access to Britain and its labour market. The proportion of Ipsos MORI's respondents naming immigration as one of the nation's most important problems rose above 25 per cent in 2003, and stayed there for the rest of Labour's second term. As we have seen, such concerns were felt most intensely by the poorer, white working-class voters who were already disaffected with Labour's economic policies. Immigration also overlapped with other concerns about identity and security, which were reinforced by urban disturbances in two northern mill towns in 2001, terrorist attacks by British-born Muslims in 2005, and the emergence of the English Defence League in 2009, all of which seemed to heighten anxieties that British Muslims were not integrating, and threatened traditional Britain's culture and values.[25]

Labour's response to working-class anxieties about migration and identity was a mix of frenetic activity and benign neglect. There was a sustained effort to deal with voters' concerns about asylum seekers by restricting their numbers, but the decision to open Britain to EU workers from Central and Eastern Europe was taken with little consultation and not revisited when both migrant numbers and public opposition proved far higher than anticipated. Central government was also slow to respond to local pressures on school places, housing and public services that followed these large migration inflows. At the same time, great effort was expended on the problem of Muslim integration, including significant funding to Muslim communities under the 'Prevent' initiative and the passage of the Race Relations (Amendment) Act, which made religious prejudice a crime. Part of the problem with Labour's response to these issues may have stemmed from the sharp differences in outlook between Labour and Whitehall political elites and the communities expressing concerns about migration. The political top flight was drawn largely from the young, highly educated middle-class section of society, which as we have seen was most open to immigration and most comfortable with diversity. The social divide that had opened up over the previous decades now found a specific political expression, as many Labour activists and politicians failed to give sufficient weight to concerns about these issues among their older working-class voters, which were often seen as expressions of ignorance and prejudice.

Labour's inaction reflected political calculations as well as differences in social values between their activists and their traditional voters. By the 2000s, Britain's ethnic minority population was a significant voting bloc, and one whose traditional loyalties to Labour were no longer certain.[26] Retaining the support of Britain's large and rapidly growing minority groups was an important pillar of Labour strategy, particularly after 2005, when British Muslims angry about the war in Iraq defected in large numbers to the Liberal Democrats and the Respect party. Liberalisation of the immigration system, the toughening of discrimination legislation, and a growing slate of ethnic minority candidates for Parliament were actions designed to appeal to Britain's growing ethnic minority population, who had often experienced the sharp end of prejudice and were understandably keen to correct decades of under-representation in the political elite. However, such efforts risked further alienating white working-class voters, who often saw this as Labour putting the interests of ethnic minorities before their own needs.

Labour's policies of economic moderation and a liberal approach to migration and minorities both made electoral sense. But neither reflected the values or priorities of their original support base: the ageing, shrinking and left behind white, working class. Over the course of a decade, the costs of this mismatch mounted. White working-class voters no longer saw Labour as a party sensitive to

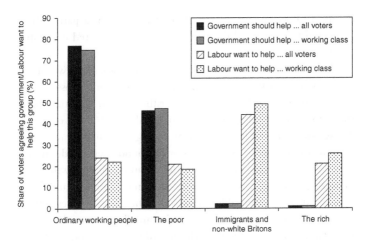

FIGURE 3.7 Views about which groups the government should help, and which groups Labour wants to help

Source: YouGov 'Euro Mega Poll', June 2009.

their concerns, but as part of the problem. The startling extent of this problem was reflected in a large poll conducted by YouGov on the eve of Labour's disastrous European Parliament defeat in 2009, which saw the party win only 15.7 per cent of the total vote, their lowest figure in the history of European elections. Voters were asked to indicate which groups the government *should* help most, and which groups the governing Labour Party *wanted* to help most – we display a selection of the answers in Figure 3.7. As the solid black and grey bars show, voters strongly prioritise government help for the poor and ordinary workers over help for the rich, immigrants and minorities. Yet when asked which groups the governing Labour Party actually *wants* to help most, shown by the striped bars, the pattern is reversed – voters had come to believe that Labour prioritised immigrants and minorities, and the rich, while neglecting the poor and ordinary workers. This divide is even clearer among working-class voters, whose responses are shown in the grey dotted bars. The message is clear: after a decade in government, New Labour were seen as a party which neglected the poor and the working class, and courted minorities and the rich.

The cumulative consequence of thirteen years of New Labour government was thus a gradual loss of faith among those on the bottom rungs of Britain's social ladder that Labour was still a party that represented, responded to and cared about their concerns. These voters responded with a mix of anger, alienation and disaffection, and the loyalties that had once bound them to the dominant left-wing party gradually withered away. This growing pool of voters, disaffected with Labour's economic approach and angry about immigration, should have provided the Conservatives with an opening. Their economic focus on the middle class would present less of a handicap with voters who regarded Labour as no different, while tough policies on immigration and assertive nationalism had worked before, winning earlier Conservative politicians, like Enoch Powell and Margaret Thatcher, a large and devoted working-class following.[27]

The Conservatives did make efforts to appeal to this electorate. They proposed a tougher line on immigration in the 2001 and 2005 manifestos, variously warning Britons that their country was turning into a 'foreign land' and that it was 'not racist to talk about immigration'. These appeals had some effect – voters who were most concerned about immigration were more likely to switch to the Conservatives in both 2001 and 2005, but the impact was not enough to offset their disadvantages elsewhere.[28] After a third straight election defeat in 2005, the Conservatives decided a drastic shift in approach was needed to win back power. They elected a young and untested leader who – much like Blair – was determined to steer his party back onto the centre ground. Just as New Labour had downplayed or tweaked tenets of their philosophy that lacked mass appeal, so too did David Cameron with his 'compassionate Conservatism' project. In his pitch for the leadership, Cameron had talked of fundamentally changing his party, warning against a rightward turn and proposing to give voters a message 'that shows we're comfortable with modern Britain'.[29] A new cadre of young and highly educated Conservatives aimed to remake the centre-right in their image, designing economically moderate and socially liberal policies, which included boosting the number of women and ethnic minorities MPs and tackling climate change, all policies designed to win over educated middle-class voters and other groups, such as ethnic minorities, who previously shunned the Conservative Party.

In contrast, the 'Cameroons' made relatively little effort to win over white, working-class voters who a previous generation of Conservatives had cultivated assiduously. This, like New Labour's lack of interest in the same group, was a deliberate strategy. Many white, working-class voters, particularly in the former industrial towns and cities of Northern England, retained an intense antipathy towards the party of Thatcher, which made them difficult to win over. Such voters also tended to concentrate in safe Labour seats, with weak or non-existent local Conservative parties. By the time Cameron took over, the Liberal Democrats were the main challenge to Labour in most of these urban Northern seats, and the Conservatives had been wiped out of local government in many large Northern cities.[30] Winning back ground in these areas would require a serious, sustained investment with a very uncertain return. This investment would also come with costs: a pitch designed to appeal to white, working-class voters – focusing on immigration, law and order and Euroscepticism – would likely resurrect the Thatcherite 'nasty party' image, and alienate other growing and electorally vital social groups, such as the young, university graduates and ethnic minorities. The changing relative sizes of the left behind groups and the degree holding middle class, thus changed the politics of the Conservatives, as it had previously changed the politics of Labour. Winning support from the army of middle-class professionals was simply more important now than attracting poorly educated and financially disadvantaged blue-collar voters.

In the end, Cameron's centrist makeover was still not sufficient to secure his party a majority, and in 2010 he entered a coalition with the Liberal Democrats. This coalition with a centrist and socially liberal party further curtailed the Conservatives' ability to appeal to left behind groups. On the one hand, the austerity agenda of tax rises and cuts to benefits and public services was likely to antagonise such voters, as they were more likely to make use of government assistance. On the other, the Conservatives' ability to offset this antagonism with a tough socially conservative line on immigration, Europe and crime was constrained by the objections of their coalition partners. Meanwhile, the Liberal Democrats, who had been making inroads in many urban working-class Labour seats, severely damaged their appeal to white, working-class voters by allying with the Conservatives and supporting the austerity agenda. The 2010 result thus cleared the field for the radical right in many areas, as white, working-class voters still alienated from Labour soon turned against the coalition parties, as well.

Conclusions: the new rebel army

Five years after Paul Nuttall had first urged UKIP to focus on disadvantaged, working-class voters, he found himself making the same argument at the party's annual conference, in 2013. By this time, however, UKIP had enjoyed unprecedented electoral growth and were more open to ideas about how to widen their appeal still further. Taking aim at the 'Westminster media' for portraying UKIP as a repository of disgruntled Southern Tories, Nuttall reiterated his belief for the party to build support rapidly among the deprived, working-class communities that had lost faith in their traditional party. 'In the days of Clement Attlee', argued Nuttall, 'the Labour MPs came from the mills, the mines and the factories. The Labour MPs today follow the same route as the Conservatives and the Liberal Democrats. They go to private school, they go to Oxbridge, they get a job in an MP's office and they become an MP. None of them would know what it's like in a working man's club.' Reflecting on this potential source of support, he continued: 'We have an opportunity to change British politics forever. We can create an earthquake next year ... but we cannot do it if we're a political party that only appeals to Conservatives in the South. We need to take the Labour vote in the North with us if we want to succeed.'

After taking a step back to look at the major political and social trends of the last few decades, our evidence suggests Nuttall was right. Over the past fifty years, a deep divide has opened up between struggling, working-class voters who have been left behind by the economic and social transformation of Britain, and the university educated middle classes, who have prospered and risen to numerical and political dominance. This divide is a matter of heart as well as head: the circumstances of the left behind voters are different, but so are their values. The long-running social surveys we have examined reveal how the degree-holding middle class and the unqualified working class are worlds apart on issue after issue, including all the core items on the radical right political agenda – national identity, immigration, Europe and views of the political system. The left behind provide a new army of potential rebels for the radical right, united by their stronger and more assertive sense of nationalism, hostility towards Brussels and immigrants, and loss of faith in mainstream politics.

Those who thought Britain was somehow different to Europe, that the radical right revolts which upended political systems across the Channel could never occur here, were simply wrong: the potential for such a revolt in Britain has existed for decades. Social and economic change has shrunk the traditional working classes, and pushed them to the margins, where they feel alienated, left behind and angry. The strategies of the two main parties have compounded this process, denying these voters a political voice and leaving them with no outlet for their distinct set of values and concerns, which that separate them from the dominant middle class. After twenty years of neglect by the two main parties, many of these voters feel little connection with the established political class, and after twenty years of battling with economic and social stagnation, many have also lost faith in the ability of the political system to resolve their problems.

The divisions between the left behind and the British mainstream have existed for decades, but until now they have had no effective political outlet. UKIP, a party formed for a very different purpose, and which initially appealed to very different voters, has, almost by accident, stumbled across this potent new social division and given it a voice. The 2009 European elections and later local campaigns in towns like Oldham in 2011 taught the party that their message had a powerful appeal to working-class voters. This was taken further in Nuttall's speech in 2013, during which he outlined how the party had come to recognise the power of these resentments they are mobilising, and the potential that lies before them among specific sections of society. Nor is there any quick fix for the main parties to bring these left behind voters back into the fold. Their alienation runs too deep. The changes which have pushed these voters to the margins will continue: the economic prospects of unskilled workers look as grim as ever, while the university educated middle classes continue to grow in size and political influence, and on Europe, immigration and identity the mainstream parties' political interests continue to lie in hewing to the values of the growing middle-class mainstream. Britain's radical right revolt has been a long time coming, and it has a long way yet to run.

Notes

1 Paul Nuttall, 'How and why UKIP can attract the Old Labour vote', *Independence* (Winter 2007).
2 Ashcroft's study suggested those who voted for UKIP at the 2010 general election tended to be male, were older than average and working class, unemployed or dependent on the state for subsistence (the so-called 'C2 and DE' categories). Support for UKIP was much lower among more prosperous, skilled and educated upper- and middle-class groups (the 'ABC1' categories). However, his data suggested that UKIP-considerers were also more likely to be male and older, but otherwise exhibited the same socio-economic profile as the general population. Lord Michael Ashcroft (2012) 'UKIP: They're thinking what we're thinking: Understanding the UKIP temptation'. Published by Lord Ashcroft. Available online: http://lordashcroftpolls.com/2012/12/the-ukip-threat-is-not-about-europe/ (accessed 3 September 2013).
3 Ashcroft 'UKIP: They're thinking what we're thinking'.

4 David Butler and Donald Stokes (1964) *Political Change in Britain: The Evolution of Electoral Choice*, London: Macmillan. Data from the BSA surveys can also be accessed online: http://www.natcen.ac.uk/series/british-social-attitudes (accessed 18 September 2013).

5 Hans-Georg Betz (1993) 'The new politics of resentment: Radical right-wing populist parties in Western Europe', *Comparative Politics*, 25(4): 413–27; Hans-George Betz and Susi Meret (2013) 'Right-wing populist parties and the working-class vote: What have you done for us lately?', in Jens Rydgren (ed.) *Class Politics and the Radical Right*, Abingdon: Routledge, pp. 107–21.

6 On the French National Front vote see Nonna Mayer (2013) 'From Jean-Marie to Marine Le Pen: Electoral change on the far right', *Parliamentary Affairs*, 66(1): 160–78. More generally see Rydgren (ed.) *Class Politics and the Radical Right*; Daniel Oesch (2008) 'Explaining workers' support for right-wing populist parties in Western Europe: Evidence from Austria, Belgium, France, Norway and Switzerland', *International Political Science Review*, 29(3): 349–73; Herbert Kitschelt with Anthony McGann (1995) *The Radical Right in Western Europe: A Comparative Analysis*, Ann Arbor: University of Michigan Press.

7 Adam Przeworski (1985) *Capitalism and Social Democracy*, Cambridge: Cambridge University Press.

8 As Hooghe *et al.* (2002) note, social democratic parties are certainly not monolithically in favour of European integration, and some contain vocal factions that are critical of this process. However, across Europe they note how majorities in centre-left parties 'have come to perceive European integration as a means for projecting social democratic goals in a liberalizing world economy'. Liesbet Hooghe, Gary Marks and Carole J. Wilson (2002) 'Does left/right structure party positions on European integration?', *Comparative Political Studies*, 35(8): 965–89; see also Liesbet Hooghe and Gary Marks (1999) 'Making of a polity: The struggle over European integration', in Herbert Kitschelt, Peter Lange, Gary Marks and John Stephens (eds.) *Continuity and Change in Contemporary Capitalism*, Cambridge: Cambridge University Press, pp. 70–97.

9 On the historic failure of the radical and extreme right-wing in Britain see Roger Eatwell (1992) 'Why has the extreme right failed in Britain?', in Paul Hainsworth (ed.) *The Extreme Right in Europe and the USA*, London: Pinter, pp. 175–92; and (2000) 'The extreme right and British exceptionalism: The primacy of politics', in Paul Hainsworth (ed.) *The Politics of the Extreme Right: From the Margins to the Mainstream*, London: Pinter, pp. 72–92; Matthew J. Goodwin (2007) 'The extreme right in Britain: Still an "ugly ducking" but for how long?' *Political Quarterly*, 78(2): 241–50.

10 Anthony Heath and S. K. McDonald (1987) 'Social change and the future of the left', *Political Quarterly*, 58: 364–77; Anthony Heath, Roger Jowell and John Curtice (2002) *The Rise of New Labour: Party Policies and Voter Choices*, Oxford: Oxford University Press, pp. 10–30; Ivor Crewe (1991) 'Labor force changes, working class decline, and the Labour vote: Social and electoral trends in postwar Britain', in F. F. Piven (ed.) *Labor Parties in Postindustrial Societies*, New York: Oxford University Press, pp. 20–46; Mark F. Franklin (1985) *The Decline of Class Voting in Britain; Changes in the Basis of Electoral Choice, 1964–1983*, Oxford: Clarendon Press; for a broader argument see also Herbert Kitschelt (1994) *The Transformation of European Social Democracy*, Cambridge: Cambridge University Press.

11 Marcel Lubbers and Peer Scheepers (2010) 'Divergent trends of Euroscepticism in countries and regions of the European Union', *European Journal of Political Research*, 49: 787–817; Catherine De Vreese and Hago Boomgaarden (2005) 'Projecting EU referendums: Fear of immigration and support for European integration', *European Union Politics*, 6(1): 59–82; Lauren McLaren (2006) *Identity, Interests and Attitudes to European Integration*, Basingstoke: Palgrave Macmillan.

12 Respondents who are in professional middle-class jobs, have degrees or were born in the 1970s or later are consistently more likely to give positive views about the effects of immigration, as well as being less likely to demand reductions in migration levels. See Robert Ford, Gareth Morell and Anthony Heath (2012) 'Fewer but Better? British Attitudes to Immigration', in Alison Park, Elisabeth Clery, John Curtice, Miranda Phillips and David Utting (eds.) *British Social Attitudes: the 29th Report*, London: NatCen

13 Robert Ford (2011) 'Acceptable and unacceptable immigrants: The ethnic hierarchy in British immigration preferences', *Journal of Ethnic and Migration Studies*, 37(7): 1017–37; Robert Ford (2008) 'Is racial prejudice declining in Britain?', *British Journal of Sociology*, 59(4): 609–36.

14 Ashcroft, 'UKIP: They're thinking what we're thinking'.

15 Geoffrey Evans and James Tilley (2012) 'How parties shape class politics: Explaining the decline of the class basis of party support', *British Journal of Political Science*, 42: 137–61.

16 Thomas Koelble (1992) 'Recasting social democracy in Europe: A nested games explanation of strategic adjustment in political parties', *Politics and Society*, 20: 51–70; also Kitschelt, *The Transformation of European Social Democracy*, cited in Evans and Tilley, 'How parties shape

class politics'; Peter Mair, Wolfgang Muller and Fritz Plasser (2004) 'Introduction: Electoral challengers and party responses', in Peter Mair, Wolfgang Muller and Fritz Plasser (eds.) *Political Parties and Electoral Change*, London: Sage, pp. 1–19.

17 The moderate in question was Labour MP Gerald Kaufman.

18 Steven Fielding (2003) *The Labour Party: Continuity and Change in the Making of 'New' Labour*, Basingstoke: Palgrave Macmillan.

19 Ibid.

20 The endorsement of the traditionally liberal, free-market magazine was itself a symbol of Labour's changed political agenda.

21 Inactivity rates among low skilled men continued to rise through most of the 2000s. Some 60 per cent of all inactive men were in the lowest quartile (25 per cent) for skills. Most of these inactive men were claiming disability benefit during the New Labour governments. See S. Nickell (2003) 'Poverty and worklessness in Britain', LSE: Centre for Economic Performance Working Paper; G. Faggio and S. Nickell (2005) 'Inactivity rates among prime age men in the UK', LSE: Centre for Economic Performance Working Paper.

22 Though Labour were also helped by the incompetence of the Conservative opposition (see Tim Bale (2011) *The Conservative Party from Thatcher to Cameron*, London: Polity Press).

23 David Butler and Dennis Kavanagh (2002) *The British General Election of 2001*, Basingstoke: Palgrave Macmillan, pp. 307–10.

24 Figures taken from Ipsos MORI Issues Index. Available online: http://www.ipsos-mori.com/researchspecialisms/socialresearch/specareas/politics/trends.aspx (accessed 17 September 2013).

25 On EDL support see Matthew J. Goodwin (2013) *The Roots of Extremism: The English Defence League and the Counter-Jihad Challenge*, London: Chatham House; also Jamie Bartlett (2011) *Inside the EDL: Populist Politics in a Digital Age*, London: Demos.

26 On support for Labour among ethnic minority voters see David Sanders, Anthony Heath, Stephen Fisher and Maria Sobolewska (2013) 'The calculus of ethnic minority voting in Britain', *Political Studies* (in print); Maria Sobolewska, Edward Fieldhouse and David Cutts (2013) 'Taking minorities for granted? Ethnic density, party campaigning and targeting minority voters in 2010 British general elections', *Parliamentary Affairs*, 66(2): 329–44; Anthony F. Heath, Stephen D. Fisher, David Sanders and Maria Sobolewska (2011) 'Ethnic heterogeneity in the social bases of voting at the 2010 British General Election', *Journal of Elections, Public Opinion and Parties*, 21(2): 255–77.

27 On Enoch Powell and working-class support see Douglas E. Schoen (1977) *Enoch Powell and the Powellites*, London: Macmillan. On the Conservatives' success with working-class voters under Thatcher, see Heath, Jowell and Curtice, *The Rise of New Labour*, chapters 3, 4 and 7.

28 Robert Ford (2008) 'British attitudes towards immigrant ethnic minorities 1964–2005: Reactions to diversity and their political effects', Oxford: Unpublished DPhil dissertation.

29 Transcript of David Cameron's speech to the Conservative conference 2005.

30 Neil O'Brien and Anthony Wells (2012) *Northern Lights: Public Policy and the Geography of Attitudes*, London: Policy Exchange.

4
THE SOCIAL ROOTS OF THE REVOLT

Meet John. He is 64 years old and was born and raised in Nottingham, where he worked for many years as a skilled machinist in the famous Raleigh bicycle factory. John started as a line worker when he was only 15 years old. 'I was never much for school, left as soon as I could. I knew Raleigh were hiring, you could walk straight into a good job in those days.' John prospered at the factory and, within a few years, he was supervising a team of ten. 'That was how it was back then. You didn't need certificates. Work hard, show you can learn, and you'd make your way.' But in 2003, John was made redundant as the last factory was shuttered. 'They said something I didn't understand about European regulations, and that we couldn't compete with the Far East. They'd work twice the hours we could, for a tenth of the money.' When John turned 50, he found himself unemployed for the first time in his life. 'I don't blame the company, they did their best, treated me fair, gave me a good pay-off. But when I went looking, there was no work.'

It was around this time that John, who used to vote for Margaret Thatcher's Conservatives before switching to Labour after she resigned, began to question his loyalties. 'Labour, right? Party of the working man, right? Well, here's my pals and me, all lifelong workers, all on the dole. What are the politicians doing? Nothing. Absolutely nothing. But when immigrants come they lay down the welcome mat.' Bouncing between a series of low-paid temporary jobs, John became angry and embittered about the state of British politics. 'There was a time when the working man was respected, when politicians listened to us, when if you kept your head down and worked hard they'd make sure you'd get a fair go. Thatcher's lot believed in that. Labour too, once. That's all long gone now. Those in Westminster don't give a toss about us.'

At the 2005 general election, John considered voting for the BNP, but decided against it. 'I agreed with a lot of what they said, but I couldn't stomach it. Nazis, they are. Fascists. My dad fought a war against that. So I bit my lip and voted for Labour.' But then things for John went from bad to worse. 'The economy went down the tubes. The pointless wars. Muslims blowing up London. All those kids running riot – don't even want to work, that lot. Just steal it all. Then more immigrants, as if we didn't have enough! The Poles. The Lithuanians. Flooding in from all over, taking all of our housing, milking our benefits, and no one in the party for workers wants to do a thing about it. The EU ordered it and our government wouldn't stand up to them. They never even bothered to ask us if we wanted it. And then the expenses thing. Politicians from all the big parties robbing us blind.' At the 2009 European Parliament elections, John switched to UKIP. He knew they were a small and untested party but he agreed with their call to 'sod the lot'. 'I saw an election broadcast. It was amazing. Finally, someone was speaking plain, common sense. I was converted on the spot.' Since then, John has stayed fiercely loyal to UKIP, backing them at every election and becoming an active member. 'Thought I'd turned my back on politics, but UKIP give me hope. They are what this country needs: common sense and a fresh start.'

John's story is representative of the hundreds of thousands of voters who have defected to UKIP over the past decade. Each of these voters has their own unique story to tell, of course. But the fictional account of John draws on the mix of social background, attitudes and views our analysis suggests is typical of UKIP's average voter. UKIP are the most successful British insurgent party in a generation. Despite campaigning in a system that stacks the deck against smaller parties, they have struck a chord, meeting a demand in politics that none of the existing parties are addressing, and perhaps which none realised existed until a few years ago.

So far, we have shown how UKIP have evolved from a single-issue, anti-EU pressure group into a more professional party with a clearly defined message. This has been focused and targeted: opposition to Europe, opposition to immigration and opposition to the established political class. Our look at wider trends in British society then showed how social and economic changes created a market for radical right politics among struggling 'left behind' voters without a voice in mainstream politics by Britain. But who have UKIP *actually* won over, and how has this changed as they have become more successful? This chapter focuses on where UKIP's voters come from – their social backgrounds and prior political attachments. The next chapter examines what they want – their beliefs and political demands. Both provide unprecedented insight into these new rebel voters.

Competing interpretations: who backs UKIP?

Journalists and academics who have tried to make sense of UKIP's rise offer contradictory accounts. Many maintain that the party's support remains primarily a matter of Euroscepticism and comes from disaffected middle-class Tories, who share their antipathy to Europe, yearn nostalgically for the days of Margaret Thatcher 'handbagging' the Eurocrats and today feel fed up with the compromises that are required by coalition government.[1] 'UKIP', writes the journalist Peter Oborne, 'is in reality the Conservative Party in exile'.[2] Tim Montgomerie, an influential Conservative commentator, concurs: 'On issue after issue Nigel Farage, the UKIP leader, is directly wooing unhappy Conservatives. UKIP's position on human rights laws, foreign aid, immigration and gay marriage all appeal to those most unhappy with the limits that coalition has put on Mr Cameron.'[3] These claims similarly emerge during interviews with Nigel Farage, who is repeatedly told by journalists like Andrew Neil that his party is 'dominated by ... disgruntled Conservatives'.[4]

This view has gained wide currency, but there is an alternative perspective that points to the strength of UKIP among working-class voters, including many who once backed Labour. As we saw in Chapter 2, since 2010 the party has actively courted disadvantaged, working-class voters, including 'Old Labour' supporters, with activists like Paul Nuttall identifying this constituency as crucial to widening UKIP's appeal. One journalist who has noted this development is Fraser Nelson, editor of *The Spectator*, who watched this pitch to Britain's working class while attending Farage's 'common sense tour' of the country in 2013. UKIP's leader, wrote Nelson, 'invokes Europe, but only when it relates to problems felt by blue-collar workers: unemployment, housing and school places. He is trying to move UKIP's politics away from the Rue de la Loi and towards Britain's housing estates.'[5] Also watching the party's advance was Glen Owen of the *Daily Mail*, who similarly observed how UKIP were launching tailored appeals to workers in Labour areas.[6] Andrew Rawnsley of *The Observer*, has similarly warned against the 'orthodox view' that UKIP poses a threat only to the Conservatives. While the party 'is probably gaining most of its new support from former Tory voters', he argues, 'it is also drawing in people who used to back Labour or the Lib Dems and adding others who normally don't turn out for elections at all'.[7] Seen from this perspective, whereas UKIP's voters dislike Brussels it is not their main or only motive for revolt. Rather, 'Europe' often functions as a symbol of other problems in society and perceived threats to the nation: unresponsive and out-of-touch elites in Brussels and Westminster; a breakdown in respect for authority and British traditions; and, most importantly, the onset of mass immigration.

The working-class dimension to UKIP support, which we explore in this chapter, has also attracted the attention of their current leader, Nigel Farage, who in interviews with the authors rejected the conventional wisdom that his party is populated only by disillusioned Tories: 'It's Fleet Street. This is *all* Fleet Street. This is their obsession and they can't get out of it. But the numbers are perfectly clear. There is now a huge class dimension to the UKIP vote.'

This ongoing debate about the roots of the revolt has also led some to draw parallels with the extreme right BNP, which also draws support from white, working-class men. While the two parties have very different histories, some argue UKIP 'feels like the BNP – only in blazers', and suggest there are significant overlaps in support for these two parties.[8] This has been voiced by Peter Kellner, President of the polling firm YouGov, who before the BNP's demise suggested the two 'nationalist parties' had tapped into the same public anxieties over immigration and Europe: 'Not surprisingly', he observed, 'potential UKIP and BNP voters feel particularly strongly about both things. However, two things are striking: the range of views among potential UKIP and BNP voters is virtually identical – and in both cases, immigration arouses even stronger hostility than Europe.'[9] As we saw in Chapter 2, Kellner's argument has been echoed by some academics who have also suggested the two parties may be 'part of the same phenomenon', while in our interviews senior UKIP activists acknowledged how since 2010 they have sought to take advantage of the BNP's collapse.[10] Such comparisons have even led anti-fascists to campaign against UKIP, arguing that while the party is not fascist it 'taps into an English nationalism and xenophobia that was once mined by Enoch Powell' (a view that led UKIP, in response, to proscribe members of the anti-fascist movement Hope Not Hate).[11] These arguments suggest that both parties have drawn support from the left behind electorate that we identified in the previous chapter: the older, white and poorly educated working class, who share strong feelings about national identity, Europe and immigration, and a lack of faith in established politics.

Yet these perspectives also tend to assume that the profile of UKIP's support has remained stable, even as the party have grown rapidly since 2010, which ignores important questions. Has the party surged by maximising support from groups who sympathised with them from the start, or have they grown by branching out and recruiting new groups of voters? The evidence from radical right parties in other Western democracies suggests that either route is possible. In France, for example, Jean-Marie Le Pen's Front National (FN) increased their support among manual workers from 8 per cent during their breakthrough in 1984, to over 30 per cent in 1995. While the party struggled to make headway into the more financially secure middle class, Le Pen's success with blue-collar voters was such that his party supplanted the Socialists as the most popular choice among workers. The Freedom Party of Austria similarly evolved into a serious electoral force by consolidating working-class support, which in twenty years grew from around 4 to 49 per cent.[12] Other countries have seen radical right parties develop a base in one part of society, and then grow by recruiting different groups. In countries like Denmark and Norway the radical right Progress Parties began by rallying opposition to high taxes and welfare provision among rural social conservatives and the self-employed, but as they grew their base diversified. Both parties increased their share of the vote from workers and the least educated voters who agreed with their criticism of immigration, Islam and, in the Danish case, the EU.[13]

Since 2010, some commentators in Britain have argued that UKIP's more recent and rapid growth is the result of a similar shift. Following their record results at the 2013 local elections, this view was expressed by the journalist John Rentoul: '[I]t is possible that most of those Tories who are tempted by UKIP had defected already, before 2012, whereas Labour's disaffected have only recently seen the attraction of Nigel Farage's lot as a protest vote.'[14] The question of whether UKIP's electoral base has changed is not merely one of academic interest. The party's future prospects are likely to be very different depending on whether they have widened their support across society or, instead, deepened their support among their already loyal 'core' groups.

In this chapter, we delve into the data to build a social profile of UKIP support, focusing on four questions. First, does UKIP's revolt have a distinctive social base and, if so, what does this look like? Second, has the party rallied similar types of voters as the BNP, or have they recruited citizens from different walks of life? Third, has the overall picture of support for UKIP remained static or changed over time as they have grown? Fourth, what is the political background of UKIP support and how is this changing? To answer these questions we make use of the most extensive dataset on UKIP supporters currently available. Before diving into the analysis, we will say a little about why we have picked this dataset, and how we plan to use it.

Painting a reliable picture: a brief note on data

Researching public support for radical parties has never been easy. Those who study supporters of established parties typically use representative sample surveys, which interview a random selection of a few thousand voters. This information can be used to make statistical inferences about a party's wider electorate, thanks to the nature of statistical sampling. If proper sampling methods are used, researchers can use their analysis of a survey sample to draw confident conclusions about the larger mass of voters from which the sample is drawn. George Gallup, one of the founders of public opinion research, explained this process by comparing sampling people to sampling soup. 'One spoonful', he said, 'will reflect the taste of the whole pot, provided the soup is well stirred'.[15] But it is far more difficult to use this method when exploring support for smaller parties such as UKIP. Until recently, only around one voter in every twenty expressed support for the party, and so a typical survey of 1,000 people would only have around fifty UKIP supporters, which is not enough for meaningful analysis.

If traditional surveys are too small to be effective, then how can we study radical right parties like UKIP? One alternative is to go hunting *only* for their supporters. Researchers might find them in areas where the party performs well at elections, at party meetings or on affiliated websites. After UKIP's strong performance at local elections in 2013, the polling company ComRes surveyed 101 UKIP councillors, with the findings taken by some as evidence that the party's wider support has come almost exclusively from disillusioned Tories.[16] This strategy can provide interesting insights but it has two important drawbacks. The first is that we have no way of knowing how representative these people are of the *average* UKIP supporter. In fact there are good reasons to expect them to be quite different! Supporters who live in stronghold areas, attend meetings, browse websites or represent the party at elections are likely to be far more informed and committed than the average supporter. In this book we want to paint a picture of UKIP supporters in general, but if we use samples like these we will end up with a portrait of the true believers.[17] A second drawback is that we cannot compare supporters recruited in this way with supporters of other parties, as the methods used to gather the two samples are too different. So, if a traditional survey is too small, and a UKIP-specific study is too unreliable, what options are left?

The option that we favour is simply to turbo-charge the traditional survey approach by using a much larger sample of voters. This sample has to be large enough to ensure that, even if only one out of every twenty voters expresses support for UKIP, we still have a sufficient number to enable meaningful analysis. The survey also needs to ask a large range of questions, so we can build a nuanced picture of supporters. One high quality and reliable survey that meets both criteria is the Continuous Monitoring Survey (CMS), conducted by the British Election Study.[18] Since April 2004, the CMS has gathered detailed information on around 1,000 British voters every month, including their backgrounds, values, views on issues and on the performance of the government and opposition parties. Combining all of the surveys fielded between April 2004 and April 2013 produces a sample of 124,000 British voters. Importantly for this book, this large sample also includes 5,593 voters who expressed intended support for UKIP at the next general election (and 1,332 BNP supporters), a large enough group to enable serious analysis. Also, where necessary we draw on our past academic studies.[19]

The size of this sample enables us to provide a reliable profile of UKIP voters, while the long time frame of the CMS enables us to also analyse how this profile of support has evolved over time. We pool together voters interviewed over a period that encompasses two general elections (in 2005 and 2010), two European Parliament elections (in 2004 and 2009), a parliamentary expenses scandal (in 2009), two changes of Prime Minister (from Tony Blair to Gordon Brown in 2007, and from Gordon Brown to David Cameron in 2010) and a change of government (in 2010). When the first surveys were filled in during the spring of 2004, Tony Blair and New Labour presided over a booming economy and an electorate whose main concerns were improving public services and the war in Iraq. When the last surveys were returned in the spring of 2013, David Cameron and a Conservative–Liberal Democrat coalition were struggling to tackle a deep financial crisis, enacting austerity cuts and the electorate's top priorities were the economy and immigration. UKIP's first major breakthrough in local elections occurred only a few days after our last surveys were returned, so the data provide a unique resource for analysing the roots of this political revolt, and how it has evolved dynamically as the rebellion gathered momentum.

There is one small caveat to bear in mind. What we are analysing here is not actual marks on the ballot for UKIP, but declarations of an intent to support the party in a future election, which may be years away. Many voters will not follow through on this intention when polling day comes, for any number of reasons. Fleeting sympathy with the radical right, or anger with the incumbents, may melt away as the ballot date approaches; latent sympathies for one of the other parties may be reactivated by the election campaign or specific events; voters may be influenced by loyalty towards a particular local candidate; or may conclude that, while UKIP would be their first choice, the rebels have no chance of winning in their local seat (see Chapter 6). While this limitation needs to be borne in mind, we are still analysing voters who have openly declared their sympathies for UKIP. We have no reason to doubt the sincerity of this declaration when it was made, even if was not acted upon in the polling booth. What our data most certainly capture is a willingness to consider backing the new radical right insurgent, and this willingness alone is enough to make waves politically, as the media and political reaction to record UKIP poll ratings in 2013 demonstrated. What we dissect here, then, is the *potential* for a mass voter revolt, a potential which may or may not be realised at future Westminster elections, but which exists in the minds of British voters, as recorded in their survey responses. We provide some further discussion of our data and their limitations in the methodological appendix at the end of the book.

A social profile of the UKIP revolt

Political parties usually rise by mobilising conflicts with society: between classes, religions, the town and the country, or the centre and the periphery.[20] Britain's contemporary parties have their origins in such divides: the divide between Labour and the Conservatives originated as a competition for power between the working class and the middle class; the Scottish and Welsh nationalist parties mobilised opposition to rule from the English centre; and the Northern Irish loyalist and republican parties mobilise and reflect divisions of religion and national identity.[21] As parties very often emerge as the political expression of social divisions, a natural question to ask is whether UKIP are performing a similar role.

We start by looking at the social profile of UKIP voters, looking at how this support is distributed across five key demographics: social class, education, gender, age and ethnicity, and compare this to the bases of support for the three main parties, the BNP, and the other large minor party, the Greens. Table 4.1 provides these details and, for ease of comparison, we have aggregated these demographic variables into broad categories. Social class is aggregated into three categories: the 'middle class' of professionals and white-collar managers in secure and high status work; the 'routine non-manual' class of clerks, sales people and service workers who populate the nation's offices and shops; and the 'working class', which consists of all those in society who do manual work plus those who do not work at all.

Contrary to those who argue that UKIP's voters are middle-class Tories, we actually find that their base is more working-class than that of any of the main parties. Blue-collar UKIP voters outnumber their white-collar counterparts by a large margin: 42 per cent of these voters work in blue-collar jobs or do not work at all, while a smaller percentage of 30 per cent hold professional middle-class jobs. This picture is reversed in the main parties, where the middle classes dominate: 44 per cent of Conservative supporters are middle class, and 28 per cent are working class; there is a similar 43–27 division among supporters of the Liberal Democrats; while

TABLE 4.1 Social distribution of radical right support compared with the mainstream parties, 2004–2013

	UKIP	BNP support (2007–13)	Cons	Labour	Lib Dems	Greens	Overall sample
Social class							
Professional/managerial middle class	30	22	44	36	43	44	39
Routine non-manual (clerical, sales, services)	27	23	28	29	29	27	28
Working class/other/never worked	42	55	28	35	27	28	33
Education: age left school							
16 or younger	55	62	36	40	31	21	38
17 or 18	21	19	24	20	19	18	21
19 or older	24	19	40	40	50	60	41
Gender							
Male	57	64	49	49	47	46	50
Female	43	36	51	51	53	54	50
Age							
Under 35	12	20	24	28	32	37	26
35–54	31	41	32	38	33	35	34
55 plus	57	39	44	34	35	28	39
Ethnicity							
White	99.6	99.5	98.9	96.3	98.4	98.3	98.0
Non-white	0.4	0.5	1.1	3.7	1.6	1.7	2.0

Source: British Election Study Continuous Monitoring Study 2004–2013.

for Labour, historically the party for workers, the middle classes have a narrow 36–35 lead. The only other party showing a similar pattern of working-class dominance is the BNP: 55 per cent of their supporters are blue-collar, but only 22 per cent are middle-class professionals.[22] This is consistent with our analysis of wider social trends in Chapter 3: support for the radical right in Britain is concentrated among the 'left behind' social class groups while the more privileged and financially secure middle classes, whose voters dominate the three established parties, as well as the Greens, are under-represented in the radical right revolt.

We find a similar pattern when we look at education. University education has now expanded to the point where graduates are the largest group in the electoral coalitions of all the mainstream parties: 40 per cent of Labour and Conservative voters are graduates, as are more than half of Liberal Democrat and Green voters. The radical right, however, is very different. UKIP's coalition is dominated by those who left school at the earliest opportunity: 55 per cent of their voters left school at 16 or earlier, while only 24 per cent attended university. BNP support has a similar profile: 62 per cent of their voters left school at 16 or earlier, while less than one in five went to university. Education has become ever more important to social and economic success in modern Britain, but UKIP, and before them the BNP, appeal most strongly to those who lack the qualifications that provide a vital passport to social mobility. These differences in support by education may also reflect differences in social attitudes. Education, particularly at the university level, is associated with a more liberal and tolerant outlook towards minorities, including immigrants, ethnic minorities and homosexuals. UKIP, and before them the BNP, may be appealing most strongly to the least educated in society, as they are also the most likely to share the social values associated with these parties.[23]

Across Europe, support for radical right revolts also shows a clear 'gender gap', with support typically splitting 60 per cent male and 40 per cent female.[24] Both British radical right parties show the same tendency: UKIP's electorate is 57 per cent male while the BNP's is even more male-dominated (64 per cent). There is no consensus on why this gender gap emerges, although several factors are likely to play a role. The most obvious is that the socially conservative, chauvinistic and anti-egalitarian ideas of the radical right may put off women who are otherwise sympathetic to these parties. There is no shortage of evidence for this in the case of UKIP, whose activists have been repeatedly criticised for sexist remarks. In the course of only a few months in 2013, the UKIP treasurer suggested women should not be promoted to company boards, a major donor argued women should not wear trousers, and a UKIP MEP belittled the achievements of feminism, argued that small businesses should not employ women 'of childbearing age' and appeared to call women at a party meeting 'sluts'. [25] It is easy to see how many women might conclude UKIP is not a party for them.

Women also tend to be more sensitive to established 'norms' in society that sanction expressions of intolerance, which may make them less willing to back parties that are seen as intolerant, even when they sympathise with their ideas. For example, research has shown that British voters are keen on policies to restrict Islamic schools, but they reject these policies when they are endorsed by the extremist BNP. Voters who express stronger attachment to social norms against intolerance, like women, are more sensitive to the reputations of parties, and less likely to back those that are ostracised in society. [26] Finally, women also tend to have lower interest in politics, knowledge about politics and political efficacy (i.e. a feeling that one's actions can make a difference) than men. As the academic Vicky Randall has argued: 'Of all the charges brought against women's political behaviour … the most solidly founded is that they know less about politics, are less interested and less psychologically involved in it than men.'[27] This political disengagement encourages a preference for more familiar and established parties and an avoidance of new parties with radical or unfamiliar ideas.[28]

Having examined gender we now turn to the age profile of voters, which can tell us much about a party's future prospects. Strong support among the young points to a promising future, while an elderly base may suggest long-term decline. Looking at the main parties, we find that the age distribution of their supporters broadly mirrors that of British society, although the Conservatives have a few more pensioners than average, the Liberal Democrats have a few more young people, and Labour have a few more middle-aged supporters. UKIP, however, are leading a grey revolt: 57 per cent of their supporters are over the age of 54, while just over one in ten are under 35. This elderly base has already attracted attention, including from Farage, who recognises it is a problem for his party: 'We are not connecting with disaffected youth. There are one million 16–24 year olds out of work. They are not all lazy and useless. A lot of them are extremely angry about the way things are and we are not reaching them. We are not reaching them. I know that, and I recognize that is potentially a very important demographic for us.'[29]

What explains the dominance of grey-haired voters among UKIP's support? Three factors may play a role here: wider changes in society; changes in the attitudes of citizens; and the timing of Britain's entry into the EU. Over the years, Britain has steadily become more educated, middle class and ethnically and culturally diverse, as we saw in Chapter 3. Today, younger Britons are less likely than their parents and grandparents to have left school early or to work in a blue-collar job, and more likely to attend university and do professional, middle-class work.[30] Affluent democracies like Britain have also seen a 'silent revolution' in the social values of their citizens, which are strongly influenced by the conditions citizens encounter as they are growing up.[31] Whereas older voters who grew up in more turbulent times tend to prize material security and social stability, younger voters who have grown up in a wealthier, more diverse, and, albeit with some notable disruption since 2008, more economically secure context, tend to focus on 'post-material' values, such as individual freedom and universal rights. British researchers have shown how younger generations are more socially liberal, more accepting of ethnic diversity and of homosexuality, less opposed to immigration and less likely to subscribe to ethnic nationalist beliefs.[32] These shifts in values have been further encouraged by the spread of education, rising ethnic diversity and personal mobility across borders. The overall pattern of values in British society is one of large generational divides, and the overall pattern of change is a slow but steady move in a cosmopolitan, socially liberal direction, as more conservative older generations die off and are replaced by more socially liberal, cosmopolitan successors.

Each of the main parties in Britain have recognised the direction of travel, and adopted more socially liberal policies. However, UKIP's positions on a range of issues – their strident nationalism, strong opposition to immigration and gay marriage, and criticism of multicultural policies that aim to support minorities – place the party firmly on the grey side of this generational divide. UKIP support is predominantly old because the party reflects the values and outlook of older voters: socially conservative; threatened by immigration; suspicious of diversity; attached to traditional, material values; and angry about the perceived breakdown of respect for authority and institutions. This is a worldview that was mainstream when UKIP's voters were younger, but has gradually become marginalised as they have aged and the values of their more liberal children and grandchildren have become the new mainstream.

The final factor that may contribute to UKIP's elderly base is the timing of Britain's entrance into the EU, as voters' views of Europe are also strongly influenced by the relationship their country had with Brussels when they were growing up (see Chapter 3).[33] This view is certainly endorsed by Farage, who explained his party's elderly base as follows:'They [younger voters] have all grown up with a series of received wisdoms … They certainly never knew Britain as a self-governing nation. It's very interesting; almost your most common UKIP member is somebody who worked abroad for thirty years and has come back to retire to Britain, has turned on the ten o'clock news and said: "What?! What do you mean?!"' Britain first joined the European Economic Community (EEC) (later the EU) in 1973. This means that respondents in our sample who are under the age of 55 will have little memory of Britain outside of the European Community: for example, a voter who was 45 years old at the time of the 2010 general election would have been just eight years old when Britain joined. By contrast, a voter who turned 65 in 2013 would have cast his or her first ballot in 1966, when integration into Europe was still a distant, and contentious, objective for a country whose foreign policy was focused on the unravelling Empire. This older voter would not find the idea of Britain outside of the EU as abstract or threatening, as this is what he or she grew up with. Indeed, older voters' nostalgia may contribute to their Euroscepticism: the sepia-toned Britain of their youth was, after all, a Britain outside Europe.

The age of their supporters is one area where the BNP departs from UKIP. Support for the BNP is highest among the middle aged but then tails off among the over 55s. This is odd, as the wider changes in British society and values that we outlined above, and which make UKIP more appealing to the old, should have a similar impact on BNP support. But this difference may also reflect the influence of voters' experiences as they were growing up. Most Britons over the age of 55 have direct or indirect experiences of the Second World War. Even if they did not see conflict, it is highly likely that their parents or other relatives did, and as a result of this experience they have remained allergic to parties that are associated with fascism.

A final characteristic worth exploring is ethnicity. The differences here are more subtle, as the ethnic minority sample in our dataset is quite small. Still, all of the main parties have more ethnically diverse electorates than UKIP. Labour have traditionally won a large majority of the votes from all minority ethnic groups, which is reflected in our sample: 3.7 per cent of their supporters are non-white, a much higher proportion than the other mainstream parties.[34] Meanwhile, 1.7 per cent of Liberal Democrat supporters in our sample were non-white and 1.1 per cent of Conservative supporters. The Conservative Party's struggles to recruit ethnic minority voters are well documented. But these minority voters find the radical right UKIP, and the extreme right BNP, even less appealing. Only 0.4 per cent of the UKIP electorate is non-white – or one supporter out of every 250 – a lower figure even than the BNP and well below the 2 per cent average across our whole sample. Although

UKIP very publicly rejects the overt racism of the extreme right, they have advocated ideas that are likely to put off ethnic minority voters, such as calls to remove benefits for migrants, end multicultural policies, prohibit the wearing of religious dress and end international aid for what one UKIP MEP described as 'bongo bongo land'.[35] That UKIP recognise and often mobilise public resentments of immigration and ethnic minorities among the white majority goes some way to explaining why non-white voters are steering well clear of them.[36]

We see, then, how UKIP's support has a very clear social profile, more so than any of the mainstream parties. Their electoral base is old, male, working class, white and less educated, much like the BNP's. The strength of these social divisions suggests UKIP may be mobilising a new cleavage in British society, splitting the older blue-collar, white voters, whom we identified in Chapter 3 as the 'left behind' electorate, away from the middle classes who now dominate British politics. But which of these social divides are central to understanding UKIP support, and which are marginal? Which social divisions are uniquely strong in UKIP's support, and which are similar to divisions found in other parties? This is hard to discern from our initial tables, for two reasons.

First, the association between social groups and political parties can be obscured by differences in the size of social groups, and the popularity of parties. For example, it is hard to compare the *relative* strength of the association between ethnicity and UKIP support with that of age and UKIP support because the age groups are very evenly sized, while on ethnicity the white group is far larger than the non-white group. Similarly, it is hard to compare class differences in support for Labour and UKIP, because the overall popularity of Labour is so much higher. So, for example, if UKIP win 10 per cent of their support from blue-collar voters and 5 per cent from white-collar voters, then they are twice as strong among the working class. If Labour wins 40 per cent from blue-collar voters, and 20 per cent from white-collar voters, they are also twice as strong among the working class: the relative strength of the link between class and party is the same even though the raw differences

TABLE 4.2 Social divisions in support for parties and in non-voting, 2004–2013

	UKIP	BNP	Cons	Labour	Lib Dems	Greens	Non-voters 1	Non-voters 2
Social class (reference: middle class)								
Working class	**1.25**	**1.77**	**0.72**	**1.08**	0.87	1.03	**1.59**	**1.54**
Education (reference: stayed in school past 16)								
Left school at 16 or earlier	**1.53**	**2.58**	**0.83**	**1.23**	**0.69**	**0.46**	**1.38**	**1.30**
Gender (ref: female)								
Male	**1.42**	**1.71**	**1.14**	**1.06**	0.95	0.91	**0.60**	**0.49**
Age (ref: under 55)								
Over 55	**2.07**	**0.74**	**1.46**	**0.79**	0.95	**0.75**	**0.41**	**0.53**
Ethnicity (ref: non-white)								
White	**4.09**	**4.41**	**2.36**	**0.45**	**1.53**	**1.61**	**0.75**	**0.62**

Source: British Election Study Continuous Monitoring Study 2004–2013.

Notes: Figures are odds ratios from logistic regression models. A figure above one means the group is more likely to support the party, below one means less likely. For example, a figure of 1.25 means that the named group is 25% more likely to support the party than the reference group, while a figure of 0.24 means the named group is 24% as likely to support the party as the reference group. Bold figures indicate statistically significant differences in support (p < 0.05). BNP support is measured from 2007–2013 as BNP were not recorded as a separate voting category before this.

in vote choices are larger, because Labour are much more popular overall. Second, the social divisions we examine overlap, making it hard to disentangle which factors are doing the work. For example, working-class citizens are less likely to have university degrees, as are older citizens. To overcome these problems, we can use a statistical technique called 'regression modelling' to disentangle these effects.

Table 4.2 presents the results of such an analysis for UKIP, the BNP, the three main parties, the Greens and for non-voting.[37] More detailed statistical models of the social drivers of UKIP support, and how this compares to support for other parties, can be found in the appendix at the end of the book. The figures in Table 4.2 present the differences in levels of support using a measure called the 'odds ratio'. A figure above one indicates the party is more popular with the named group than with the reference group, while a figure below one indicates the party is less popular. For example, the figure of 1.25 for UKIP among the working class indicates that working-class voters are 25 per cent more likely to support UKIP than middle-class voters, after allowing for all the other differences between the two groups. But in contrast the figure of 0.48 for white voters and Labour, which is below one, indicates that white voters are half as likely to be Labour supporters as otherwise similar non-white voters, or conversely that non-white voters are twice as likely to back Labour as similar white voters.

Two main messages emerge from this table. First, both radical right parties show very strong social divisions in their support, and second, these are much stronger than those found in the bases of support for the three main parties. UKIP show stronger age, gender, ethnic and educational divides than any of the main parties, while for the BNP social divisions are even stronger still on all dimensions other than age. The social class division in UKIP support is stronger than that in either Labour or the Liberal Democrats, and only slightly weaker than the Conservatives' class division, which runs in the opposite direction. Far from being 'the Conservative party in exile', UKIP attracts voters from the opposite side of the traditional class political divide to the Conservatives. Our models also highlight one class division that is much stronger than that in

UKIP support – the division over whether to vote at all. The 'left behind' working-class voters back UKIP, but they are even more over-represented among the voters who plan to stay home on polling day, underscoring their marginal status and disconnection from mainstream politics. On all measures except age, the social divisions in BNP support are in the same direction as those for UKIP, but are even stronger.

When we use statistical modelling to separate out the overlapping social effects, we find it is a voter's age, education and ethnicity that tell us the most about their propensity to back UKIP, though class and gender do add to the story. White voters are four times as likely to support UKIP as otherwise similar non-white voters; those over 55 are more than twice as likely to back UKIP as younger voters; while voters who left school at the first opportunity are 53 per cent more likely to be UKIP backers than otherwise similar voters who stayed on in education. Both social values and economic circumstances are likely to contribute to this pattern of effects. This overall pattern of effects certainly fits with our expectations in Chapter 3, where we tracked wider trends within British society; that UKIP's revolt on the right appeals strongest to the older, disadvantaged and least educated groups in Britain, who are furthest from mainstream values, and feel left behind and threatened by the changes going on around them.

Support for the right-wing revolt: fixed or fluctuating?

The social profile of UKIP and the BNP resembles a throwback to an earlier era of socially polarised politics – both parties do very well among the left behind groups, but barely register with the more privileged. But does this profile reflect the UKIP of 2013 as accurately as the UKIP of 2004? Support for the rebels has risen rapidly over the past decade, particularly since 2010, while the party has transformed their organisation over the same period, becoming a more disciplined and electorally focused machine. Has UKIP's evolution enabled them to grow by *broadening* their reach out to new groups of voters, or have they simply become more effective at *deepening* their support from their already core groups? We can answer this question by tracking trends in the social distribution of UKIP's support.

In Table 4.3 we divide our sample into four time periods: the end of the Blair government (2004–2007), the government of Gordon Brown (2007–2010) and the early (2010–2011) and late (2012–2013) periods of the coalition government. We divide the coalition government into two periods so as to test the impact of the sharp rise in UKIP's support since 2011. We focus on the five demographic characteristics that we have already examined, showing the party's popularity among their 'core' and 'peripheral' groups in each period, and also showing the odds ratios in relative support produced by regression models for each period.

The social mix of UKIP supporters does shift, though there is also evidence of long-term stability in their core appeal. The first comparison – between Blair's final years in office and Gordon Brown's premiership – is interesting because of what does *not* happen to UKIP support. During this period, British politics was upended, as the financial crisis refocused the minds of voters and politicians on the economy. At the same time, UKIP suffered a protracted internal crisis, stemming from the acrimonious departure of Robert Kilroy-Silk and their lacklustre performance at the 2005 general election. Despite all of this dramatic upheaval, the profile and overall level of the party's support remained stable, concentrated among older, white, working-class men. However, when we look at the next transition, from Gordon Brown to the early period of David Cameron's post-2010 coalition government, we see a much more dynamic picture. UKIP's support rises almost equally among all social groups, and the odds ratios fall, indicating lower levels of social division. What this suggests is that, in the early years of the post-2010 coalition government, UKIP succeeded in reaching out beyond their core voters to a broader base.

This may have been a by-product of Britain's first coalition government in seventy years. By transitioning from an outsider protest party into a governing party, the Liberal Democrats left UKIP as the

TABLE 4.3 Social profile of UKIP support across four time periods

	Blair (2004–7)	Brown (2007–10)	Cameron I (2010–11)	Cameron II (2012–13)	Change (2004–13)
Class					
Working class	4.7	3.8	4.9	12.3	+7.6
Middle class	3.0	2.5	3.7	8.9	+5.9
Odds ratio	1.34	1.25	1.22	1.18	–0.16
Education					
Left school 16 or earlier	5.1	4.3	5.6	15.4	+10.3
Stayed in school past 16	2.5	2.1	3.3	7.2	+4.7
Odds ratio	1.69	1.65	1.33	1.69	0.00
Gender					
Men	4.2	3.5	4.6	12.2	+8.0
Women	3.0	2.4	3.7	8.1	+5.1
Odds ratio	1.38	1.45	1.24	1.60	+0.22
Age					
Over 55s	5.1	4.4	6.1	15.8	+10.7
Under 55s	2.7	2.0	2.9	6.2	+3.5
Odds ratio	1.70	1.92	1.99	2.47	+0.77
Ethnicity					
White	3.6	3.0	4.2	10.3	+6.7
Non-white	0.6	0.3	0.8	1.7	+1.1
Odds ratio	3.92	7.13	3.94	4.15	+0.23

Source: British Election Study Continuous Monitoring Study 2004–2013.

only viable option for voters who felt unhappy with the incumbent government, but who also disliked Labour, the main opposition party. But it might also reflect UKIP's change of strategy, which since 2009 stressed the importance of offering voters a wider platform of issues, building more intensive, locally focused campaigns, and engaging more forcefully with the media, local elections and by-elections.

The profile of UKIP support then changes again as we move from the early years of coalition to the later period, when the party reached their highest level of support to date. Unlike the earlier growth in 2010–11, this late surge was not fuelled by a broadening of support, but the opposite. From 2011 until 2013, support for UKIP rose by close to 10 percentage points among pensioners, skilled workers and those who left school at 16 or earlier, while gains among their peripheral groups were more modest. As a result, the odds ratios rise to record highs in the final period on all the variables except social class, indicating social divisions in UKIP support were stronger than ever. In 2013, as in 2004, white older men with relatively little formal education dominated UKIP's base. But by 2013 UKIP were receiving a far larger share of the votes available from these groups, enough to make them competitive with the mainstream parties. Among pensioners, the least educated and the working class, UKIP had overtaken the Liberal Democrats as the third party in British politics, and were closing in on second place. For example, among the over 65s in 2012–2013, the Conservatives lead with 38.5 per cent, Labour are a distant second with 22 per cent and UKIP are a close third with 18.9 per cent.[38] The Liberal Democrats are a distant fourth with 6.2 per cent. Among the under 35s we see a very different picture: Labour lead with 42.1 per cent, the Conservatives trail with 24.4 per cent and the Lib Dems hold third place with 9.3 per cent. UKIP are far behind, with only 3.7 per cent, barely ahead of the Greens. All of this points clearly to the conclusion that the surge of public support for UKIP during 2012–2013 was driven by the party *deepening*, rather than *widening*, their support.

TABLE 4.4 Recalled vote of UKIP supporters in previous election

	Blair 2004–5	Blair 2005–7	Brown 2007–10	Cameron I 2010–11	Cameron II 2012–13
UKIP voters' recalled vote					
Conservatives	21	18	20	29	45
Labour	32	14	24	5	7
Lib Dems	6	6	8	13	11
Other	21	52	33	44	27
Abstain	18	9	14	10	9
N (weighted)	800	911	1,139	813	1,703
Conservative voters' recalled vote					
Conservatives	63	68	60	82	83
Labour	13	8	14	2	2
Lib Dems	4	7	6	7	5
Other	3	3	3	1	1
Abstain	17	13	16	7	9
N (weighted)	4,505	9,218	12,874	6,137	4,940
Labour voters' recalled vote					
Conservatives	1	1	1	3	5
Labour	81	80	79	66	60
Lib Dems	2	4	3	18	18
Other	1	1	1	1	2
Abstain	15	14	15	11	19
N (weighted)	4,915	10,489	12,766	7,543	5,743
Lib Dem voters' recalled vote					
Conservatives	6	3	3	3	6
Labour	33	14	22	4	2
Lib Dems	36	65	52	79	76
Other	1	1	2	1	1
Abstain	22	17	19	12	16
N (weighted)	3,228	5,512	5,763	2,032	1,304

Source: British Election Study Continuous Monitoring Study 2004–2013.

Political roots: who have UKIP taken their votes from?

We now know that UKIP supporters share a distinct profile, but what about their political profile? Uncovering the social profile of these voters tells us a great deal about the party's appeal, but if we want to know how UKIP are impacting on British politics then we need to know which parties they are taking votes from. To do this, we can look at the 'recalled vote' of their supporters – who they said they voted for at the last general election. This is a very commonly asked question, but it has some limitations. Our memories of who we voted for in the past are notoriously imperfect, and subject to several biases: we might remember voting, when we did not; we might think we voted for the winner, when we voted for the loser; and we might project our current preference back to earlier elections, when we may have voted for someone else.[39] Voters backing smaller parties are also more likely to forget their choice, or misremember it, than those who back one of the 'big two'. These recollections of past voting, therefore, need to be taken with a large pinch of salt, and, where possible, assessed against other sources of data.

Bearing these caveats in mind, Table 4.4 charts the 'recalled vote' at the previous general election for current UKIP supporters and backers of the three main parties. The recalled vote question on our survey did not offer a separate UKIP option, but did allow voters to opt for 'other', and it is reasonable to assume that most current UKIP voters giving this response probably backed UKIP at the previous election. Even using this maximum estimate of past support we can see UKIP have a much smaller 'core' of loyal voters than any of the main parties. While most Labour, Conservative and Liberal Democrat voters typically recall backing the same party at the last election, most UKIP voters recall backing someone else. This is unsurprising given that UKIP is a small and young party, which has tripled in size since 2004. Parties grow by picking up support from elsewhere in the political landscape, and when small parties grow rapidly new recruits will dominate.

The preponderance of converts in the UKIP coalition has important implications. The big established parties are stabilised by their

TABLE 4.5 Recalled vote of each party's supporters, excluding loyalists

	Blair 2004–5	Blair 2005–7	Brown 2007–10	Cameron I 2010–11	Cameron II 2012–13
UKIP					
Conservatives	35	47	38	62	70
Labour	53	36	45	10	10
Lib Dems	11	15	14	27	18
N	482	358	1,139	813	1,704
Conservative					
Labour	62	42	60	22	22
Lib Dems	22	41	26	60	60
Other/Don't know	16	17	14	18	17
N	932	1,707	3,095	663	411
Labour					
Conservatives	22	11	13	12	20
Lib Dems	55	70	57	80	71
Other/Don't know	22	19	30	8	9
N	173	640	828	1,851	1,567
Lib Dems					
Conservatives	14	14	11	38	60
Labour	80	73	71	42	26
Other/Don't know	6	12	11	20	13
N	1,334	1,021	1,717	181	124
Overall sample					
Conservatives	27	27	28	35	40
Labour	52	43	49	32	28
Lib Dems	13	29	15	24	21
Other	7	9	9	8	9
N	12,325	25,997	32,634	17,634	14,888

Source: British Election Study Continuous Monitoring Study 2004–2013.

large pool of loyalists, while the character and priorities of smaller insurgent parties can be rapidly transformed by a wave of new recruits. We can see how this happened to the Liberal Democrats in 2004–5, when the party benefited from an influx of disillusioned former Labour voters. In this period, the Lib Dems had almost as many former Labour voters (33 per cent) in their support base as Lib Dem loyalists (36 per cent). UKIP have picked up an even more politically diverse and shifting mix of recruits. The party always wins over significant support from former Conservative voters, but these are certainly not the only source of new votes. During the New Labour governments of Blair and Brown, former Labour voters were as common in the UKIP coalition as former Conservatives. Under the coalition, Conservative recruitment increased, but so did defection from the Liberal Democrats. Across all time periods, UKIP also picks up a lot of support from voters who said they abstained at the last election, and this source of support may well be underestimated as abstention is typically underreported in surveys. This initial look at the past voting patterns of UKIP voters suggests that while their social profile is very stable, their prior political loyalties are not.

The small size of UKIP's loyal electorate does, however, make it difficult to compare the pattern of recruitment into UKIP with those of the other parties, so in Table 4.5 we run a new comparison, excluding loyalists who supported their current party at previous elections, and those who report abstaining or being too young to vote at the last election. This allows us to focus only on where each party is winning its new recruits from, and how these recruitment patterns change over time. At the bottom of the table, we also provide details of the overall pattern of recalled votes, to allow comparison of each party's recruits with the overall political mix in the sample.

The Conservatives are always a big source of UKIP recruits, but they are not consistently the main source, in fact there is clear evidence that UKIP mobilizes discontent with whichever party is in charge. The party won many recruits from Labour during the Blair and Brown governments, indeed more UKIP voters in this period came from Labour than from the Conservatives. Since the advent of the coalition, however, new recruits to UKIP have been mainly ex-Conservative voters, and recruitment from the Liberal Democrats has also picked up, particularly during the early coalition period when overall Liberal Democrat support fell sharply. Most of this support switched to Labour, who experienced a strong inflow of Liberal Democrat voters in the first eighteen months of coalition, but UKIP also benefited: 27 per cent of their new recruits in this period were former Liberal Democrat voters, suggesting UKIP received an electoral boost from people who may previously have backed the Liberal Democrats as an anti-establishment option.

The broader patterns of recruitment are also interesting. During the Labour government, when UKIP were weaker, there was a steady increase in direct defections from Labour to the Conservatives as the popularity of the government declined. This is particularly evident during Gordon Brown's troubled premiership, when a large cohort of former Labour voters switched to the Conservatives – nearly 6 per cent of the whole sample in this period were Labour to Conservative switchers. The dynamics under the coalition have been quite different. The austerity agenda has not been popular, and both governing parties have leaked support, but to different rivals. There has been very strong recruitment of former Liberal Democrats by Labour – around 8 per cent of all the voters with a party preference surveyed since the coalition began say they voted Lib Dem in 2010, but now back Labour. UKIP has been similarly effective at recruiting disaffected Conservatives – over 8 per cent of those polled since the beginning of 2012 are defectors from the Conservatives to UKIP. Yet there has been much less movement from the Conservatives to Labour under the coalition than there was in the opposite direction when Labour were in government, suggesting UKIP's success in mobilising discontent with the government may come at the expense of the main opposition party.

Commentators who argue UKIP have advanced by recruiting discontented Conservatives thus have a point; their recent recruits have mostly been former Conservative voters. Such commentators are mistaken, however, when they assume that these Conservative defectors are stereotypical affluent, professional and middle-class Tories. As we have seen, UKIP have recruited a distinct social segment – older, white, working-class voters with low education levels. Their revolt has peeled off the blue-collar section of David Cameron's electoral support, which means that his centre-right party is now even *more* dominated by educated and affluent middle-class voters than previously. This raises two interesting questions.

First, has UKIP's emergence prevented Labour from rebuilding support with the left behind voters, who stand to suffer most from falling real incomes and declining public spending, and might therefore be expected to turn to the centre-left which has traditionally protected the economically vulnerable? Second, what are the longer-term leanings of the 2010 Conservative voters from left behind groups who have driven UKIP's surge in support? Are these 'Old Labour' voters who were once loyal to Labour on economic grounds, but lost faith in the party once it moved to the centre, and who were recent recruits to Cameron's Conservatives? Or are these longstanding working-class Conservatives, who have been alienated from their traditional preference for the centre-right by the more socially liberal policies of 'Cameroon' Conservatism?

In Table 4.6 we look at whether UKIP have damaged Labour's progress among left behind groups. We do this by examining the change in support for the three main parties and UKIP between the last year of the Labour government (i.e. April 2009–April 2010) and the last available year of the coalition government (i.e. April 2012–April 2013), among UKIP's strongest ('core') and weakest ('periphery') social groups. We find some clear shifts in voting behaviour. The Conservatives do worse in UKIP's periphery groups, losing on average 4.4 percentage points, with particularly large falls in support among women and the under-35s. Among UKIP's core groups, the Conservatives are down by less, on average 1.7 points. The Conservatives lose some ground with whites, the least educated and pensioners while holding steady with the working class and

TABLE 4.6 Change in party support levels from last year of Labour government to last available year of coalition, by UKIP core and periphery groups

	Lab	Con	LD	UKIP
UKIP Core groups				
Working class	+4.1	−0.2	−9.8	+9.1
Left school 16 or earlier	+3.3	−3.0	−9.0	+11.3
Men	+1.9	−0.4	−9.2	+9.1
Over 65s	+0.1	−1.8	−10.9	+12.5
Whites	+6.0	−3.0	−10.1	+7.5
Mean: UKIP core	*+3.1*	*−1.7*	*−9.8*	*+9.9*
UKIP Peripheral groups				
Professionals and managers	+4.7	−2.3	−10.5	+7.2
Attended university	+8.3	−2.7	−11.5	+5.0
Women	+10.5	−5.6	−10.7	+5.9
Under 35s	+17.2	−8.1	−11.2	+2.3
Ethnic minorities	+10.0	−2.2	−5.6	+1.6
Mean: UKIP periphery	*+10.1*	*−4.2*	*−9.9*	*+4.4*

Source: British Election Study Continuous Monitory Study 2009–2013.

men. The shift away from the Conservatives is thus not larger in the groups where UKIP support has surged. In fact, the opposite is true: the Tory vote has tended to hold up slightly better in the core UKIP groups. Nor does the surge in UKIP support come at the expense of the junior coalition partner: the sharp decline in Liberal Democrat support is similar across both sets of social groups.

Instead, the strongest evidence for a UKIP effect is found in Labour's performance. Since their low ebb in 2009–2010, Labour have registered an average 10 per cent rise in support among the social groups where UKIP are weakest: middle-class professionals, degree holders, women, ethnic minorities and the young. But among core UKIP groups, support for Labour has risen by only 3 percentage points on average, with modest rises among whites, the working class and the less educated, a tiny rise among men and no increase at all among pensioners. This performance gap may, in part, be the direct result of more effective competition for Labour voters by a more active and effective UKIP, who have increasingly targeted these voters (see Chapter 2). It might also be due to the mix of attitudes, such as hostility to immigration or dissatisfaction with mainstream political elites, which make UKIP's core demographic groups more reluctant to support Ed Miliband's Labour, and more receptive to the radical right revolt (we will explore these attitudes in the next chapter). Whichever mechanism explains the difference, it is striking that during an economically right-wing administration that is pursuing an austerity agenda, the left behind social groups who stand to lose the most show greater enthusiasm for UKIP's radical right insurgency than for the party traditionally associated with state support for the most vulnerable. The performance gap we see both reflects and reinforces the growing social divide between the left behind groups and the middle-class dominated political mainstream.

Where do UKIP's recruits fall in terms of the partisan divide between Labour and the Conservatives, which has framed British political competition for seventy years? The left behind groups who provide the most support to UKIP should have economic interests that would align them with the centre-left. These are voters who are likely to benefit from income redistribution, have a greater need of state provided services and welfare benefits, and work in professions that once had strong links with Labour, particularly through trade unions. Yet as we saw in Chapter 3, these left behind voters also have a distinct set of attitudes which are more closely aligned with the Conservatives, particularly the assertive nationalism, social conservatism and Euroscepticism of the Thatcher government.

In short, UKIP's base is blue-collar, socially conservative, and conflicted – their 'heads' are Labour, as this is where their economic interests lie, but their 'hearts' are often with the social values of the Conservatives. So which way did these voters break before UKIP's emergence? This is a difficult question to resolve, as the surveys available do not give the long-term voting information we need to answer it. We know how UKIP voters recall voting in the previous election, but not in earlier elections. We also do not have questions on economic ideology, which might help us gauge the strength of UKIP voters'

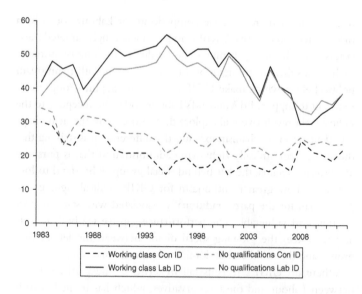

FIGURE 4.1 Party identification of working-class respondents and respondents with no qualifications, 1983–2012

Source: British Social Attitudes survey.

sympathy for Labour's traditional economic policies. But while we do not have a straightforward way of directly assessing the relative balance of sympathy UKIP voters had for Labour and the Conservatives in the past, we can at least assess this indirectly. In Figure 4.1, we track the proportions of left behind voters who say they identify with Labour and with the Conservatives over the past thirty years.

What the figure shows is the decline of mainstream party loyalties in general, and 'Old Labour' loyalties in particular, among left behind voters. In the 1980s and 1990s, working-class and voters with no educational qualifications were 'locked in' to the two-party system: a large majority identified with Labour or the Conservatives and both groups sided heavily with Labour. Then, in the 2000s, many of these voters lost faith in Labour, but rather than attaching themselves to the Conservatives they instead ceased to identify with either of the main parties: barely half express a party allegiance by the end of the 2000s. This loss of political faith provided a clear opening to UKIP, as we shall see in more detail in the next chapter, and suggests disaffected 'Old Labour' voters may be an important source of support for the rebels. However, we can also see from the figure that a significant minority of left behind voters – typically about a quarter – have always identified with the Conservatives. It is quite likely that UKIP have gained a lot of their support from this 'blue-collar Tory' group as well. But without more information about the past voting habits and current ideological leanings of UKIP voters, it is hard to say for certain which group predominates among UKIP voters. The simplest, and most plausible, conclusion to draw is that UKIP's emergence has drawn working-class support away from both Labour and the Conservatives, and made it harder for either mainstream party to recruit or retain support from the left behind voters.[40]

Conclusion: UKIP's grey-haired, blue-collar revolt

We began this chapter by asking three questions: Does the right-wing revolt have a distinct social base? Have UKIP rallied similar types of voters as the extreme right-wing BNP? And has the character of support for UKIP changed over time? After a deep dive into our dataset, we can now give clear answers.

A useful starting point is UKIP's own analysis of their support. During one interview, Paul Nuttall, who became UKIP's Chairman in 2008, reflected on what he saw as their main weakness: 'We need more women on the front-line. We need more working-class voices. We need people from ethnic backgrounds. We need more young people to be able to put them on TV, because at the moment it is all very white and very middle-class.' Nuttall was talking more about members than voters, but as we have seen in this chapter, much of his analysis is mirrored in our findings on UKIP's electorate, with the important exception of class.

UKIP's radical right revolt is anchored in a clear social base: older, blue-collar voters, citizens with few qualifications, whites and men. In earlier years, the extreme right BNP also drew the bulk of their support from these same groups in society, but was less success-ful overall. These are the social groups we identified in Chapter 3, who were left behind by the economic boom of the late 1990s and early 2000s, and have been pushed to the margins of politics by the centrist convergence on the middle-class electorate that began with Tony Blair and New Labour, and has continued under David Cameron. These older blue-collar voters with obsolete skills and few formal qualifications have struggled in a post-industrial econ-omy and face a bleak future in austerity Britain. We will explore their attitudes in the next chapter, but we can hazard a guess that they probably do not see any solutions to their problems coming from the established parties.

These working-class voters have begun to turn to a radical right party who reject the established political class and provide them with someone to blame for their problems. The social mix of UKIP supporters has not changed dramatically as the party has become more successful at elections, and as a result the polit-ical weight of UKIP varies enormously between social contexts. In UKIP's core of older and working-class men, by 2013 Nigel Farage was competing on nearly equal terms with the mainstream parties. Yet, at the same time, his party was barely registering with young Britons, graduates and ethnic minorities, and continued to struggle with women. Interestingly, Farage himself is keenly aware of his party's strong appeal to the working class, as he explained during one of our interviews: 'It's a completely different party to 2010. It's a completely different atmosphere. It's a completely different feel. In four or five years' time, if you come to see me, UKIP will be a party that has far more Labour support than Tory support. That's where it's going. I can see it. *I can feel it.* Maybe it's the old traditional Labour socialist party that's got the biggest problem in this country.'

The older, blue-collar white men who are now backing UKIP are voters who find themselves marginalised in a political debate where their voice was once one of the loudest and most respected. This is reflected in their partisan attachments: these groups once had strong party affiliations, primarily with Labour. In the 2000s, a large number ceased to identify with Labour, but found little to like about the Conservatives. They dropped out of the political battle, expressing no affiliation to either side, and became more receptive to a radical alternative. In this sense, the UKIP vote, in part, reflects longstanding limitations to representative democracy: parties need to focus on winning and holding support from the largest and most rapidly growing social groups in order to win elections. As a result the main parties tend to converge in terms of their policies and ideas on the preferences of the groups that control the centre of British politics, and also tend to recruit their activists and politicians from these groups. Those who find themselves at the margins socially often also find themselves voiceless, politically.[41]

In Chapter 3, we contended that the UKIP revolt may mark a response to wider trends in British society and the economy, which have created a left behind electorate who have lost out from both economic and political change. In this chapter we have uncovered more evidence. We have seen how UKIP have mobilised support from precisely these voters. However, understanding the social roots of this revolt is only a start. While these are clearly concentrated among the left behind, even in the friendliest social milieux, the majority of voters reject UKIP. To understand what drives only some of these older working-class men, like John at the start of the chapter, to join the revolt while similar voters in similar circumstances remain loyal to the main parties, we need to take a closer look at the hopes, fears and demands that are motivating UKIP's supporters. Having established the roots of the revolt, we now need to get inside the rebels' heads, to try and understand their motives and how, if at all, these set them apart from other voters in similar social circumstances. This is the task we turn to in the next chapter.

Notes

1 Such nostalgia tends to misrepresent Thatcher, who was more pragmatic about Europe than her image suggests – for example, she signed the Single European Act, which significantly enhanced the political powers of the European Community, in 1986.

2 Peter Oborne, 'As the landscape starts to shift, UKIP can create political havoc', *The Daily Telegraph*, 3 November 2011.

3 Tim Montgomerie, 'David Cameron ignores UKIP at his peril', *The Times*, 11 April 2012.

4 BBC One, *Sunday Politics*, 7 July 2013.

5 Fraser Nelson, 'Margaret Thatcher listened to voters – now it's Nigel Farage who hears their despair', *The Daily Telegraph*, 11 April 2013.

6 Glen Owen, 'Now UKIP leader Nigel Farage sets his sights on working-class Labour voters', *Mail on Sunday*, 25 May 2013.

7 Andrew Rawnsley, 'Local elections: It's not just the Tories who should beware UKIP', *The Observer*, 21 April 2013.

8 Gaby Hinsliff, 'It feels like the BNP – only in blazers', *The Observer*, 30 May 2004; 'Baroness Warsi sparks UKIP fury over BNP suggestion', *BBC News*, 4 May 2012.

9 Peter Kellner, 'Cameron outflanked', *Prospect*, 20 June 2012.

10 Peter John and Helen Margetts (2009) 'The latent support for the extreme right in British politics', *West European Politics*, 32(3): 496–513.

11 Nick Lowles, 'Opposing UKIP, we could but should we?', *Hope Not Hate Blog*, 9 May 2013.

12 Daniel Oesch (2008) 'Explaining workers' support for right-wing populist parties in Western Europe: Evidence from Austria, Belgium, France, Norway, and Switzerland', *International Political Science Review*, 29(3): 349–73; Jocelyn A. J. Evans (2005) 'The dynamics of social change in radical right-wing populist party support', *Comparative European Politics*, 3(1): 76–101.

13 Jørgen Goul Andersen and Tor Bjørklund (1990) 'Structural changes and new cleavages: The Progress Parties in Denmark and Norway', *Acta Sociologica*, 33(3): 195–217.

14 John Rentoul, 'Labour lost more votes than Tories as UKIP surged', *The Independent*, Eagle Eye Blog, 5 May 2013. Available online: http://blogs. independent.co.uk/2013/05/04/labour-lost-more-votes-than-tories-as-ukip-surged/ (accessed 26 July 2013).

15 The origins of this aphorism are a little obscure. Gallup seems to have used the analogy frequently in the early 1930s, and the story is widely quoted by public opinion researchers, but we were unable to trace its first usage.

16 'UKIP is not a Tory right splinter group, says Farage', *BBC News*, 7 July 2013. ComRes poll for BBC Sunday Politics. Available online: http:// www.comres.co.uk/poll/957/bbc-sunday-politics-ukip-councillors-survey.htm (accessed 18 July 2013).

17 See, for example, Paul Whiteley and Patrick Seyd (2002) *High-Intensity Participation: The Dynamics of Party Activism in Britain*, Ann Arbor: University of Michigan Press.

18 For the most recent British Election Study see the official website http://www.bes2009-10.org/. Also Paul Whiteley, Harold D. Clarke, David Sanders and Marianne C. Stewart (2013) *Affluence, Austerity and Electoral Change in Britain*, Cambridge: Cambridge University Press.

19 Robert Ford, Matthew J. Goodwin and David Cutts (2012) 'Strategic Eurosceptics and polite xenophobes: Support for the United Kingdom Independence Party in the 2009 European Parliament elections', *European Journal of Political Research*, 51(2): 204–34; Robert Ford and Matthew J. Goodwin (2010) 'Angry white men: Individual and contextual predictors of support for the British National Party, *Political Studies*, 58(1): 1–25; Matthew J. Goodwin (2011) *New British Fascism: Rise of the British National Party*, Abingdon: Routledge; David Cutts, Robert Ford and Matthew J. Goodwin (2011) 'Anti-immigrant, politically dissatisfied or still racist after all? Examining the attitudinal drivers of extreme right support in Britain at the 2009 European elections', *European Journal of Political Research*, 50(3): 418–40.

20 Seymour Martin Lipset and Stein Rokkan (1967) 'Cleavage structures, party systems, and voter alignments: An introduction', in S. M. Lipset and S. Rokkan (eds.) *Party Systems and Voter Alignments: Cross-National Perspectives*, New York: Free Press, pp. 1–64.

21 Echoes of a long dormant divide over religion can still be seen in support for the Liberal Democrats, who continue to perform strongest in places like South-West England, where 'dissenting' Protestant churches once opposed the dominance of the Church of England 'Tories' by backing the Liberals. On class as the origin of Labour–Conservative competition, see D. Butler and D. Stokes (1974) *Political Change in Britain* (2nd edition), Basingstoke: Macmillan; on the Scottish and Welsh nationalists see J. Mitchell, L. Bennie, and R. Johns (2011) *The Scottish National Party: Transition to Power*, Oxford: Oxford University Press and C. Ragin (1979) 'Ethnic political mobilization: The Welsh case', *American Sociological Review*, 44(4): 619–35; on Northern Ireland see J. Tonge and J. Evans (2009) 'Social class and party choice in Northern Ireland's ethnic blocs', *West European Politics*, 32(5): 1012–30 and J. Tilly, G. Evans and C. Mitchell (2008) 'Consociationalism and the evolution of political cleavages in Northern Ireland 1989–2004', *British Journal of Political Science*, 38(4): 699–717.

22 On BNP voters see also Ford and Goodwin, 'Angry white men', and Goodwin, *New British Fascism*, Chapter 5.

23 On immigrants see Robert Ford (2011) 'Acceptable and unacceptable immigrants: The ethnic hierarchy in British immigration preferences', *Journal of Ethnic and Migration Studies*, 37(7): 1017–37; Robert Ford, Gareth Morrell and Anthony Heath (2012) '"Fewer but better?" British attitudes to immigration', in A. Park *et al.* (eds.) (2012) *British Social Attitudes: The 29th Report*, London: NatCen. On ethnic minorities see Robert Ford (2008) 'Is racial prejudice declining in Britain?' *British Journal of Sociology*, 59(4): 609–36. On homosexuals see Geoffrey Evans (2003) 'In Search of Tolerance', in A. Park *et al.* (eds.) *British Social Attitudes: The 19th Report*, London: Sage, pp. 213–30.

24 On the gender gap and radical right parties see Terri Givens (2004) 'The radical right gender gap', *Comparative Political Studies*, 37(1): 30–54; also Rosie Campbell and Gareth Harris (2010) 'Why are these men so angry?' Paper presented to the Elections, Public Opinion and Parties Conference, University of Essex; Nonna Mayer (2013) 'From Jean-Marie to Marine Le Pen: Electoral change on the far right', *Parliamentary Affairs*, 66(1): 160–78; on women becoming more left wing over the years see, for example, Pippa Norris and Ronald Inglehart (2003) *Rising Tide: Gender Equality and Cultural Change Worldwide*, New York: Cambridge University Press.

25 Nigel Morris, 'UKIP faces renewed accusations of sexism as Stuart Wheeler claims women are not as competitive as men', *The Independent*, 15 August 2013; Nicholas Watt, 'UKIP donor brands women "hostile" for wearing trousers', *The Guardian*, 17 May 2013; Martin Wainwright, 'UKIP's bloomer over women's rights', *The Guardian*, 21 July 2004; quote from 'Feminists mocked by "Bongo bongo" UKIP man Godfrey Bloom', *The Daily Telegraph*, 21 August 2013; BBC News, 'UKIP's Godfrey Bloom under fire over "demeaning" joke'. Available online: http://www.bbc.co.uk/news/uk-politics-24175041 (accessed 1 October 2013).

26 Scott Blinder, Elisabeth Ivarsflaten and Robert Ford (2013) 'The better angels of our nature: How the anti-prejudice norm affects policy and party preferences in Great Britain and Germany', *American Journal of Political Science*, 57(4): 841–57.

27 Vicky Randall (1987) *Women and Politics: An International Perspective*, Chicago: University of Chicago Press, p. 78.

28 Elisabeth Gindengil, André Blais, Neil Nevitte and Matthew Hennigar (2005) 'Explaining the gender gap in support for the new right: The case of Canada', *Comparative Political Studies*, 38(10): 1171–95; see also Cas Mudde (2007) *Populist Radical Right Parties in Europe*, Cambridge: Cambridge University Press, pp. 113–118.

29 It is worth noting that the party's elderly membership has also attracted attention, though party voters and members often have quite different

profiles. One journalist who attended the party's conference observed how the seniority of delegates 'can be judged by the fact that their favourite theme is the war – against Germany, not Iraq – and their most common heckle is "speak up!"' Helen Rumbelow, 'There's talk of war and a leadership battle', *The Times*, 4 October 2004. This grey membership was also noted by activists in interviews, for example. 'In 2006, at the age of 38 or 39, I was picked to speak at Conference as the representative of UKIP youth. There were four students in the room.'

30 Thomas F. Pettigrew (1997) 'Generalized intergroup contact effects on prejudice', *Personality and Social Psychology Bulletin,* 23(2): 173–85. For a wider review of 'contact theory' and the effects of intergroup contact on prejudice see Thomas F. Pettigrew and Linda R. Tropp (2006) 'A meta-analytic test of intergroup contact theory', *Journal of Personality and Social Psychology*, 90(5): 751–83.

31 Ronald Inglehart (1977) *The Silent Revolution: Changing Values and Political Styles among Western Publics*, Princeton: Princeton University Press; Karl Mannheim (1952) 'The problem of generations', in Paul Kecskemeti (ed.) *Essays on the Sociology of Knowledge by Karl Mannheim*, New York: Routledge & Kegan Paul, pp. 276–320.

32 On social liberalism, see James Tilley (2005) 'Libertarian-authoritarian value change in Britain 1974–2001', *Political Studies*, 55(2): 442–53; on diversity and racial attitudes see Ford, 'Is racial prejudice declining in Britain?'; on acceptance of homosexuality see Evans, 'In search of tolerance'; on attitudes to immigration see Robert Ford (2012) *Parochial and Cosmopolitan Britain: Examining the Social Divide in Reactions to Immigration*, report for the George Marshall Foundation 'Transatlantic Trends: Immigration' project and Ford, 'Acceptable and unacceptable immigrants'; on nationalism see Anthony Heath and James Tilley (2005) 'British national identity and attitudes towards immigration', *International Journal on Multicultural Societies*, 7(2): 119–32 and James Tilley and Anthony Heath (2007) 'The decline of British national pride', *British Journal of Sociology*, 58(4): 661–78.

33 Ian Down and Carole Wilson (2012) 'A rising generation of Europeans? Life-cycle and cohort effects on support for "Europe"', *European Journal of Political Research*, 52: 431–56; see also Lauren McLaren (2006) *Identity, Interests and Attitudes to European Integration*, Basingstoke: Palgrave Macmillan.

34 David Sanders, Anthony Heath, Stephen Fisher and Maria Sobolewska (2013) 'The calculus of ethnic minority voting in Britain', *Political Studies* (in print); see also Maria Sobolewska (2013) 'Party strategies and the descriptive representation of ethnic minorities: The 2010 British general

election', *West European Politics*, 36(3): 615–33 and Maria Sobolewska (2005) 'Ethnic agenda: Relevance of political attitudes to party choice', *Journal of Elections, Public Opinion and Parties*, 15(2): 197–221.

35 'UKIP MEP Godfrey Bloom has regret over "Bongo Bongo" phrase', *BBC News*, 7 August 2013.

36 Michael Skey (2013) 'Belonging and entitlement: Britain's "ethnic majority" and the rise of UKIP'. Available online: http://www.opendemocracy.net/ourkingdom/michael-skey/belonging-and-entitlement-britains-ethnic-majority-and-rise-of-ukip

37 Very few respondents in the YouGov survey report a settled intention to abstain from voting – fewer than 5 per cent of the total. Given that abstention rates in recent elections have run at 30 per cent or more, this means that self-reported intentions to vote are seriously overstated. Those who express no voting preference, even after being pushed for a party they 'lean' towards are perhaps the least likely group to turn out in elections, so we also measure abstention with these included as a partial effort to correct for the bias in self-reported voting intentions.

38 Note that these shares are calculated including non-voters (8.1 per cent of the total in this group). If we exclude non-voters (as the commercial pollsters do when reporting poll results), the shares are Conservatives 41.9 per cent, Labour 24.0 per cent, UKIP 20.5 per cent, and Lib Dems 6.7 per cent.

39 Hilda Himmelwit, Marianne Jaeger Biberian and Janet Stockdale (1975) 'Memory for past vote: Implications of a study of bias in recall', *British Journal of Political Science*, 8: 365–84.

40 The past party allegiances of older voters are more evenly divided – those born between 1925 and 1945 (who would constitute the bulk of the over 65s in our 2004–13 sample) tend to show almost equal levels of party identification with both Labour and the Conservatives over the past thirty years. Working-class or low education voters from this cohort, however, break heavily to Labour. The patterns of partisanship in this group would also fit with an interpretation of UKIP recruiting disaffected 'Old Labour' voters alongside socially conservative 'blue-collar Tories'. However, without more evidence it is hard to know the relative mix of prior loyalties in the UKIP voting coalition.

41 For a related argument, see Heinz Brandenburg and Robert Johns, 'The declining representativeness of the British party system, and why it matters', *Political Studies* (Available in early view online: http://onlinelibrary.wiley.com/doi/10.1111/1467-9248.12050/abstract).

5
THE MOTIVE FOR REBELLING

When John first decided to vote for UKIP he wasn't simply registering a protest. 'Of course I was hacked off with the politicians', he laughs, 'but who isn't these days?' Along with his discontent with 'the usual suspects', John was also worried about his country, and how it was changing. Although UKIP talks a lot about Britain's relationship with the EU, John's concerns stretched beyond this particular issue, as he explains: 'I do want us out of the EU. The whole thing is total madness. But it's not just about Europe, is it? There's a bigger picture here. We're taking in more immigrants than the country can cope with, and the economy's a mess. None of the usual lot has any idea what to do about it. I don't think they even care. It doesn't hurt them. Nigel [Farage] always says to us, you can't separate these problems, immigration, the economy, from Europe. They are all part of the same problem. I think he's right.'

In John's mind, the EU and immigration present the biggest threats to Britain since the Second World War. But unlike this earlier era, he argues that the main parties today cannot resolve the problems. 'The Conservatives used to be good on immigration; at least I think they were. Maggie was all right, she said we should have strict limits and she meant it. But with Europe, and all the red-tape, none of them can do anything to stop it. Look at Cameron. He says he wants to stop migrants coming, but he just can't do it while we are in Europe! The Bulgarians and the Romanians can now come too, and he won't do anything about it. Not that Labour are any better: we're still dealing with the mess that lot made when they threw open the floodgates!'

John was once loyal to Labour but is now heavily critical of their record on immigration. 'Labour were the worst, the absolute worst. Ruined this country. They just let everyone come in; gave them benefits from the get-go and didn't even ask us. *They didn't even ask their own people!* They weren't open about it, and they certainly weren't honest about what was happening. Look at that lady in Rochdale. She mentions it, and they call her a bigot.'

These concerns are not just focused on the impact of migration on jobs and welfare, but stem from a deeper anxiety that John feels about Britain's general direction, and the effects of the EU and immigration on the national community, identity and way of life. 'It's difficult to define, isn't it? British. But whatever it was, it's on the way out now. People don't understand what it is we are losing. I think it's about a sense of fair play, decency, hard work and respect for traditions. Nigel always says you see it best at Remembrance Day parades. But the Eurocrats want rid of national identities, don't they? And the immigrants don't understand our traditions. It's a different culture, isn't it? It's a different way of life. You can't learn it in … what are they calling it now? Citizenship tests. So when I first voted UKIP', recalled John, 'it was like coming home. I finally realised, here was this party, that shared my values, was on the side of people like me and had its heart in the right place.' For John, UKIP talks about the issues that other parties do not want to address and speaks for the ordinary people. 'It's like on immigration', he explains. 'You know what UKIP say? It's not racist to talk about it; it's *realist*. They actually want to listen to us, and stand up for us despite all the crap they get from the politicians. You know what? That's British! Standing up for what you believe.'

It is no wonder John has so much to say about why he backs UKIP. Switching to an untested rebel party is a big step for a voter in Britain. UKIP have no Members of Parliament, have never governed anything more significant than a few rural councils, and their leaders have not held high office. Supporting such a party is a leap into the unknown, and such a radical shift requires strong motives. But what is driving UKIP supporters like John? In the previous chapter we began to shed light on the nature of UKIP's revolt by examining its social roots, showing how it appeals most strongly to financially struggling, older and white male workers who have been 'left behind' by the economic and social changes of the past thirty years. In this chapter, we turn to examine their attitudes and values.

Two routes to revolt: endorsement and rejection

Gavin, one of the activists we interviewed, started supporting UKIP in 2006. 'When I joined UKIP', he recalled, 'it was like when you clamber up a hill and you have a nice view. You feel good about it. Then you take your rucksack off, and you suddenly feel *really* good about it. Leaving the Tories and joining UKIP was like when you take that rucksack off. Suddenly, I could be honest. I could actually say what I believed.' Gavin's account encompasses both of the classes of motive that might lead someone to support an insurgent party: his *rejection* of an established party, which he felt no longer represented his beliefs; and his *endorsement* of a new party, UKIP, whose ideas he felt were closer to his own views and priorities.

If the motive driving UKIP's supporters is mainly an endorsement of their ideas, then we need to understand which of these ideas are most effective at recruiting voters. UKIP's key policy is their longstanding demand that Britain withdraw from the EU, but is this 'hard' brand of Euroscepticism the only motive behind their support? UKIP have grown rapidly in a period when opinion polls consistently show that Europe ranks very low on the list of concerns for voters, suggesting that other motives may also be at work. This view is certainly held by some commentators, who have tentatively explored the party's voters. 'Recent focus groups', noted one, 'couldn't actually get Nigel Farage's supporters to talk about Brussels. While the party's activist members do obsess about Europe, UKIP's voters want to talk about immigration, crime, their perceptions of Britain "going to the dogs" and their strong belief that all politicians are essentially the same – dishonest, corrupt and incompetent.'[1] Such accounts point to other motives that may be fuelling the revolt, including concerns over immigration, a pessimistic outlook and a deep sense of frustration with the performance of mainstream politicians. As we saw in Chapter 2, since 2010 Nigel Farage has attempted to merge these domestic concerns in the public imagination with his party's founding issue of Euroscepticism. While UKIP's activists may be more obsessed with the EU, their voters may be motivated more by concerns which have fuelled radical right revolts elsewhere in Europe, in particular hostility to immigration and to established politicians.

Alternatively, voters may be turning to UKIP not to endorse but to *reject* other parties. Rather than lump these concerns together as 'protest voting', it is important to understand what is making voters unhappy. Is it dissatisfaction with how political leaders are performing? Or does this unhappiness stem more from a sense of anger about how the main parties have managed some of the big issues facing Britain? Since 2005, commentators have pointed to David Cameron's more socially liberal and centrist brand of Conservatism as a key recruiting tool for UKIP. 'On issue after issue', writes Tim Montgomerie, 'Nigel Farage is directly wooing unhappy Conservatives. UKIP's position on human rights laws, foreign aid, immigration and gay marriage all appeal to those most unhappy with the limits that coalition has put on Mr Cameron.'[2] Others also point to UKIP's stance on immigration, selective grammar schools, their scepticism about global warming and demand to end the smoking ban in pubs as evidence that their programme 'is a land grab of terrain ceded by Tory modernisers'.[3] There is no doubt that these divisions have been targeted by Farage, who in 2012 wrote an open letter to voters disgruntled with Cameron: 'Conservatives are used to a party that is patriotic, supports business and believes in aspiration', he railed. 'Today they are led by people obsessed with wind farms and introducing gay marriage and happy to open the door to 29 million Romanians and Bulgarians.'[4] So is UKIP a means for social conservatives to voice their dissatisfaction with Cameron, or have they capitalised on discontent with how his Conservative Party approaches the key issues?

Alternatively, it may be that UKIP's rise is more the product of persistent discontent with the Labour Party's leadership and their performance during a long period in government, between 1997 and 2010, hostility which has lingered even after Labour were ejected from office. The anger that John voices about Labour's policy on immigration reflects a widespread and deep public discontent with how the centre-left managed this key issue. At the time of the 2010 general election, for example, only 15 per cent of the electorate thought Labour were the best party to manage immigration, while a poll by Angus Reid revealed 75 per cent regarded Labour immigration policies as a failure.[5] As Farage moved to exploit divisions on the centre-right, he also targeted this discontent on the left, writing another open letter 'to everybody out there who will feel the effects over the coming years of an open-door policy to migrants when the country is struggling to get back on to the straight and narrow after years of a wasteful and careless Labour rule'.[6] But which of these interpretations are correct; is UKIP's support driven by an endorsement of the radical right agenda, rejection of a failed political mainstream, or a little bit of both? We can first gather some useful ideas about what we might find by looking to mainland Europe, where support for the radical right has existed for decades and has been researched extensively. We then explore whether the same pattern of motives is fuelling UKIP's revolt, and how factors that are more specific to Britain – such as David Cameron, Labour, Europe and immigration – fit into this picture.

Radical right revolts across the channel: four possible motives

Across Europe, academics have traced support for radical right parties that are similar to UKIP to four particularly important motives: Euroscepticism; hostility towards immigration; populist dissatisfaction with established parties; and a pessimistic and dissatisfied outlook on life.[7] The first, which is obviously relevant to UKIP, is Euroscepticism. Not all radical right parties in Europe were initially hostile towards the EU, as some saw European integration as a bulwark against the more pressing threat of communism. But since the collapse of communism and the Maastricht Treaty, which accelerated political integration, the radical right has turned against the European project, attacking the EU as a threat to national sovereignty and identity.[8] Popular opposition to the EU has now become an important driver of radical right support, leading some to conclude that radical right parties are now 'a decisive force in swaying popular opinion against Europe by mobilizing the growing uncertainties about the future of European integration among the mass public'.[9] This was echoed in an eighteen-country study, which found that Euroscepticism explained support for the radical right 'over and beyond' other views.[10] Given that UKIP are even more intensely Eurosceptic than most of their European cousins, and operate in one of the most Eurosceptic countries in the EU, it is logical to suppose that Euroscepticism will play a large role in explaining the party's support.[11]

Opposition to immigration, which is prominent in UKIP's campaigns, also plays a central role in driving support for the European radical right. 'This research', summarises Jens Rydgren, 'has convincingly shown that immigration scepticism (i.e. wanting to reduce immigration) is among the principal factors for predicting who will vote for a radical right-wing party.'[12] In fact, some consider this motive so central to the radical right's appeal that they describe them as 'anti-immigrant parties'.[13] But these concerns about immigration may not be as distinct from Euroscepticism as some assume. It has been shown that scepticism towards the EU is closely related to beliefs that the nation and 'native' group are under threat. Seen from this perspective, Euroscepticism and support for parties like UKIP is driven less by views about the EU as a set of political institutions, and more by a general belief that the EU and its accompanying institutions threaten national sovereignty and national identity. Immigration contributes to this feeling of 'symbolic threat' from the EU, which is seen as a source of migrants and a force that prevents national politicians from restricting their arrival.[14] On this basis we would expect to find Euroscepticism *and* opposition to immigration to be closely aligned in the mindset of UKIP voters.

Another motive highlighted in this research, and which we noted at the outset of this chapter, is political dissatisfaction, and the argument that the appeal of radical parties may be more about what they

oppose than what they stand *for*. As one academic notes, 'the populist rhetoric of the radical right is believed to tap into deep-seated
public disaffection with the political system, an erosion of trust in
the institutions of representative government, and the expression of
disgust against "all of the above"'.[15] It is true that across Europe people who vote for the radical right are often more dissatisfied with
politicians than supporters of other parties, and are also less likely
to trust their elected officials. Parties like UKIP have met these discontents with a populist narrative, which urges voters to 'sod the
lot' and sets the common sense of the ordinary people against the
political class, who are framed as corrupt, complacent and out of
touch. This would lead us to expect that those who vote for UKIP
are similarly motivated mainly by their dissatisfaction with mainstream British politics and leaders, and that this political discontent
is as important as their views about particular issues.

But there is also more than one form of political dissatisfaction.
Voters may reject the political class as a whole, or they may have
specific resentments concerning failures of leadership and management. These last two ideas play a large role in contemporary politics,
which is less about grand social visions than providing good day-to-
day management. Today's politics is often treated as a battle between
management teams over who can 'deliver the goods' that citizens
want, such as a healthy economy and high quality public services,
and effective responses to new issues, such as immigration, as they
emerge. In the study of politics, this perspective is known as 'valence
politics', which some academics argue is the best way to understand
British political competition.[16] For the main parties, the advantage
of this shift is that it enables them to build broad political coalitions,
drawing in voters from all walks of life, by focusing on delivering
the things that all voters value. The disadvantage, however, is that
voters do not have as much reason to stay loyal to a management
team as they do to an ideological vision of society, or a tribal identity. Allegiances in modern British politics are therefore weaker and
more contingent than they were in earlier years, and a party that has
based its appeal on good management has little to fall back on if voters decide that they have failed to provide it.

Another downside to 'politics as management' is that parties are inevitably constrained by the limits on governing in a modern society, which means often they cannot give voters what they want. A government hemmed in by economic austerity, budget deficits and EU-wide treaties cannot deliver, or even promise, rapid growth, large public investment programmes or radical shifts in immigration policy. But radical right parties face no such constraints. They can promise voters the solutions they want without having to worry about delivering results. This 'populist valence' politics is likely to operate particularly in areas of policy where voters have demands that the political class regard as irresponsible or unachievable, such as large-scale reductions in immigration or a sudden withdrawal from the EU. When mainstream politicians are unable or unwilling to respond to these demands, or offer more moderate 'half a loaf' reforms that do not satisfy voters, public faith in the management skills of their leaders may be eroded, thereby opening space for an insurgent party that is free from the shackles of office.[17]

A final driver of radical right support is a more general sense of pessimism about the current state of society. The radical right in Europe have made the biggest gains with voters who are the most dissatisfied about the direction of their country, the most pessimistic about their future and the least trusting of others.[18] The political scientist Roger Eatwell describes these voters as the *pessimistariat*: 'mainly male working class voters who are extremely pessimistic about the future and place little or no faith in mainstream parties and institutions'.[19] While it may seem obvious that new parties will appeal to citizens who feel discontented with the status quo, this is not always the case. Another great wave of party change in post-war Europe was the emergence of socially liberal 'New Left' parties, who appealed to optimistic young university graduates who were motivated by progressive ideas like human rights, tackling global warming or championing Internet freedom.[20] Europe's radical right revolt has been the opposite, driven by older, poorly educated and financially insecure voters yearning to restore the 'good old times', which in their eyes were defined by greater respect for authority, traditional gender roles and assertive nationalism.[21] At the heart of this counter-revolution is a deep-seated gloom about the fallen state of society, and a distrust of alien and threatening modern values. Radical right populists provide scapegoats to blame for society's decline, stoking fond memories of a lost, golden era. Perhaps it is no accident that UKIP's campaigns often feature rural villages and country pubs, symbols of an idealised traditional England that voters like John may yearn for, or in the words of the past Conservative leader John Major, 'the country of long shadows on county [cricket] grounds, warm beer, invincible green suburbs, dog lovers and pools fillers'.[22]

The radical right agenda and support for UKIP

We begin by looking at the impact of the four motives outlined above: Euroscepticism; hostility to immigration; populist dissatisfaction; and a pessimistic outlook.[23] Readers who are interested in how we have measured these motives can find a full description in the appendix to this book. Figure 5.1 gives us a first sense of the power of these four motives, by showing how support for UKIP changes when we move from the lowest to the highest score on the main measure of each.[24] The motives are ranked from left to right in terms of the strength of their effects. Euroscepticism has the strongest impact on UKIP support. Overall, one-fifth of the British electorate are deeply unhappy with Britain's membership of the EU, and support for UKIP among this group is 15.6 percentage points higher than it is among the 13 per cent who are very happy with Britain's EU membership. Hostility to the EU, the issue that first led Alan Sked to launch UKIP in 1993, remains a key driver of support for the party today. But it is not the only motive fuelling the revolt.

Support for UKIP is also strongly linked to the three other motives. Their support is 8.9 points higher among the 20 per cent of Britons who are very dissatisfied with how Britain's democracy operates than it is among the 5 per cent who are very satisfied. Hostility to immigration shows a similarly strong connection: UKIP support is seven points higher among the 42 per cent of Britons who rate the importance of immigration at ten out of ten, than

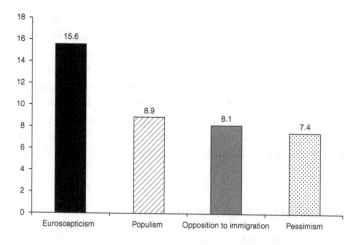

FIGURE 5.1 Impact of four motives on UKIP support, bivariate relationships

it is among the 13 per cent who rate its importance at five out of ten or below. Similarly, support for the party is around seven points higher among citizens who are the most negative about economic prospects than it is among the most optimistic. As the baseline level of support for UKIP in our sample is about 4 per cent, these differences suggest that support for the party is two to four times as high among voters who express these radical right motives most strongly.

This initial look suggests that Euroscepticism is the most powerful motive driving the UKIP revolt, with political dissatisfaction, anti-immigration and economic pessimism playing important, supporting roles. But this first cut also overlooks two important issues. First, these motives overlap in voters' minds. Those who take a dim view of the EU will often also oppose immigration, distrust politicians who they feel have failed them on these issues and feel insecure and pessimistic about the future. Second, these motives may change over time, as the agenda in British politics shifts and as UKIP have evolved. To address the first issue of overlapping motives, we employ the statistical 'regression' technique used in the previous chapter to separate out

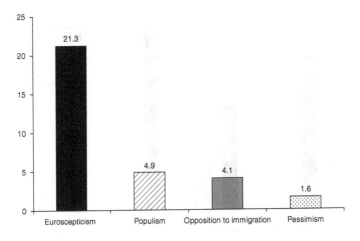

FIGURE 5.2 Impact of four motives for UKIP support, logistic regression model

the influence of overlapping social groups. Using this method we can isolate the impact of one motive from the effects of the others.

As we can see in Figure 5.2, Euroscepticism stands out as a dominant motive when all of these attitudes are examined together. Support for UKIP among voters who are the most strongly dissatisfied with Britain's EU membership is nearly 20 percentage points higher than among those who are the most satisfied. This is not a huge surprise given that Europe is UKIP's core issue. Nevertheless, it underscores the party's impressive hold on the most strongly Eurosceptic voters. Consider this: in our overall sample, UKIP wins support from less than one voter in twenty, but among strong Eurosceptics they win one in five. These hard Eurosceptic attitudes are relatively widespread in Britain, more so than in almost every other EU member state, and UKIP are the beneficiary, as Farage recognises: 'They [UKIP voters] hate the European thing. I am some kind of Europhile compared to most of them. They hate it. They want nothing to do with it.'

Populism and opposition to immigration are less important when we control for the overlap between attitudes, but they are

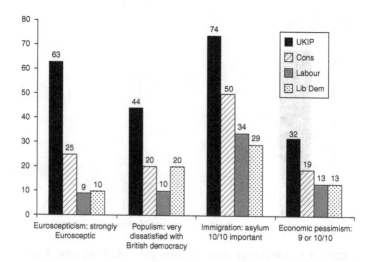

FIGURE 5.3 Popularity of radical right motives among UKIP supporters and mainstream party supporters

still significant. General pessimism, however, drops out entirely as a motive when we control for the other three, which suggests that, while UKIP voters are typically gloomy, such pessimism is not what drives their choice. This pattern, whereby Euroscepticism is the main driver of support for UKIP, with populism and anti-immigration feeling playing supporting roles, is the opposite to the pattern typically found in Europe, where in most cases concerns over immigration have taken centre stage. This may reflect the unusual power of British Euroscepticism, in an island nation that has never warmed to the EU, as well as UKIP's unusual beginnings as an explicitly anti-EU pressure group. But it might also reflect the changed political context since 2004, which has included a surge of migration from Central and East European states and a protracted financial crisis in the single currency Eurozone. As a result, the EU is now linked in voters' minds with the two 'problems' they say they care about most: the poor state of the economy, and high immigration. This may explain why, while Euroscepticism dominates, all four motives are expressed more frequently and intensely by UKIP voters than by any other party's supporters, as Figure 5.3 shows. This charts the proportion of each party's support base expressing the most intense level of support for each motive. Nearly three-quarters of UKIP voters rate the importance of immigration as a political problem at 10 out of 10; almost two-thirds describe themselves as 'strongly Eurosceptic', nearly half say they are 'very dissatisfied' with the state of British democracy and almost a third rate themselves as extremely pessimistic about the economy. This is an intensely motivated electorate: angry, fed up and ready for a radical alternative.

'Brussels plus': how radical right motives interact to drive UKIP support

Euroscepticism is more than just one motive among many for UKIP voters – it is so universal, and so central to the party's identity, that it is better seen as a necessary condition for considering a UKIP vote: 95 per cent of UKIP voters disapprove of Britain's EU membership, while less than one in two hundred of those who *approve* of Britain's EU membership back UKIP. However, while almost all of UKIP's supporters are Eurosceptic, most Eurosceptics are not UKIP supporters. The rebels win the support of only 9 per cent of the Eurosceptic voters in our overall sample, and 16 per cent of those who are strongly Eurosceptic. Most of these Eurosceptics who were interviewed over our nine-year survey period continued to back one of the main parties, particularly in the earlier years of our sample, before UKIP's post-2010 surge.[25] Euroscepticism is thus a necessary condition for UKIP support, but not a sufficient one. Their voters do not tend to be single-issue Eurosceptics, but can instead be characterised as 'Brussels-plus', fusing hostility to the EU with potent domestic concerns.

We illustrate this Brussels-plus pattern in Table 5.1, which shows how UKIP's appeal is strongest for voters who combine Euroscepticism with at least one of the other two core radical right motivations: populism and opposition to immigration. On both issues, radical right attitudes are much more widespread among UKIP supporting Eurosceptics than among Eurosceptics who don't back the rebels. UKIP can only get its foot in the door with voters who oppose

TABLE 5.1 The attitudes of Eurosceptics in and outside of the UKIP revolt

	UKIP Eurosceptics	Non-UKIP Eurosceptics	Europhiles
Populism			
Dissatisfied with democracy	81	64	43
Pop Scale 1: Govt not honest/ trustworthy	85	70	56
Pop Scale 2: Govt doesn't treat people like you fairly	87	72	48
Pop scale 3: Big gap between what you expect and what you get	79	74	58
No political influence★	64	54	42
Immigration			
Immigration MIP (spontaneous)	35	25	9
Importance of asylum (scale)★★	75	60	24
Very negative view of asylum situation	81	69	32
Three or four negative emotions about asylum seekers	52	40	15
Share of the sample	5	44	51

★ Scored 0 or 1 on ten-point scale; ★★ scored 10 out of 10 importance.

Britain's EU membership, but to close the sale they also need to tap into other concerns: resentment of an unresponsive and out-of-touch political elite, or opposition to mass immigration. It is, therefore, misleading to debate whether UKIP's support is 'really' about the EU, anger at the government or hostility to immigration. Most UKIP voters tend to hold some combination of all three motives, which form different facets of their overall worldview.

We now have a picture of overall UKIP support, but how is the party changing over time? As is clear in Figure 5.4 below, UKIP have grown in part by consolidating support from the 20 per cent of voters who say they strongly disapprove of Britain's EU membership. The Conservatives were once the overwhelming favourites of this group, winning nearly half of their votes, but since entering government in 2010 Cameron's party have rapidly lost ground to

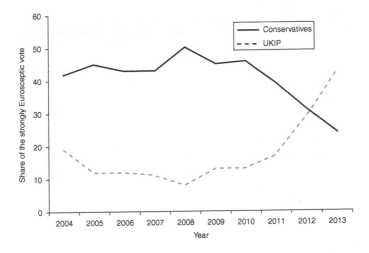

FIGURE 5.4 Conservative and UKIP vote share among strong Eurosceptics

the rebels. By 2013, UKIP were the favoured choice of this group, and Nigel Farage was winning as much backing from the group as Cameron had been just four years earlier.

While UKIP have consolidated much of the strong Eurosceptic vote, their growth has also come by a fuller mobilisation of the Brussels–plus voters, as Table 5.2 illustrates. When Tony Blair's time in office drew to a close, 14–15 per cent of strong Eurosceptics who also had populist or anti-immigration attitudes backed UKIP; this rose to 16–20 per cent in the first two years of coalition and then surged to 35–58 per cent in 2012–13. Over the same period, support for UKIP among weak Eurosceptics with populist or anti-immigration motives grew from 5 to 15 per cent, but support among populists or anti-immigrant Europhiles hardly increased at all. By 2013, UKIP were the dominant party among strongly Eurosceptic Brussels–plus voters, which is a large group that represents some 15 per cent of all voters. In fact, UKIP were winning about as much support from these Brussels–plus voters as the Labour and Conservative parties combined. They had also tripled their support among voters with only weakly Eurosceptic views, but who shared their views about immigration or the established political class.

TABLE 5.2 UKIP support levels among different groups, by time period

	Strong Eurosceptics	Weak Eurosceptics	Europhiles
Populism – dissatisfied with democracy			
Blair: 2004–7	15	5	0.6
Brown: 2007–10	12	5	0.6
Cameron I: 2010–11	20	5	0.4
Cameron II: 2012–13	38	15	1
Share of sample	*14*	*18*	*21*
Immigration – rate importance of immigration 10 out of 10			
Blair: 2004–7	14	6	1
Brown: 2007–10	11	5	0.8
Cameron I: 2010–11	16	5	0.8
Cameron II: 2012–13	36	14	2
Share of the sample	*15*	*16*	*11*

These results suggest that the shifts in UKIP's strategy we examined in the opening two chapters have played an important role in raising their support. What began as a single-issue, anti-EU rebellion has grown into a potent force by consolidating voters who say 'no' three times: no to Brussels; no to political elites in Westminster; and no to immigration. The Eurosceptic core of this 'Brussels-plus' message is also more than a means to recruit voters. It provides the party with a coherent ideological core, which attracts and motivates the grassroots army of activists that any party needs to do the grunt-work. UKIP can also present themselves as a vehicle for anti-immigration and anti-establishment politics, without being defined only by these positions. Their criticism of Europe is accepted by all as a legitimate topic for mainstream British political debate, which gives the party a ready defence to charges of intolerance, or what the political scientist Elisabeth Ivarsflaten refers to as a 'reputational shield'.[26] UKIP can then build outwards from this Eurosceptic core, recruiting politically dissatisfied and anti-immigration voters while retaining their image as a legitimate party. Journalists may mock UKIP on occasion, but very few of them treat the party in the same way that they treat the extreme right BNP. As a result, the party enjoys much wider and less critical access to the media than their more extreme rivals, coverage that they can use to disseminate their populist and anti-immigrant arguments. Paradoxically, then, the core radical right ideology of populism and hostility to immigration can be more powerful when it is offered by a party who are primarily about something else.

The contrast with the BNP is instructive. Unlike UKIP, since their establishment in 1982 the racial nationalist party mobilised on the far more contentious ground of racial immigration and identity, and infused their campaigns with ethnic nationalism and white, racial supremacism. Whereas in their early years UKIP were forging links with centre-right think tanks and emphasising the economic costs of EU membership, the BNP were preaching about the need to separate different racial groups, sterilise mentally ill citizens, refute the events of the Holocaust and forcibly remove migrants from the country.[27] As a result, the extreme right party became heavily dependent on a smaller rump of activists, many of whom were previously active in the National Front, and driven by openly racist and anti-democratic motivations. Though in later years the BNP recognised the importance of political legitimacy as a prerequisite for mass support, their efforts to project a more moderate image were repeatedly undermined by their openly racist and violent past, and by the behaviour of their activists.

Unlike UKIP, the BNP were never accepted as a legitimate player in the political system and, having emerged from an undercurrent of neo-Nazism and racial nationalism, lacked the reputational shield that UKIP enjoy. This was reflected in the front cover of one national newspaper that read 'Bloody Nasty People', and in the views of voters. Even at the time of their electoral peak at the 2009 European Parliament elections, one survey revealed that 72 per cent of Britons felt negatively towards the BNP, with 62 per cent feeling 'very' negative towards the party. In marked contrast, only 38 per cent felt negatively, and only 18 per cent felt very negatively, about UKIP, while almost three times as many voters felt positively about UKIP as had warm feelings about the BNP.[28] Such findings reflect how, even though many voters may sympathise with extreme right ideas, a strong social norm against prejudice, racism and extremism often leads them to reject parties who take these ideas too far.[29]

UKIP have also prospered under the coalition due to an unusually favourable political context in which none of the other parties were in a position to compete effectively with them on radical right issues. The implosion of the BNP removed any lingering competition for the populist anti-immigrant electorate from the extreme right.[30] Meanwhile, the formation of the coalition initially limited the ability of the Conservatives to move onto UKIP's territory of Europe and immigration, as the centre-right party found themselves constrained both by their own leader, David Cameron, who has remained anxious to avoid a sharp right-wing drift, and the pro-EU and pro-immigration positions of their Liberal Democrat coalition partners. The entrance of the Liberal Democrats into government has removed competition for another source of support for UKIP: moderate voters without any strong political agenda, but who are angry with the government and looking for an outlet for their discontent. The Liberal Democrats performed this role in British politics for decades, but as part of government they can no longer be the catch-all voice of political dissent. This presented Farage and UKIP with an opportunity to diversify further, from an alliance of anti-EU, anti-elite, anti-immigration radicals into a catch-all party of discontents.

A vehicle for protest votes? UKIP and performance politics

Voters often base their political choices on expectations of good performance, and will turn against parties they think are doing a bad job, a tendency encouraged by the focus of modern parties on management and delivery, rather than big ideological visions.

Voters who are frustrated with the government are, however, only likely to consider a radical alternative if they have also ruled out the main opposition party. If you think the main opposition has some potential, why risk supporting an untested insurgent party? But, alternatively, if you think that *both* the government and the opposition are incompetent on the issues that really matter to you, and you do not want to stay at home on polling day, then where else can you turn? UKIP should therefore do best of all among those voters who think that both mainstream parties have failed to deliver good management.

We also need to bear in mind the central role that Euroscepticism plays in UKIP's electoral appeal. As we have shown, currently UKIP only connect with the half of the British electorate who disapprove of the EU. An initial look at the impact of attitudes towards the performance of parties reveals the same pattern: UKIP makes no impression on pro-European voters, regardless of how they rate the main parties' performance. This confirms the 'Brussels-plus' dynamic that we have identified: Euroscepticism is so central to UKIP's political identity that they can only appeal to voters who share it. As such, our analysis of these performance effects will now focus on the Eurosceptic half of the electorate only.[31]

We start by looking at whether governing party performance matters overall. Do UKIP do better among those who think that Labour and the Conservatives have failed on the key issues?[32] We look at perceptions of performance on six issues. Five of these – immigration, crime, terrorism, the NHS and education – are available for the full run of our data, while a question about performance on the financial crisis was asked from late 2008 onwards.[33] As with radical right motives, judgements about parties' performance tend to overlap – voters who think the Conservatives are doing a bad job on the economy will often also think the party is doing poorly on education or health. Many voters' judgements are driven as much by their view of the party's performance in general as by views about particular issues. To isolate the impact of particular issues from these more global assessments, we once again employ the statistical technique of regression analysis.

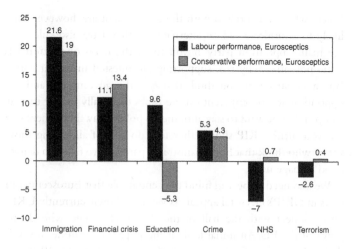

FIGURE 5.5 Issue performance effects on UKIP support, 2008–2013

Figure 5.5 shows how support for UKIP among Eurosceptic voters changes as we move from the most positive to the most negative rating of the two main parties' performance on each of six issues, while holding views on the other issues constant.[34] Two issues clearly stand out: immigration and the financial crisis.[35] Citizens who hold strongly negative judgements of mainstream performance on either are far more likely to back the rebels. Support for UKIP is 21 percentage points higher among Eurosceptics with the most negative views of Labour's record on immigration than among those who are most positive. For the Conservatives, this difference is 19 points. Support for UKIP is also 11 points higher among Eurosceptics who are the most critical of Labour's performance on the financial crisis than it is among the most positive voters. A similar swing in sentiment about Conservatives' performance produces a 13 point rise in support for UKIP. The two highest profile issues on the political agenda in the past five years have been immigration and the financial crisis, and on both issues UKIP have done very well among Eurosceptic voters who think the mainstream parties have failed to deliver.

The other four issues covered in our survey had less consistent effects. UKIP does best among voters who are unhappy with Labour's performance on education and those who like Tory education performance. This may suggest sympathy among UKIP voters for the Conservatives' approach to education, and may explain why UKIP have heavily promoted a traditional Conservative approach to education, emphasising grammar schools and traditional teaching methods, in their campaigns (see Chapter 2).

UKIP typically wins over those who are angry over poor performances, but when we turn to the NHS this pattern is reversed: the party does best among voters who approve of Labour's record on healthcare. This may reflect the demographics of UKIP supporters, which we examined in Chapter 4. These are mainly older, working-class voters who will most likely have had more experiences than the average voter with the NHS, and who feel more attached to the health service.[36] The fact that these voters are willing to defect to UKIP despite their strong approval of Labour's NHS record should concern Labour strategists, given the central role that healthcare often plays in their campaigns. UKIP's older working-class voters recognise that Labour 'delivered the goods' on healthcare but this is not enough to win or retain the loyalty of these voters whose attention has shifted to concerns about immigration and the economy.

The final two issues are terrorism and crime, which were high up the political agenda in the early 2000s, but featured much less in voters' minds between 2008 and 2013. Crime shows a similar pattern of effects to immigration and the financial crisis: UKIP does better with those who are critical of the performance of both of the main parties. But these effects are modest, reflecting the low importance of the issue in the minds of voters. Terrorism has even less impact, and no significant effects on UKIP support.

So, what is this telling us about the party's appeal? We have already seen that while nearly all of UKIP's voters are Eurosceptic, most Eurosceptics do not back UKIP. Euroscepticism is not enough, on its own, to prompt many voters to back the rebels. They need an extra push. In the last section we showed how hostility to immigration and populist anger at mainstream politics

TABLE 5.3 Support for UKIP among Eurosceptics by views of party performance (on immigration, and on the financial crisis)

	Negative about both parties	Negative about Lab, satisfied with Con	Negative about Con, satisfied with Lab	Neutral or positive about both parties
Performance on immigration				
Blair	12	6	1	5
Brown	11	5	2	2
Cameron I	15	3	2	3
Cameron II	27	8	7	5
Share of sample				
Performance on the financial crisis				
Brown	15	6	5	6
Cameron I	19	7	3	5
Cameron II	36	16	9	10
Share of sample				

could each provide this extra incentive to rebel. Now, we can add perceptions that the established politicians have failed to manage immigration or the financial crisis to the mix of motives that can tip the balance. In particular, as can be seen in Table 5.3, the recent surge of support for UKIP has been driven by mass defections among the large and growing portion of the electorate who feel that *both* Labour and the Conservatives have failed on these two key issues. Such voters are not making an emotional and unfocused protest, but are voicing their intense unhappiness with the established parties' performance on the issues at the top of the national political agenda.

The worldview of the average UKIP voter is becoming clearer. He (because they are mainly men) wants Britain out of the EU and immigration brought under tighter control. He is also angry with both of the two main parties in Britain for failing repeatedly to deliver good management on the two defining issues of the day: immigration and the financial crisis. As a result, he has lost faith in the political system, which he thinks serves the interests of wealthy and powerful elites and ignores ordinary voters like him. Europe is an overarching symbol of this failure: the EU is the source of the immigrants causing problems in Britain, and is an economic failure in constant crisis, yet Britain's politicians refuse to listen to the voters and leave.

But what about his views of the political leaders themselves? Is our average UKIP voter also motivated by a personal hostility to David Cameron, Ed Miliband or Nick Clegg? All three are young, highly educated, socially liberal and middle-class career politicians. All three are examples of the new political and social elite, resented by the 'left behind' voters attracted to UKIP. But each of these leaders also brings unique personal qualities to their role, which may attract or further repel such voters. Have Cameron's widely publicised arguments with his own party over Europe and gay marriage alienated traditional right-wing voters, encouraging them to turn to UKIP? Have perceptions that Ed Miliband is too left wing and indecisive put off voters who are angry with Cameron and the Conservatives, thereby helping to encourage a switch to Nigel Farage and UKIP? Has hostility to Nick Clegg, the most unpopular Liberal Democrat leader in modern history, prevented his party from picking up voters disaffected with the 'big two'? Our final section considers what role, if any, these mainstream leaders have played in fuelling UKIP's revolt.

Mainstream leaders and UKIP support: don't like Ed and never liked Dave?

The decisions that voters make at elections are often driven more by their views of individual party leaders – who they see and hear on a daily basis – than by the less familiar details of party policy or ideology. Leaders provide voters with what psychologists call a 'heuristic device', an accessible shortcut for making decisions about complex issues. Leaders provide this shortcut because they provide the most readily available piece of political information that voters have when they decide who to back. Academics have shown that leaders' judgements are central to explaining the behaviour of voters at elections: 'Leader *images* – people's feelings of like or dislike of leaders and the standards of judgements that they bring to bear on leader performance – exert significant direct effects on party support.'[37]

In recent British history, Tony Blair has been most prominent example of this. In the early years of his leadership Blair's widespread popularity helped win Labour votes from citizens who would not otherwise have backed the party. Later on, however, the more divisive post-Iraq Blair became an electoral liability for Labour, repelling left-wing voters who might otherwise have backed Labour.[38] However, because of their status as the most prominent symbol of a party, judgements of leaders will also be strongly influenced by voters' other views and performance perceptions. Many voters will, for example, dislike David Cameron because of their views of the party he leads, and what it has done, rather than due to his personal qualities. What we want to know is whether voters' views of Cameron and other leaders have any 'added value' in helping to explain defections to UKIP, which cannot otherwise be explained by the other attitudes we have examined.

We therefore again employ statistical techniques to 'control' for the impact of voters' other attitudes, focusing on what effect judgements of leaders have on top of this. As we do not have data on views of the UKIP leader, our picture of leadership effects is necessarily incomplete, as we cannot test for the effect that views of Nigel Farage, or UKIP's earlier leaders, had on their support.[39] This is likely to result in a substantial underestimate of leadership effects on UKIP performance, as Farage, in particular, has proved to be an effective and well-known frontman for his party. As before, we focus on the Eurosceptic half of the electorate who are willing to give UKIP a hearing, as preliminary analysis confirmed that pro-EU voters do not consider UKIP even when they loathe the main party leaders.[40]

The Eurosceptic half of our sample were asked to rate the main parties' leaders on a 0–10 scale. Figure 5.6 shows the simple relationship between these ratings and UKIP support levels with lower ratings on the right hand side of the graph. The lines all slope upwards, meaning that UKIP perform better among Eurosceptic

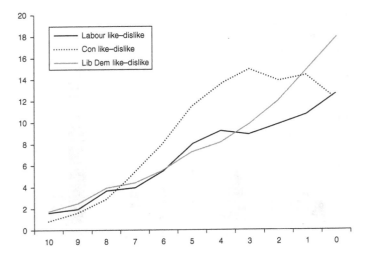

FIGURE 5.6 Views of party leaders and UKIP support, 2004–2013

voters who dislike each of the main party leaders. The relationship is strongest, though, for the Conservatives. UKIP does poorly among Eurosceptics who give the Tory leader a strong positive rating, but their support rises sharply as the ratings of the Conservative leader drop into the negative half of the scale. The intensity of hostility to Cameron, however, does not seem to matter: UKIP does not do any better among Eurosceptics who rate the Conservative leader at zero than those who rate him at four. While all of the main parties face a potential problem from UKIP competition when voters dislike their leaders, this problem is most acute for the Conservatives. Eurosceptics do not have to despise the Conservatives' leader to defect to UKIP; even those giving him a lukewarm four out of ten are willing to switch in large numbers.

The overall relationship glosses over two important distinctions, however. First, all the parties have changed leader over the decade we consider, and the role each party's leader plays has also changed, as the Conservatives and Liberal Democrats have replaced Labour in government. Second, much of the relationship between leadership

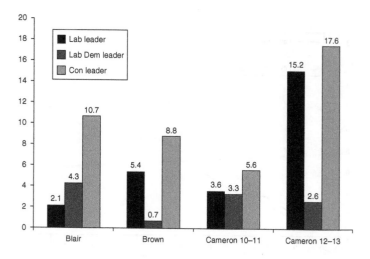

FIGURE 5.7 Modelled leader effects on UKIP support over four time periods

ratings and UKIP support may be partly driven by the other factors we have analysed. In Figure 5.7, we show the impact party leaders have when we control for all the other motives driving UKIP support, in each of our four time periods. As before, the analysis is restricted to Eurosceptic voters.

The strong link between Conservative leader ratings and support for UKIP holds up in this analysis. Ratings of the Conservative Party leader have the largest and most consistent connection to UKIP support, even when all other attitudes are controlled. During Tony Blair's premiership, support for UKIP among Eurosceptics who loathed David Cameron (and his predecessor, Michael Howard) was nearly 11 points higher than support among those who were most positive about him. Views of the Liberal Democrat leaders in this period (Charles Kennedy and Menzies Campbell) show a weaker but significant relationship with UKIP support, which rises over 4 points as we move from the highest to the lowest rating.

What about the role of Labour's leaders in fuelling support for UKIP? Among Eurosceptic voters, views of Tony Blair show virtually no relationship at all with support for UKIP. Although many voters were angry with Tony Blair by the end of his premiership, few expressed their anger by decamping to UKIP. Support for UKIP among those who were the most hostile towards Blair was only 2 points higher than among Blair's most ardent supporters. Gordon Brown was a more effective recruiting agent for UKIP: their support is over 5 points higher among his strongest critics than among his most loyal supporters. Yet under Brown, as under Blair, it was views of the Conservative leader that had the strongest effects: support for the rebels is nearly 9 points higher among those who are the most critical of David Cameron. Views of Nick Clegg had no effect at all on UKIP support in this period.[41]

Leadership effects are weakest during the first eighteen months of the coalition government, perhaps reflecting a brief 'honeymoon' period for the two leaders of the new coalition government, and the new leader of the Labour opposition, Ed Miliband. Hostility to Cameron still had an impact though: support among Eurosceptics with the most negative views of the new Prime Minister was over 5 points higher than among his strongest supporters. The impact of leaders really takes off again during the later period of coalition, when UKIP support was surging. Voters hostile to Cameron's leadership became much more willing to back the rebels while the party also became more adept at winning over Eurosceptics with a dim view of Ed Miliband's Labour leadership. In this period, UKIP succeeded in being a catch-all opposition party, winning strong support from voters unimpressed by both mainstream party leaders.

The strengthening link between views of David Cameron and support for UKIP since 2010 is puzzling. Under Cameron, the Conservative-led coalition government have adopted a range of policies designed to restrict immigration and have, despite the objections of the Liberal Democrats, adopted a consistently soft Eurosceptic approach, with the promise of harder Euroscepticism from the Conservatives if they are able to govern alone.[42] Given the motives that we have shown are animating UKIP voters, in theory such proposals should win them over. This is where Cameron's personal image may be important – UKIP voters may agree with the

Conservatives on these issues, but our findings suggest that they just do not like or trust David Cameron. Many may see Cameron as a symbol of the university-educated, socially liberal and economically privileged political class that dominates the country and excludes them from the political conversation. This deep-seated distrust may limit Cameron's ability to win UKIP voters round with policy appeals. UKIP's ability to mobilise hostility to Ed Miliband may stem from a similar source – he is seen by UKIP-leaning groups as another politician from the 'Westminster bubble' who does not understand the needs of ordinary voters, and they are therefore reluctant to give him a hearing. We cannot know from our data what mix of motives makes the rejection of Cameron such a potent driver of UKIP support, but its power presents the Conservatives with a serious strategic problem. At the time of writing, their leader is a man who consistently outpolls his party with the electorate overall, yet is also a man who inspires such furious hostility among the Eurosceptic, left behind electorate that he alone is often sufficient to tip the balance in UKIP's favour with such voters.

Conclusions: putting the pieces together

On a hot summer's evening in August 2011, Lord Pearson called Nigel Farage to inform him of his decision to stand down as party leader. Having only resigned from the role two years previously, and now realising he would be one of the leading candidates to succeed Pearson, Farage met the news with horror. He had felt under-appreciated during his first term as leader, and was still recovering from injuries that he suffered in a plane crash on the eve of the 2010 general election. The next month, at UKIP's annual conference in Torquay, Farage was due to give the keynote speech and had to confirm whether or not he planned to return. The night before the speech, he found himself awake in the early hours, seemingly unable to reach a decision. 'Do I want to go back to the life that I walked away from a year ago? Am I well enough? Am I strong enough, physically, to do it?' While grappling with these questions, his mind drifted back to a journey that he had shared with a London taxi driver: 'He said to me: "Well, look Nigel, with David Cameron as leader of the Tories, a man who is not even a Tory, this is a great time for you. You've got to go back".'[43]

Farage's taxi driver was an astute political observer. In the past few years, the British political context has provided UKIP with an unprecedented opportunity. In the previous chapters, we showed how wider political and social changes over recent decades produced a large 'left behind' electorate of ageing, white, working-class voters who are alienated from mainstream politics, and how UKIP have emerged as a voice for this bloc of voters. Now we have filled out this picture by showing the mix of motives which have driven these citizens into the UKIP rebellion: strong Euroscepticism combined with hostility to immigration, rejection of the political class and a deep dissatisfaction with the poor management provided by the mainstream parties.

The taxi driver was also right to point to David Cameron as an important source of support for UKIP's insurgency. Since his election as Conservative leader in 2005, commentators have pointed to Cameron's more socially liberal, centrist brand of Conservatism as a potential recruiting tool for UKIP: his strong support for gay marriage, perceived equivocation over the EU, and perceived failure to tackle immigration have all led his critics to claim Cameron's 'train has left the Conservative station'.[44] Typical of this view is Conservative elder Norman Tebbit, who argued that voters 'are so fed up with the Cameron Coalition that they will turn to Ukip as the party which comes closest to a traditional Conservative agenda, and a reasoned position on the European issue. One can hardly blame them for that.'[45] Our analysis shows Tebbit has a point: public hostility to Cameron is a powerful asset for UKIP, and has become an important source of support for the party.

Aside from dissatisfaction with Cameron, however, the UKIP electorate is motivated by a clear agenda – the party have fused their core Euroscepticism with potent appeals on domestic issues. The 'left behind' voters flocking to UKIP are angry about immigration and the failure of the mainstream parties to manage it, and alienated by a political class which they feel does not listen to them, and has done little to make their lives better. These individual elements are facets of a populist and anti-politics worldview: a perception that changes wrought by the EU and immigration threaten British identity and sovereignty, and a loss of faith in the ability of mainstream politics to recognise or solve these problems. We can summarise the motive of the average UKIP voter as 'Brussels-plus'. While hostility to Europe is ever present, it is combined with a shifting mix of other concerns: strong opposition to immigration; anger with the mainstream parties for failing to control it; a belief that British democracy is no longer functioning to protect their interests; that the established political class is corrupt and self-serving; that mainstream parties have poorly managed the financial crisis, or are no longer able to resolve the problems that face Britain; and, since 2011, dissatisfaction with the Labour Party and Ed Miliband's leadership of it. These attitudes explain most of the differences that we saw in the social profile of UKIP voters in Chapter 4. The older, blue-collar, white and working-class men with little formal schooling who we identified as the core UKIP voters are also the voters who hold this mix of motives.[46]

The pattern of motives that has fuelled support for UKIP is also, on the whole, stable. Opposition to immigration, populist hostility to mainstream politics, perceptions of poor management on immigration and the financial crisis and negative views of the party leaders – all of these factors contribute to UKIP support in 2013 in much the same way as they did in 2004. UKIP's growth in this period has not come through mobilising new concerns, but through a dramatic increase in their effectiveness at winning the voters who already share their worldview. In the mid-2000s, UKIP was a minor player even among their core electorate of strong Eurosceptics and 'Brussels-plus' voters. But by 2013 the party had become the most popular choice among both of these groups. UKIP has become a significant player by building a more effective party organisation to consolidate support from the large section of the electorate who share their outlook, but they remain very weak with the majority of voters who do not.

UKIP, then, have risen by developing a distinctive appeal, which has mobilised longstanding and latent divisions within British society. Yet the concerns that are now being organised into politics by this revolt still have no voice in the halls of power. Britain's most successful political insurgency in a generation has, as of 2013, not a single Member of Parliament in Westminster. Here, UKIP face a challenge unknown to most of their European cousins: an electoral system that is heavily stacked against insurgent parties with support spread evenly across the country. In most European countries, a party consistently polling 10–15 per cent would be widely expected to play a significant role in the next Parliament, but in Britain most are sceptical that this level of support can deliver UKIP a single MP. In the next chapter, we turn to consider the challenge posed to the rebellion by the electoral system, and UKIP's efforts to meet it.

Notes

1   Tim Montgomerie, 'The PM can rise above the battle of the tiddlers', *The Times*, 1 October 2012.
2   Tim Montgomerie, 'David Cameron ignores UKIP at his peril', *The Times*, 11 April 2012.
3   'The UKIP insurgency', Bagehot's notebook, *The Economist*, 7 June 2012.
4   Nigel Farage, 'An open letter from UKIP leader Nigel Farage MEP', *The Daily Telegraph*, 20 May 2013.
5   Angus Reid, 'Labour's immigration policies seen as failure by most Britons'. Available online: http://www.angusreidglobal.com/polls/43024/labours-immigration-policies-seen-as-failure-by-most-britons/ (accessed 19 September 2013).
6   Nigel Farage, 'Ed Miliband's running scared – and now UKIP will go after him and Labour', *Daily Mail*, 27 January 2013.
7   For reviews of this literature see Jens Rydgren (2007) 'The sociology of the radical right', *Annual Review of Sociology*, 33: 241–62; Cas Mudde (2007) *Populist Radical Right Parties in Europe*, Cambridge: Cambridge University Press; Matthew J. Goodwin (2011) *Right Response: Understanding and Countering Populist Extremism in Europe*, London: Chatham House.
8   See Mudde, *Populist Radical Right Parties in Europe*, pp. 159–60.
9   Catherine E. De Vries and Erica E. Edwards (2009) 'Taking Europe to its extremes: Extremist parties and public Euroscepticism', *Party Politics*, 15(1): 5–28 (6).
10 Hans Werts, Peer Scheepers and Marcel Lubbers (2012) 'Euro-scepticism and radical right-wing voting in Europe, 2002–2008: Social cleavages, socio-political attitudes and contextual characteristics determining

voting for the radical right', *European Union Politics*, 14(2): 183–205. For further evidence on the importance of Euroscepticism to radical right support see Elisabeth Ivarsflaten (2005) 'What unites right-wing populists in Western Europe? Re-examining grievance mobilization models in seven successful cases', *Comparative Political Studies*, 41(1): 3–23; Wouter Van der Brug, Meindert Fennema and Jean Tillie (2005) 'Protest or mainstream? How the European anti-immigrant parties developed into two separate groups by 1999', *European Journal of Political Research*, 42(1): 55–76; Kai Arzheimer (2009) 'Contextual factors and the extreme right vote in Western Europe, 1980–2002', *American Journal of Political Science*, 53(2): 259–75; Margarita Gomez-Reino and Ivan Llamazares (2013) 'The populist radical right and European integration: A comparative analysis of party–voter links', *West European Politics*, 36(4): 789–816.

11 In the regular Eurobarometer survey, which tracks these attitudes across EU member states, British voters have long been the least likely to view their country's EU membership positively. The last time they were asked, in 2011, just 26 per cent said that Britain's membership of the EU is a 'good thing' Available online: http://ec.europa.eu/public_opinion/index_en.htm (accessed 24 July 2013). On British Euroscepticism see Chris Gifford (2010) 'The UK and the European Union: Dimensions of sovereignty and the problem of Eurosceptic Britishness', *Parliamentary Affairs*, 63(2): 321–38; Geoffrey Evans (1998) 'Euroscepticism and Conservative electoral support: How an asset became a liability', *British Journal of Political Science*, 28(4): 573–90; Andrew Geddes (2003) *The European Union and British Politics* (Chapter 9), Basingstoke: Palgrave Macmillan; Stephen George (2000) 'Britain: Anatomy of a Eurosceptic state', *Journal of European Integration*, 22(1): 15–33; Anthony Forster (2002) *Euroscepticism in Contemporary British Politics: Opposition to Europe in the Conservative and Labour Parties since 1945*, London: Routledge; Menno Spiering (2004) 'British Euroscepticism', *European Studies: A Journal of European Culture, History and Politics*, 20(1): 127–49.

12 Jens Rydgren (2008) 'Immigration sceptics, xenophobes or racists? Radical right-wing voting in six West European countries', *European Journal of Political Research*, 47: 737–65. See also Pippa Norris (2005) *Radical Right: Voters and Parties in the Electoral Market*, Cambridge: Cambridge University Press; Geertje Lucassen and Marcel Lubbers (2012) 'Who fears what? Explaining far right-wing preference in Europe by distinguishing perceived cultural and economic ethnic threats', *Comparative Political Studies*, 45(5): 547–74.

13 Meindert Fennema (1997) 'Some conceptual issues and problems in the comparison of anti-immigrant parties in Western Europe', *Party Politics*, 3(4): 473–92; see also Ivarsflaten (2005) 'What unites right-wing populists in Western Europe?'

14 Catherine De Vreese and Hago Boomgaarden (2005) 'Projecting EU referendums: Fear of immigration and support for European integration', *European Union Politics*, 61(1): 59–82; Marcel Lubbers (2008) 'Regarding the Dutch "nee" to the European constitution: A test of the identity, utilitarian and political approaches to voting "no"', *European Union Politics*, 9(1): 59–86; Jocelyn Evans (2000) 'Contrasting attitudinal bases to Euroscepticism amongst the French electorate', *Electoral Studies*, 19(4): 539–61.

15 Norris, *Radical Right*, p. 13.

16 Valence politics is typically traced to the work of Donald Stokes, and was subsequently developed in a series of books by members of the British Election Study team. Donald Stokes (1963) 'Spatial models of party competition', *American Political Science Review*, 57: 368–77; Harold Clarke, David Sanders, Marianne C. Stewart and Paul Whiteley (2004) *Political Choice in Britain*, Oxford: Oxford University Press; Harold Clarke, David Sanders, Marianne C. Stewart and Paul Whiteley (2009) *Performance Politics and the British Voter*, Cambridge: Cambridge University Press.

17 This strategy has backfired on populist radical right parties when they have succeeded in entering government, and find themselves facing the same limitations of governing parties. See, for example, R. Heinisch (2003) 'Success in opposition, failure in government: Explaining the performance of right wing populist parties in government', *West European Politics*, 26(3): 91–130.

18 See, for example, Norris, *Radical Right*, p. 158; Jaak Billiet and Hans De Witte (1995) 'Attitudinal dispositions to vote for a "new" extreme right-wing party: The case of "Vlaams Blok"', *European Journal of Political Research*, 27(2): 181–202; Pierre Bréchon and Subrata Kumar Mitra (1992) 'The National Front in France: The emergence of an extreme right protest movement', *Comparative Politics*, 25(1): 63–82.

19 Roger Eatwell (2010) 'Responses', in Roger Eatwell and Matthew J. Goodwin (eds.) *The New Extremism in Twenty-First Century Britain*, Abingdon: Routledge, pp. 211–30.

20 Ferdinand Müller-Rommel (ed.) (1989) *New Politics in Western Europe: The Rise and Success of Green Parties and Alternative Lists*, Boulder: Westview Press.

21 Piero Ignazi referred to this as the 'silent counter-revolution'. Piero Ignazi (1992) 'The silent counter-revolution: Hypotheses on the emergence of extreme right-wing parties in Europe', *European Journal of Political Research*, 22(1): 3–34; see also William Kornhauser (1960) *The Politics of Mass Society*, London: Free Press; Michael Billig (1978) *Fascists: A Social Psychological View of the National Front*, London: Harcourt.

22 Quoted in 'What a lot of tosh', *The Independent*, 25 April 1993.

23 The specific measures we use to capture each of these motives is provided in the appendix at the end of this book.

24 For each motive, we have selected the measure which shows the strongest relationship to UKIP support. The overall picture is not affected by the choice of measure – a table detailing the effect of each individual measure is provided in the appendix at the end of this book.

25 The Conservatives are the most popular party with strong Eurosceptics, though they do not dominate either. Among strong Eurosceptics the overall breakdown of support in our sample is Conservatives 42 per cent, Labour 16 per cent, UKIP 16 per cent, Don't know 14 per cent, Liberal Democrats 7 per cent. Among weak Eurosceptics the breakdown is Conservatives 41 per cent, Labour 26 per cent, Liberal Democrats 12 per cent, Don't know 11 per cent, UKIP 5 per cent. Notice that, as we saw in the demographics chapter, it is Labour which weakens most when UKIP strengthens.

26 Elisabeth Ivarsflaten, 'Reputational shields: Why most anti-immigrant parties failed in Western Europe, 1980–2005'. Paper presented at the Annual Meeting of the American Political Science Association, Philadelphia, 2006.

27 Matthew J. Goodwin (2011) *New British Fascism: Rise of the British National Party*, Abingdon: Routledge, Chapter 2.

28 On 'Bloody Nasty People', see *The Sun*, 15 July 2004. The Channel 4/YouGov opinion poll was undertaken between May 29 and 4 June 2009, and asked voters: 'Do you generally feel positive or negative toward the following political parties?' Overall, 28 per cent said they felt positively about UKIP (7 per cent 'very' and 21 per cent 'fairly'), 27 per cent felt neither positive nor negative, 38 per cent felt negative about UKIP (19 per cent 'fairly' and 18 per cent 'very') and 7 per cent didn't know. Meanwhile, 11 per cent felt positively about the BNP (3 per cent feeling very positive and 8 per cent feeling fairly positive), 13 per cent felt neither positive nor negative and 72 per cent felt negatively towards the party (11 per cent fairly, and 62 per cent very negative), with the remainder not knowing.

29 For academic research on the power of these social norms against prejudice see Scott Blinder, Elisabeth Ivarsflaten and Robert Ford

(2013) 'The better angels of our nature: How the anti-prejudice norm affects policy and party preferences in Great Britain and Germany', *American Journal of Political Science*, 57(4): 841–57.; also Tali Mendelberg (2001) *The Race Card: Campaign Strategy, Implicit Messages, and the Norm of Equality*, Princeton, NJ: Princeton University Press.

30 As we saw in the demographics chapter, the social profile of UKIP and BNP voters is very similar. Additionally, all three of the radical right motives we find to predict UKIP support also strongly predict BNP support. Indeed, BNP voters are motivated even more by populism and hostility to immigration. The implosion of the far right's main party since 2010 has therefore made it much easier for UKIP to recruit voters with these motivations.

31 Models comparing performance effects on UKIP support among Eurosceptic and Europhile voters can be found in the appendix. Asylum and immigration is the only issue that encourages significant defection from Europhiles. Pro-EU voters who felt Labour had failed on this issue were more likely to back UKIP, but the overall size of the effect is quite modest, with UKIP support rising by around 2 per cent when we move from the most positive to the most negative judgements on the issue.

32 Note that voters continue to be asked about the Conservatives' performance after the coalition starts. We unfortunately do not have any questions asking about the Liberal Democrats' performance in government, or the overall performance of the coalition.

33 This is, of course, not an exhaustive list of the issues that matter to voters and on which they judge politicians' performance. However, we can only look at the effects of issues where we have data. Performance on other issues, most obviously relations with the EU, may also have important effects.

34 We restrict ourselves to the 2008–13 data for this overall analysis, as the question about financial crisis performance only began in 2008. The overall pattern of effects for the other five issues is largely the same if we use the full 2004–13 dataset.

35 The CMS asks about asylum rather than immigration, as asylum was more politically salient when the survey first began and the investigators were reluctant to change the question wording. We treat this measure as a proxy for more general immigration attitudes, for three reasons. First, the item remains a potent predictor of voter behaviour even in 2013, despite sharp declines in asylum settlements. Second, other research suggests that asylum seekers are the most salient group of migrants in the minds of voters (Blinder *et al.*, 'The better angels of our nature'). Third, to the extent that this decision introduces bias, it is

in a downward direction – the impact of a measure asking about immigration more broadly would be even larger.

36 Working-class voters and those born before the NHS was founded, show considerably higher support for the institution, perhaps reflecting greater awareness of the value of the NHS among those with direct or indirect memories of healthcare before its introduction, and among those from poorer social classes who have greater reliance upon it. See research by Ipsos MORI on the NHS: http://www.ipsos-mori.com/researchpublications/researcharchive/2975/Public-Perceptions-of-the-NHS.aspx and on political generations: http://www.ipsos-mori-generations.com/nhs

37 Clarke *et al., Political Choice in Britain*, p. 28.

38 Robert Andersen and Geoffrey Evans (2003) 'Who Blairs wins? Leadership and voting in the 2001 election', *British Elections and Parties Review*, 13(1): 229–47; also Clarke *et al., Political Choice in Britain*. On the effects of Blair's declining popularity see Geoffrey Evans and Robert Andersen (2005) 'The impact of party leaders: How Blair lost Labour votes', *Parliamentary Affairs*, 58(4): 818–36.

39 While individual opinion polls should always be treated with caution, during the spring of 2013 one poll by YouGov indicated that 44 per cent of the electorate thought that Farage was 'doing well' as leader of his party, compared to the equivalent figures of 39 per cent for Cameron, 29 per cent for Miliband and 21 per cent for Clegg. However, as Farage is often excluded from opinion polls and surveys (that often subsume UKIP under 'other') it is difficult to paint an accurate picture of voters' views towards the UKIP leader. YouGov/Sunday Times Opinion Poll, 25–26 April 2013.

40 Details of this analysis are provided in the appendix.

41 Liberal Democrat leader ratings in this period also cover the end of Menzies Campbell's leadership and the brief interim leadership of Vince Cable. Excluding these has no impact on the pattern of effects.

42 Philip Lynch and Richard Whittaker (2013) 'Where there is discord, can they bring harmony? Managing intra-party dissent on European integration within the Conservative party', *British Journal of Politics and International Relations*, 15(3): 317–39; P. Lynch and R. Whittaker (2013) 'The Conservatives and European intergration: Electoral strategy, party competition and modernization', paper presented at the American Political Science Association annual conference, Chicago.

43 Interview with Nigel Farage, 22 July 2013.

44 Cited in Peter Oborne, 'On gay marriage and Europe, David Cameron is far closer to the British public than his critics are', *The Daily Telegraph*, 20 May 2013.

45 Normal Tebbit, 'If the Tories want to win back UKIP voters, they should stop insulting them', *Daily Telegraph Blog*. Available online: http://blogs.telegraph.co.uk/news/normantebbit/ (accessed 29 July 2013).

46 Attitude differences cannot explain the gender gap in UKIP support, however. Older, working-class women with little schooling have very similar views to men from the same background on Europe, the political class, immigration and so on, yet are much less willing to switch to the UKIP revolt. It is not clear at present why this is – it may relate to lower political interest or efficacy among female voters, or to their greater reluctance to consider untested or possibly extreme parties.

6
OVERCOMING THE BARRIERS TO ENTRY

In September 2013, José Manuel Barroso, President of the European Commission, and so a bête noire for Eurosceptics, provided UKIP with an unexpected publicity boost when he predicted the party would win the 2014 European Parliament elections, and despite David Cameron's promise of a referendum on Britain's EU membership. 'When it comes to being against Europe', Mr Barroso argued, 'people prefer the original to the copy.'[1] Nigel Farage was delighted with the compliment paid by his old rival, but he and his party were already looking beyond the 2014 European elections, where they knew they could perform well, towards the greater challenge of the 2015 general election. UKIP's goal was now to become a credible force in domestic politics by winning seats in Westminster, and towards the end of 2013 they laid out how they planned to achieve it: by fighting every constituency at the general election in 2015. Elaborating on the strategy, Farage had a clear message for voters: 'If you really want a referendum you make sure that UKIP win the Euro elections next year to keep the pressure on and then you make sure that UKIP has decent representation in the House of Commons.'[2]

But as senior Ukippers were also painfully aware, the quest to win seats in Westminster would once again bring them face-to-face with a formidable barrier that had broken many political revolts in British history: the first-past-the-post electoral system. This is not like systems used in many European countries, or in British elections to the European Parliament, because it takes no account of parties' overall popularity. Voters choose one candidate in their local constituency, and the candidate who wins the most votes gets the seat. Parties who fail to win local contests receive no representation at all, regardless of their overall haul of votes. This presents a profound challenge for insurgents like UKIP, who have to build, or discover, concentrated pools of support that are sufficient to win locally. If, for example, UKIP won 20 per cent of the national vote but this was spread evenly across the country with no constituency victories, they would still finish with no seats and no voice in Westminster, despite having won support from one voter in five. On the other hand, a small party like Plaid Cymru in Wales, whose vote *is* concentrated in a small number of local strongholds, can achieve a presence in Westminster despite winning only a tiny share of the overall national vote.

The problem posed by this system is also one of psychology, as well as geography. Decisions about who to vote for are not made in isolation: voters have a basic understanding of how the system works, and this knowledge influences the choices they make. They are reluctant to back parties they think have no chance of winning locally, even if the party is their first choice in national politics. Voters are also less likely to vote for their national favourite if this boosts the local chances of another party they dislike. This is why many Britons vote 'tactically' at a general election, backing their second choice party, who have a chance of winning locally, rather than their first choice party who have no hope at all. Small and untested parties like UKIP are especially vulnerable to being seen as a wasted vote. This was reflected in one survey in 2012, which found that 42 per cent of all voters saw UKIP as a wasted vote, including 33 per cent of their own supporters![3] There are also other psychological effects. Donors will be more reluctant to invest in parties that have little chance of victory, while the experience of being defeated locally time and again, and shut out of Westminster, is demoralising for party foot soldiers, making it harder to keep them motivated and loyal.

For these reasons, Britain's disproportionate system really does present a major barrier to new insurgents. Even if they have wide support for their ideas, passionate leaders and committed activists, most wither and die in the face of this obstacle. In this penultimate chapter, therefore, we explore what this barrier means for UKIP, how their responses to it have evolved, and what challenges the party will need to overcome if they are to take their revolt to Westminster. Before this, we begin with the story of an earlier failed revolt, which illustrates the scale of the challenge facing UKIP.

A lesson from history: the failed revolt of the SDP

Three decades before UKIP's revolt had gathered pace, the Social Democratic Party launched the strongest insurgency in postwar British politics. The SDP were established in early 1981 by four Labour moderates who were unhappy with their party's shift towards the radical left. They had an immediate impact on public opinion. Helped by the high profile of their founders, who brought the new party attention and credibility, the SDP were polling over 30 per cent within months of their foundation, far higher than UKIP's peak in the polls so far. By the end of 1981, the SDP, now allied with the much older Liberal party, had moved into first place in most polls, an unprecedented surge of support for a new party.[4] It was this remarkable level of support that prompted David Steel, leader of the Liberals, to tell his activists to 'go back to your constituencies and prepare for government'.[5]

Although their lead in the polls was fleeting, evaporating when Britain's victory in the Falklands fuelled a Conservative resurgence, the SDP–Liberal Alliance remained a serious force, running neck and neck with Labour on between 20 and 30 per cent right through to polling day, in 1983. For a brief moment, it looked as though the rebels would achieve their aim to 'break the mould' of British politics. Activists held their breath. At the 1983 general election the Alliance finished in a virtual tie with Labour on votes. Their revolt attracted one out of every four voters, the strongest performance by any party other than Labour or the Conservatives since 1923. But now the electoral system kicked in: the similar shares of the vote for the SDP–Alliance and Labour on polling day did not translate into similar political influence the day after.

As Table 6.1 illustrates, despite slumping to their lowest share of the vote since 1918, Labour returned more than 200 MPs to the House of Commons. The SDP, however, who won almost as many

TABLE 6.1 Impact of the electoral system on SDP–Liberal Alliance and Liberal Democrat representation, 1983–1992

	Votes (million)	Seats	Votes per seat (thousand)	Share of vote	Share of seats
1983					
Conservatives	13.0	397	33	42.4	61.1
Labour	8.5	209	41	27.6	32.2
SDP/Liberal Alliance	7.8	23	339	25.4	3.5
1987					
Conservatives	13.8	376	37	42.2	57.9
Labour	10.0	229	44	30.8	35.2
SDP/Liberal Alliance	7.3	22	332	22.6	3.4
1992					
Conservatives	14.1	336	42	41.9	51.7
Labour	11.6	271	43	34.4	41.6
Liberal Democrats	6.0	20	300	17.8	3.1

votes, won only 23 seats, barely one-tenth of Labour's total. These strikingly different outcomes reflected the critical role of geography in the British electoral system. Labour's support was concentrated heavily in longstanding strongholds, like industrial cities in northern England, inner London and urban Scotland, where the party was assured of local victory despite their national weakness. The Alliance's support, however, was spread far more evenly across the country.[6] While they racked up a record number of second places, their votes were not sufficiently concentrated to take seats. As they soon discovered, second place is nothing in British politics.

This failure to convert popularity into power doomed the SDP, who found themselves afflicted by the dreaded 'wasted vote syndrome'. Even though a lot of voters agreed with their ideas, many now concluded that the party simply could not win, as the academics Ivor Crewe and Anthony King observed: 'Thousands of Liberal sympathizers – knowing their Liberal candidate was unlikely to win and knowing, too, that the Liberals nationally were unlikely to be in a position to form a government – were unwilling to

"waste" their vote. The two-party system was thus self-sustaining.'[7]
A further problem was that the SDP's appeal was not rooted in
clear social or ideological divisions. Whereas Labour had a tribal
link to the blue-collar workers who filled Britain's factories and
workshops, and clustered together in local communities, the SDP's
vote was soft, featureless and distributed more evenly across the
landscape. 'People thought it a wasted vote to back the Liberals',
continued Crewe and King, 'not only because the Liberals had no
chance of winning but also because the party was not sufficiently
different from the major parties to be worth wasting a vote on'.[8]
The SDP–Liberal Alliance was unable to muster locally dominant coalitions of voters, and so the 'cost' of each seat they won in
the House of Commons, the number of votes won for each seat
gained, was dramatically higher than that of the established parties.
In 1983, each seat won by the SDP had cost more than a third of
a million votes, compared to 41,000 for Labour and 33,000 for the
Conservatives.[9]

The SDP's failure to overcome the electoral barrier destroyed
any hope for a political realignment. Almost eight million voters in
1983 had voiced their desire for change, in vain. The other parties
and the media lost interest, and voters drifted back to the established parties that were seen as having a credible chance. Ironically,
the system that had blocked the Alliance's rise now eased their fall.
Although the party lost almost a quarter of their vote between
1983 and 1992, they held on to almost all of the seats they had won
in 1983. As Crewe and King concluded, while the SDP had set
out with plans to transform Britain, in the end their brief history
resembled that of an experimental plane: they began by soaring into
the sky, glided for a while but then crashed into a muddy field.[10]
The party had barely dented let alone broken the mould of British
party politics. With only a handful of seats in Parliament, they had
next to no influence, despite the support of millions. They had not
displaced Labour, forced electoral reform or ushered in a new era
of multiparty politics. Their rise and fall had scarcely altered the
established system, which still revolved around a competition for

power between Labour and the Conservatives, as it had for decades before.

The same electoral system has also continued to handicap the Alliance's successors, the Liberal Democrats, in their efforts to challenge the 'big two'. The Liberal Democrats have steadily increased their presence in Westminster, but the system continues to place them at a massive disadvantage. The 2010 general election may have seen the party enter government for the first time in over seventy years, but their 23 per cent share of the vote translated into only 9 per cent of Commons seats. Had seats been awarded in proportion to their national share of the vote, as is common elsewhere in Europe, then the 2010 Coalition of 306 Conservative MPs and 57 Liberal Democrats would be made up of 228 Conservatives and 145 Liberal Democrats.

UKIP represent the most popular political insurgency since the SDP but face the same daunting challenge that defeated their illustrious predecessor. In fact, in several key respects the challenge that faces UKIP is even more formidable. The SDP had political credibility from the outset: their leaders were veteran Labour politicians who forged an alliance with another long established party, the Liberals. They had a Westminster presence from the start, as two of their founders were already sitting in the House of Commons when the party launched, and were soon joined by defectors. This credibility helped the party build an activist base at lightning speed, recruiting over 50,000 members in their first two months. Armed with resources and activists the SDP were able to fight every parliamentary seat at their first general election and racked up a number of wins. UKIP face the same barrier but have none of these advantages. They emerged from a Eurosceptic movement with little experience of fighting domestic elections. They are often shunned or ridiculed by the major parties, and lack the talent and experience that were available to the SDP. But do these disadvantages mean that UKIP are doomed to fail in domestic politics? What would it take for an outsider to win in Britain? And in what types of areas might UKIP be able to break through?

No alternative: why UKIP needs domestic success

For most of their history, UKIP's response to this electoral barrier was to avoid a serious commitment to general elections, as we saw in Chapter 1. They stood hundreds of candidates but their campaigns were driven more by hope and improvisation than coordinated strategy or serious, grassroots effort. This decision reflected the party's underlying obsession with Europe, and a recognition of the difficulties in overcoming the system, as Jeffrey Titford, who led UKIP between 2000 and 2002, explained: 'Everybody [in UKIP] saw Europe as the big issue. Europe was the big issue and therefore go for the European elections. One or two people felt that on the strength of that we could go and win seats in Westminster, but of course it isn't proportional representation but first-past-the-post. It's a bloody hard climb to try and get through that system.' Aside from the mechanics of the system, Titford, like other activists, was also acutely aware of its effects on voters: 'People didn't quite believe we had other policies. "What are you doing in a general election? You're a one issue party." It was very hard. This was against us all the time.' These reflections highlight how UKIP's exclusive focus on Europe had generated a vicious circle: domestically, the party were not treated as credible due to their single-issue outlook, but domestic failure only encouraged a focus on Europe. Ironically, the party whose main goal has been to withdraw Britain from the EU was dependent on the EU's main democratic institution to provide it with a political outlet.

In a further irony, the European Parliament that gave UKIP a platform to mobilise opposition to the undemocratic and unaccountable EU, had itself been created to make the EU more democratic and accountable. An elected European Parliament was designed to remedy the EU's 'democratic deficit', by providing voters with a stronger role in the EU political system. But European voters did not warm to pan-European politics and treated the European Parliament as a 'second-order' national election, an opportunity to voice discontent with their national politicians or with the EU itself in what they saw as a low stakes competition.[11] Survey evidence confirms that British voters similarly do not take European elections as seriously as other elections: one study found that less than half of voters cared who won, and not many more thought the outcome made any difference, much lower figures than for general or even local elections.[12] Voters have also been more willing at European elections to experiment with new parties as an outlet for their discontent or Euroscepticism, making European elections a powerful opportunity for rebel parties across the continent. This was evident in focus groups with UKIP voters held by Lord Ashcroft, who observed: 'Voters readily distinguish between elections that matter and those that matter less. In our research people compared European elections to the Eurovision Song Contest; some cheerfully said that voting UKIP in these elections was just a way to "give Europe a slap".'[13]

In 1999, a decision by New Labour also unintentionally further increased the appeal of smaller parties. In Britain, European elections had always been fought under the first-past-the-post-system used for Westminster elections. Concerned about the possibility of heavy defeat in the 1999 poll, the Labour government switched to a regional list proportional representation system.[14] MEPs would now be elected as part of a 'closed list' from each region of Britain, with seats awarded in proportion to the total regional vote each party received. The new system, commonly used in Europe, makes it much easier for smaller parties, and those with evenly distributed support, to win representation. If each region elects six MEPs then a party winning 18 per cent of the vote in any region will elect an MEP, whereas under first-past-the-post they would win nothing.

The British electorate recognised and responded to the changed incentives offered by the new system, backing smaller parties in far larger numbers now they were freed from the 'wasted vote syndrome'. In 1994, the last election fought under the old system, the 'big three' parties won 89 per cent of the votes cast. This fell to 76 per cent in 1999, and kept falling in each subsequent election, reaching 57 per cent in 2009. The major party stranglehold on seats was also broken as the share of the seats won by the 'big three' fell from 98 per cent in 1994 to 71 per cent in 2009.[15] UKIP were the biggest beneficiaries of the change and, by 2009, had become the second largest party on votes and seats. But, while these elections provided a valuable platform, European representation cannot help UKIP achieve their ambitions in domestic British politics.

UKIP's main policy goals – withdrawal from the EU, sharp cuts to immigration and radical changes to education, taxation and regulation – can only be achieved through legislation in the Westminster Parliament. Their political ambitions also require a domestic focus. To win new recruits, motivate their activists and sustain the interest of politicians and the media, UKIP need to overcome the wasted vote syndrome and appear as a credible choice at general elections. Victories or near-victories are essential as they can trigger a virtuous cycle: boosting credibility; which attracts more media interest; which further raises the party's profile; which brings in new activists and politicians; who in turn deliver further victories. Success in domestic politics is thus essential if UKIP want serious political influence.

While UKIP know that domestic success is important, in the past they struggled to translate European victories into domestic support, as we saw in Chapters 1 and 2. The voters they attract at European polls often drift away as Westminster elections approach. This cycle is illustrated in Figure 6.1, which tracks the month-by-month levels of support for UKIP before and after of the 2004 and 2009 European elections. During both of these campaigns the party's support surges, and elevated support persists for several months after the election, reflecting the wave of media attention that followed their success. In 2004, support for UKIP quadrupled from under 2 per cent in the pre-campaign period to over 8 per cent around the election. In 2009, it jumped from 2 to 6 per cent.

But in both cases, support then faded away fast: in 2004 UKIP were back to their pre-European Parliament election support levels by the end of the year, while in 2009 they lost half of their new support in four months, though they managed to retain some new backers all the way through to the 2010 general election. By including the BNP in our chart, which campaigned on similar issues and attracted a similar base of support, we also see how this 'European Parliament effect' is peculiar to UKIP. The BNP saw no similar increase in support during the 2009 European elections, or from a

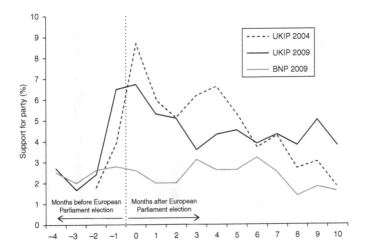

FIGURE 6.1 Monthly support for UKIP and the BNP around European Parliament elections

Source: Continuous Monitoring Survey.

surge of media interest that followed their historic capture of two seats at that election. This effect, then, is unique to UKIP and suggests that at the last two European elections they were effective at attracting a large Eurosceptic coalition, but were then unable to retain these new recruits at general elections.

The party not only struggled to retain the interest of voters. Figure 6.2 charts how many times the party were mentioned in UK-based newspapers in the three months before and after European elections in 1999, 2004 and 2009. In all three elections, media interest in UKIP surged as the European polls approached, and interest rose in each cycle, reflecting the party's earlier successes. At the height of the European election campaign in 1999 the party were only mentioned in 57 articles. By 2004, however, this peak increased to over 1,200 articles and, in 2009, over 1,800. But UKIP could not sustain this interest once the European elections passed, and press mentions soon slumped after polling day had come and gone. In the shadow of these elections, attention switched back to domestic politics where UKIP had no voice, and the voters who

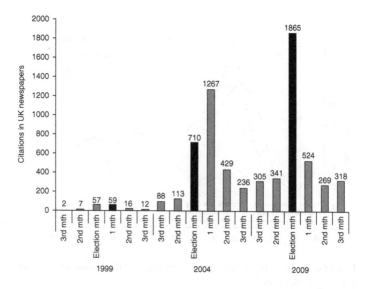

FIGURE 6.2 Media attention to UKIP, 1999–2009

Source: Nexis UK newspaper archive.

were attracted by a new party at an unconventional election lost interest.

Why UKIP struggle at Westminster: four problems

Why have UKIP been unable to hold on to the extra supporters they win in European Parliament campaigns? Decling media attention certainly contributes, but some more fundamental factors have also held UKIP back: the different social background and motives of their European election voters; their poor domestic campaigning and organisation; their message, which often focused too heavily on only one issue; and the even, geographical distribution of their support, which means UKIP lack the local 'stronghold' areas where they could appear as a credible choice.

A first problem for the party is that their European recruits often look quite different to their domestic voters. This can be seen by comparing 'strategic' UKIP voters, who only back the party once every five years at European elections, with their 'core' voters, who remain loyal at different sets of elections. The key differences between these two groups of voters, and also between them and Conservative voters, are highlighted in Table 6.2, which makes use of a large survey by YouGov after the 2009 European elections.[16] Those who only support UKIP in a strategic fashion, once every five years, differ in several key respects from core UKIP loyalists.

Consistent with our findings in Chapter 5, both groups are intensely Eurosceptic, far more so than those who vote for the Conservatives (or any of the other mainstream parties' voters). But strategic are less concerned about other issues that also motivate core UKIP backers: their opposition to immigration is less intense, and they do not share the feelings of political alienation that are held by UKIP's most loyal voters. The social backgrounds of strategic UKIP voters are also different: they are more likely to be middle class, financially secure and to have grown up in Conservative-voting households, and they are less hostile to the Conservatives. In other words, strategic UKIP voters look like strongly Eurosceptic, but otherwise typical, Conservative voters. They turn fleetingly to UKIP at European elections, voice their hostility to the EU in an election they regard as otherwise unimportant, and then return to the mainstream fold at general elections, when other issues dominate. UKIP has been unable to sustain their loyalty as these voters do not share the populist and anti-immigration motives that the party mobilise domestically, and so do not have strong reasons to risk a 'wasted' vote on UKIP.

What are the implications of this division? As we showed in Chapter 5, UKIP have grown domestically by 'deepening' their support among groups who are already sympathetic towards their agenda. But their European growth is quite different: the party instead 'broadens' their support, winning over new voters who share their intense Euroscepticism but who do not have much interest in their other ideas. We find a similar, broadening pattern in our monthly survey data – if we look at the profiles

TABLE 6.2 Social background and attitudes of 'core' and 'strategic' UKIP voters in the 2009 European Parliament elections

	Core UKIP	Strategic UKIP	Con*	Full sample
Social class				
Middle class	28	39	42	37
Working class	**34**	25	19	23
Political background				
Parents voted Conservative	28	**34**	**47**	27
Parents voted Labour	**48**	38	**25**	41
Economic expectations				
Not enough money to live comfortably	**65**	54	50	52
Euroscepticism				
EU promotes prosperity throughout Europe (disagree)	**71**	**74**	**45**	35
UK should withdraw completely from EU	**84**	**79**	**45**	39
Opposition to immigration				
All further immigration to UK should be halted	**91**	**84**	**68**	61
Britain benefited from recent arrivals from different countries and cultures (disagree)	**65**	**58**	**44**	39
Immigration has helped economy (disagree)	**74**	**69**	**56**	48
Local councils allow immigrants to jump the queue for council housing	**77**	**77**	**64**	56
Government should encourage immigrants to leave Britain	**49**	**39**	31	27
Populism				
Most politicians are personally corrupt	**75**	61	50	54
Don't trust local MP to tell the truth	**77**	**70**	60	62
Disaffection about main parties				
Conservatives never cared about people like me	**39**	22	2	36
Labour never cared about people like me	28	**38**	**42**	23
No difference between the main parties	**76**	**48**	**25**	46
N (weighted)	2,117	2,484	6,355	32,268

Note: All figures are weighted percentages. Bold figures are significantly different from the overall sample mean ($p < 0.05$). *Conservative

Source: YouGov 'Euro Mega Poll', June 2009.

and attitudes of UKIP voters who were interviewed around the time of the European elections we find they are more middle class, economically secure, less populist and anti-immigration than Ukippers interviewed at other times. The European elections in 2004 and 2009, therefore, gave UKIP a tantalising vision of a broad-based Eurosceptic coalition capable of shaking the established political order. Yet the problem for the party is that this coalition only comes together at European elections, when otherwise indifferent voters back UKIP as a way of 'throwing an egg' in the face of the EU and the established political class, in an election which does not matter to them. In this respect, UKIP's popular anti-EU coalition behaves like the mythical town of Brigadoon: it emerges from the mist for one day every five years, generates great excitement, but then fades from view again as soon as polling day passes.

UKIP's transition from European to domestic campaigning has also been hampered by their weak and conflict-prone internal organisation. The party squandered the surge of media and public interest after their advances at the 1999 and 2004 European elections by indulging in high-profile bouts of internal warfare, as we saw in Chapter 1. New voters attracted to the party were soon given reasons to reconsider. In 2000, they lost their early leader, Michael Holmes, and nearly collapsed. Four years later, their celebrity recruit, Robert Kilroy-Silk, attempted a coup before departing to form his own party. The pattern continued after the 2009 European elections. UKIP again changed leaders, installing the controversial and gaffe-prone Lord Pearson whose strategy of allying Conservative Eurosceptics alienated many of his activists, leading to further damaging infighting.

Linked closely to this internal weakness is a third factor: a narrow and unbalanced political message. At least until 2010, UKIP lacked a broader policy offer for voters. The party had a lot to say about Europe, but little to say on core domestic issues such as public services, the economy and immigration, which have dominated recent general elections. It was not until Nigel Farage's second term as leader that his party began to seriously invest in other issues like immigration. Prior to this, activists had pounded the streets at general elections armed with literature that focused heavily on the EU, but in battles where most voters had put this issue behind a list of other concerns.

A final problem for UKIP is the geography of their support. New parties can overcome first-past-the-post if their support is locally concentrated. Examples include the Scottish and Welsh nationalists, and the Liberal Democrats who, learning from the SDP's failure, increased their presence in Parliament by putting this principle into action. Modern Liberal Democrat campaigns revolve around geography: they carefully identify target seats and build strength through sustained and intensive activism in local politics, demonstrating their credibility to local voters. Consistent application of this strategy helped the Liberals triple their number of seats between 1992 and 2005, despite no increase in their overall vote share. The 'cost' of each seat they won fell from 300,000 votes to 97,000 votes, as they focused on concentrating their support in areas where they could win.[17] The impact of this strategy is evident in Figure 6.3, which plots the distribution of constituency vote shares for the Liberal Democrats in 2010. While in most seats the party attracted between 10 and 20 per cent of the vote, not enough to be a serious contender, there is also a long 'tail' of seats where the party scored 30 per cent or more, enough for a first or second place finish. To win seats at general elections, third party insurgents need a 'tail' like this: seats where their local share runs far ahead of their national average, giving them a credible chance of victory.

How does UKIP's support fare on this measure? In Figure 6.4, we similarly plot the distribution of UKIP's constituency shares in 2010. This shows how UKIP received between 0 and 5 per cent of the vote almost everywhere they stood, with no similar evidence of a 'tail' of local strongholds. Despite a decade of rising support and repeated breakthroughs at European elections, in 2010 UKIP were not credible local competitors anywhere in the country. Their best performances in 2010 were barely an improvement on those in 2001. While UKIP were certainly much more popular in the polls

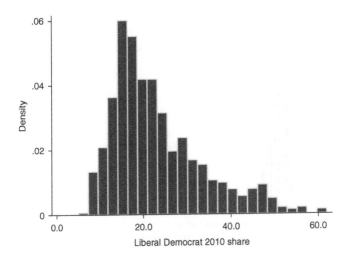

FIGURE 6.3 Distribution of Liberal Democrat vote shares in 2010

Source: 2010 constituency election results, Great Britain.

in 2010, and added half a million votes to their tally in 2001, they moved no closer at all to a seat in Westminster.

This problem is thrown into sharp relief when we take a closer look at UKIP's performance at the three general elections in 2001, 2005 and 2010. No UKIP candidate managed a second place finish, while only five candidates managed to finish third, one of whom was Farage who fought the Speaker's seat of Buckingham, which due to historic convention is not contested by the main parties.[18] In fact, across each of these three general elections UKIP's best showing in a seat that *was* fully contested by the main parties was 10.4 per cent in Staffordshire South, which only secured a distant fourth place finish. Their next best result was 9.6 per cent and third place in Boston and Skegness in 2005, 22 percentage points behind the second place challenger. After ten years of steady advances in national polling, UKIP still lacked a single seat where they could be taken seriously as Westminster challengers. Their weakness is also reflected in the party's 2010 performance in the ten seats where they had scored highest

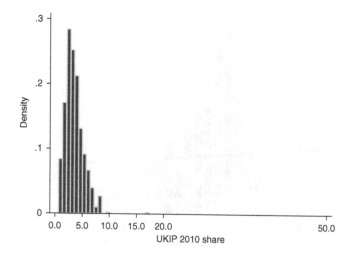

FIGURE 6.4 Distribution of UKIP vote shares at the 2010 general election

Source: 2010 constituency election results, Great Britain.

in 2005. As can be seen in Table 6.3, rather than build on their 2005 results through sustained local activism, the party fell back in eight of these ten seats, while they did not bother to stand again in the ninth and added just 0.3 per cent to their share in the tenth.

Last among minnows: UKIP's performance compared to other minor parties

The problems outlined above have consistently undermined UKIP's attempts to make an impact in the domestic arena. Yet several other minor challengers have been more successful, despite facing similar obstacles, and lower levels of national support. The Greens and Respect have achieved the Westminster success that has eluded the Eurosceptics, while the extreme right BNP, though never winning a seat, managed a string of strong local performances despite a poisonous public image. The key to stronger domestic showings for all three of these insurgents lay in their better awareness of the constraints of first-past-the-post, and the strategies that can overcome them. Each of these parties pursued a three-pronged strategy: early identification of promising target seats; sustained and intensive campaigns, including a heavy investment in local elections; and the strategic use of leaders and effective campaigners to further boost their local chances.

At the 2010 general election, the Greens' success in Brighton Pavilion came through intelligent use of all three factors. The Greens do best among young, university educated, secular, public sector workers who share their agenda on issues such as environmentalism and civil liberties.[19] Brighton, with its large population of students and young, socially liberal university graduates, was naturally favourable territory. The Greens recognised this early on, making the area a main focal point of their new, locally focused 'Target to Win' strategy, developed after they had failed to make an impact at the 1992 general election.[20] It soon produced results in Brighton, with the Greens winning their first council seat in 1996. The party then built on their local presence by standing the leader of their council group, Keith Taylor, at the 2001 general election. Taylor's strong profile in Brighton helped boost the Greens' share of the vote by seven points to 9.3 per cent, well ahead of their average constituency share of 2.7 per cent. A Green local stronghold was born.

The Greens cemented their local presence by standing the same candidate again in 2005, by which time Taylor's local profile had grown further. In 2003, Taylor had doubled the Greens' council group from three to six councillors, and was elected as one of the party's two national 'principal speakers' in 2004.[21] Taylor made effective use of his profile and his party's growing local resources, more than doubling the Green share of the vote to 22 per cent at the 2005 general election, leaving the party in third place, just 2 per cent behind the second placed Conservatives. This exceptional result provided the Greens with new strategic options for uniting a local, left-of-centre coalition behind their candidate. They could appeal for tactical votes from the fourth placed Liberal Democrats;

TABLE 6.3 UKIP's 2010 performance in top ten 2005 seats

Constituency	Region	2005	2010	Change
Staffordshire South	West Midlands	10.4	5.5	−4.9
Boston and Skegness	East Midlands	9.6	9.5	−0.1
Bognor Regis and Little Hampton	South East	8	6.5	−1.5
Plymouth Devonport	South West	7.9	6.5	−1.4
Staffordshire Moorlands	West Midlands	7.9	8.2	+0.3
Torbay	South West	7.9	5.3	−2.6
Louth and Horncastle	East Midlands	7.7	4.3	−3.4
Totnes	South West	7.7	6	−1.7
Castle Point	Eastern	7.5	N/C	n/a
Devon South West	South West	7.5	6.2	−1.3

Source: 2010 constituency election results, Great Britain.

pitch for disaffected votes from the incumbent Labour party, who were struggling nationally; or appeal to voters' local pride and sense of history by encouraging them to help elect the first ever Green MP. To maximise the opportunity, the Greens switched candidates for the 2010 general election, standing their leader and strongest media performer, Caroline Lucas, who went on to win the seat with 31.3 per cent of the vote.[22] The result reflected well over a decade of local, intensive campaigns and party building in Brighton, which the party had identified early as one of their best targets.[23]

The Respect Party's successes came more quickly but with a similar mix of ingredients. Though founded as a broad coalition of left-wing interests opposed to the New Labour government and the 2003 war in Iraq, Respect soon found that British Muslims opposed to the war were their primary source of support.[24] This provided an early advantage, as the British Muslim population is heavily concentrated in a small number of areas, providing Respect with natural electoral targets such as Bethnal Green and Bow, Bradford West and Birmingham Sparkbrook, seats where Muslims made up more than a third of the local electorate.[25] At the 2005 general election,

Respect made the most of the opportunity, standing their most charismatic and politically experienced candidate, the firebrand former Labour MP George Galloway, in Bethnal Green and Bow, an East London seat with one of the largest concentrations of Muslim voters in Britain. The seat had other advantages. It was in one of the few areas where Respect already had electoral credibility, having won 20 per cent of the vote in the borough of Tower Hamlets in the 2004 Greater London Assembly elections. Galloway campaigned intensively and focused on appealing to alienated younger Muslim voters and emphasising that he was a better representative of Muslim interests than the non-Muslim Labour incumbent, Oona King. Respect, which had never stood before, delivered a political earthquake, taking the seat from Labour with 35.9 per cent of the vote. Meanwhile, another Respect candidate, Salma Yaqoob, pursued a similar strategy in Birmingham Sparkbrook, campaigning as a progressive, left-wing Muslim candidate who opposed the murky, clannish politics of the local, Muslim-dominated Labour branches.[26] Yaqoob finished second with 27.5 per cent of the vote, nearly matching Galloway's success despite a much lower profile. She then built a powerful presence for Respect on Birmingham council after the 2006 local elections, winning a string of victories in heavily Muslim wards. Running with a much higher local profile and as Respect's deputy leader, she came very close to victory in the 2010 general election, most likely falling short due to extensive boundary changes which forced her to run in unfamiliar territory, against an established Labour MP and in a seat with a reduced share of Muslim voters.[27]

Respect suffered a serious internal split in 2007, and fielded only eleven candidates at the 2010 general election, where they lost their only seat in Bethnal Green and Bow after Labour fielded a charismatic young Muslim with strong local roots. Galloway had also decided to campaign elsewhere. Yet while they looked a spent force, at a parliamentary by-election in Bradford West in March 2012 Galloway was swept back to Westminster, seemingly coming from nowhere to win 56 per cent of the vote in a seat with the second largest Muslim electorate in Britain. The victory was less shocking than it looked: Respect had been quietly cultivating support from young British Muslims who were unhappy with the 'biraderi' clan networks that dominated Bradfordian politics, as well as from women's groups that met in local mosques, white pensioner groups unhappy with Labour's shift away from traditional working-class values, and local tenants' and residents' associations.[28] Like the Greens, Respect achieved Westminster success by identifying pockets of geographically concentrated support, in this case high-density Muslim populations, deploying their most talented candidates in these areas, and campaigning intensively over multiple elections.[29]

Although they are both regarded as radical parties, from the beginning the Greens and Respect have been accepted as a legitimate part of British politics. In sharp contrast, the British National Party's attempts to break through were hampered by their status as political pariah: an extremist party with a violent and fascist past, who were rejected by the other parties and the entire media. Yet despite this huge handicap, the BNP still managed stronger showings at Westminster elections than the much larger, and more legitimate UKIP, as we saw in Chapter 2. The BNP relied on a similar strategy to the other two successful minor parties: sustained intensive campaigning in promising target seats. Their first targets were made clear in 2001, when riots broke out in two economically declining, ethnically diverse northern towns. At the general election shortly afterwards, the BNP stood their leader, Nick Griffin, in Oldham, where some of the worst rioting had occurred, and focused on mobilising white working-class voters threatened by the riots, and by changes associated with immigration and the growth of the local Muslim population. Griffin secured 16.4 per cent of the vote, a record for a British extreme right candidate, and a wave of media attention followed.

The Oldham campaign set the template for BNP challenges: intensive local campaigns, often over several local election cycles, that targeted poor, white working-class areas in close proximity to ethnically diverse towns and cities, where white residents felt under threat from Muslims and immigrants.[30] The formula never delivered a Westminster seat, in part because the BNP's extreme reputation led to counter-mobilisation by other parties and civil society groups wherever it became successful, but it was nonetheless effective: the BNP won swathes of council seats in these areas, and managed to top 10 per cent of the constituency vote nine times between 2001 and 2010, easily out-performing UKIP. The BNP's strategy of 'community activism' was integral to this support, with the party attracting more votes in areas where they had more members, a history of local election success and where voters said they had been contacted by the party.[31]

Despite a larger, more legitimate organisation, far more candidacies and greater national support, for much of their history UKIP never managed to match the performances of the Greens in Brighton, Respect in Bethnal Green and Bradford, or the BNP in Oldham and Barking. Obsessed with Europe, and overly focused on European elections, the party never developed a strategy to build up local concentrations of support, and did not focus resources, activists or prominent candidates on target areas. UKIP could not fight locally, and seldom tried. But from 2010 onwards this began to change.

A new dawn? UKIP's domestic strategy since 2010

After failing, once again, at the 2010 general election to translate European success into Westminster power, UKIP overhauled their approach to domestic elections. The goal was to win parliamentary seats, and the new strategy was based on two key pillars, as Farage explained in a 2013 interview: '[F]irst-past-the-post is devilishly hard, and for us to win two things have to happen. First we have to do what the Reform Party of Canada did and that is to win a by-election. Second we have to win clusters of district and county council seats. The Lib Dems built up from about a dozen seats in Parliament to about 60 by building up local centres of excellence.'[32] UKIP had belatedly discovered the strategy that had been employed for years by their fellow insurgents.

Farage had initially experimented with this new approach in 2009, at a by-election in Norwich North where activists were encouraged to focus on highlighting the candidate rather than the party, and stressing immigration rather than Europe. 'But when we face the impact of 1,000 new arrivals every single day', read one leaflet, 'it's time someone asked the question: How can Britain cope?'[33] The party took 11.8 per cent of the vote, at that time their best ever result at a by-election. With Farage now back as party leader, the first opportunity to sharpen the strategy came two years later and two hundred miles north, in a parliamentary by-election in Oldham East and Saddleworth in January 2011, where an election court had annulled the general election result after finding the Labour MP, Phil Woolas, guilty of knowingly making false statements about his Liberal Democrat rival. Having been active in UKIP since the beginning, Farage was aware of the need to radically overhaul the approach to by-elections. 'It was just abysmal', he recalled, 'a completely amateur approach to it all.' Yet Oldham presented a triple challenge for UKIP, which had no local branch and little electoral experience in the town. First, it was an ethnically diverse, northern, urban and working-class seat, which was unfamiliar territory for a party that had grown used to competing in sleepy, white and middle-class southern suburbs. Oldham East and Saddleworth was also a hard fought Labour–Liberal Democrat marginal, meaning that both mainstream centre-left parties had strong local infrastructure and were investing significant national resources in the by-election. Finally, since the riots of 2001 Oldham had been a relative stronghold for the BNP: the extreme right party had won over 10 per cent in both Oldham seats in 2001, and polled well ahead of UKIP in the town at all three general elections since 2000, though they were now struggling.[34] 'The BNP were in a bit of trouble, and we knew that', recalled Paul Nuttall, 'but they were still a power. To finish them off, and stick the knife in we had to go onto their patch and beat them.'

The by-election also presented another, more practical challenge. Polling day would be held in the first two weeks of January, meaning UKIP's activists had to work the streets in snow and freezing cold. But they battled on, putting to use for the first time many of the familiar elements deployed by more successful challengers in British politics, as Farage recalled: 'I said, "We are going to do this properly. We are going to take an office in the high street. We are going to pick a candidate that actually wants to try. We are going to spend some money. We are going to do some public research. We are going to have a serious crack at this."' They stood a high profile, experienced and resourceful candidate, their deputy leader Paul Nuttall, a native son of the North-West, and arrived early in the town, opening an office, and spending heavily to establish a local presence. Nuttall and Farage also sought to turn the BNP's previous strength in the area to their advantage, by winning over the extreme right's intensely dissatisfied electorate, who had already demonstrated a willingness to back political insurgents (see Chapter 2). They campaigned intensively with large-scale billboards, leaflets and door-knocking, focusing not on the EU but on the domestic issues of crime and immigration. UKIP's advance was relatively modest, increasing their vote share by 1.9 per cent and retaining their deposit, but it was enough to overtake the BNP and convince Farage that a by-election strategy could be made to work.

More emphatic proof came less than two months later, when UKIP applied the same methods in Barnsley Central, where the incumbent MP was removed following conviction for parliamentary expenses fraud. Barnsley offered several advantages for UKIP: a large concentration of older, white working-class voters, the core UKIP demographic; limited activity from the other parties in a very safe Labour seat; and a weaker and less successful local BNP branch. UKIP once again fielded an experienced, local candidate, Jane Collins, a Yorkshire native who contested Scunthorpe in the 2010 general election, and backed her up with an intensive pavement politics campaign. The result was a new record vote share of 12.2 per cent, twice the level of support for UKIP in national polls at the time, and a first ever second place finish for the party. The Oldham and Barnsley campaigns demonstrated that the same methods that had worked for other minor insurgents could work for UKIP, too. Hard working local candidates who were backed by more intensive, street-by-street campaigning had delivered record results in parts of the country that UKIP had historically avoided, and barely bothered to fight for at the 2010 general election.[35] Nuttall now had evidence to back his argument that UKIP's future lay in these more northern and deprived constituencies.

After this initial progress, however, the next wave of by-elections showed UKIP how hard campaigning and good candidates can only take an insurgent so far in territory with a more challenging mix of voters (Table 6.4). Between June 2011 and March 2012, UKIP fought three by-elections in seats with large ethnic minority populations – Feltham and Heston, Bradford West and Leicester South – and made little impact in any of them. In Bradford, George Galloway's earthquake showed them what a charismatic campaigner with a geographically concentrated and well-mobilised electorate could achieve, winning the seat for Respect with a 36.6 point swing from Labour – the third largest by-election swing in British history.[36] UKIP's result in the June 2011 Inverclyde by-election was even worse: they finished fifth, with barely 1 per cent, underscoring UKIP's persistent weakness in Scotland.

Despite these setbacks, UKIP persevered with the new strategy and in November 2012 two new golden opportunities appeared. High-profile Conservative backbencher Louise Mensch vacated her seat of Corby, an East Midlands ultra-marginal where she had won a majority of just 1,351 over Labour. Corby presented UKIP with two firsts: a first opportunity to deploy their new by-election strategy in a Conservative seat; and a first chance to fight a seat in the East Midlands, which had been a strong region for the party since Kilroy-Silk's European candidacy in 2004 (see Chapter 2). UKIP again stood a politically experienced candidate, local businesswoman and long-term resident Margot Parker, and ran an intensive, locally focused campaign that saw Farage putting his celebrity to work by campaigning in the seat. Now that UKIP were back on favourable territory their new strategy delivered: a new record share of 14.6 per cent and a third place finish, trouncing the Liberal Democrats and bolstering UKIP's claim to be the new third force in British politics.

TABLE 6.4 UKIP by-election results since 2010

Seat	Incumbent	Result	Vote share	Position
Oldham East and Saddleworth 13/01/11	Labour	Labour hold (+10.2%)	5.8% (+1.9%)	4th
Barnsley Central 03/03/11	**Labour**	**Labour hold (+13.5%)**	**12.2% (+7.5%)**	**2nd**
Leicester South 05/05/11	Labour	Labour hold (+16.6%)	2.9% (+1.4%)	4th
Inverclyde 30/06/11	Labour	Labour hold (−2.2%)	1.0% (−0.2%)	5th
Feltham and Heston 15/12/11	Labour	Labour hold (+10.8%)	5.5% (+3.5%)	4th
Bradford West 29/03/12	Labour	Respect gain (+52.8%)	3.3% (+1.3%)	5th
Manchester Central 15/11/12	Labour	Labour hold (+16.4%)	4.5% (+3.0%)	4th
Corby 15/11/12	**Conservative**	**Labour gain (+9.8%)**	**14.3% (+14.3%)**	**3rd**
Cardiff South and Penarth 15/11/12	Labour	Labour hold (+8.4%)	6.1% (+3.5%)	5th
Rotherham 29/11/12	**Labour**	**Labour hold (+1.8%)**	**21.7% (+15.8%)**	**2nd**
Middlesbrough 29/11/12	Labour	Labour hold (+14.6%)	11.8% (+8.1%)	2nd
Croydon North 29/11/12	Labour	Labour hold (+8.7%)	5.7% (+4.0%)	3rd
Eastleigh 28/02/13	**Liberal Democrat**	**Lib Dem hold (−14.4%)**	**27.8% (+24.2%)**	**2nd**
South Shields 02/05/13	Labour	Labour hold (−1.6%)	24.2% (+24.2%)	2nd

Note: Results in bold show new party vote share records.

Toward the end of the same month, a by-election in the West Yorkshire town of Rotherham provided an even better opportunity. Just days before voters went to the polls, in a by-election that had once again been triggered by the resignation of a scandal-tainted Labour MP, the national media reported that two children from Eastern Europe had been removed from their foster parents due to the parents' support for UKIP.[37] The decision by the Labour-run local council caused a national storm and attracted sharp criticism from across the political spectrum, including Labour leader Ed Miliband. UKIP were well placed to take full advantage of the windfall. They had an experienced local candidate, Jane Collins, who was previously UKIP's record-breaking candidate in nearby Barnsley, and a strong local organisation that was supported by Farage's growing national media presence. UKIP broke the record they had set just two weeks earlier, finishing in a strong second place on 21.7 per cent of the vote, and winning three times as many votes as the two coalition parties combined.

Three other by-elections on the same day as Rotherham underscored both the strengths and limits of UKIP support. The party posted another second place in Middlesbrough, once again showing how they could provide a serious challenge to Labour in economically struggling and mainly white, working-class seats. But they put in much weaker performances in Croydon and Cardiff, underscoring the party's continued struggles in more ethnically diverse seats and outside of England.

By 2013, UKIP had demonstrated that they were serious by-election contenders, having come second on three occasions and won double-digit vote shares in Labour and Conservative held seats. But they had yet to really convince voters and pundits they had what it took to win a Westminster seat. Even in their strongest showing at Rotherham, they fell over 25 percentage points behind the victorious Labour candidate. A chance to change this came in early 2013, when the criminal conviction of former Cabinet member and Liberal Democrat leadership contender Chris Huhne triggered a by-election in Eastleigh. The seat was a tantalising prospect with a colourful history. The Liberal Democrats had first won the seat in a sensational 1994 by-election victory, triggered after the incumbent Conservative MP Stephen Milligan was found dead in his flat. The victorious Liberal Democrats achieved a 17-point swing, and the Conservatives slumped to third place.

The Liberal Democrats built a powerful local machine on the back of their by-election upset, taking over the local council and winning over former Labour voters by presenting themselves as the only viable local opposition to the Conservatives. By 2013, the Liberals had held the Westminster seat for nearly twenty years and controlled all but four seats on the council. Despite this formidable local machine, there were many reasons for UKIP to be optimistic about their prospects in Eastleigh. For the first time since beginning their intensive locally focused strategy, they would be contesting a seat near the south coast, where UKIP members and activists were plentiful, and they were fighting an incumbent party who were languishing behind them in the national polls, and tainted locally by scandal. There was much speculation that Farage himself would stand, but in the end UKIP continued with their focus on local candidates, standing experienced local campaigner Diane James. James delivered yet another record result, winning 27.8 per cent, enough to push the Conservatives into third place in a seat they had hoped to win. It was not, however, quite enough to beat the masters of local electoral campaigns. Though damaged by local scandal and national unpopularity, the well-oiled Liberal Democrat machine saw them through. UKIP's search for a first by-election victory went on, but at Eastleigh the party did enough to convince a lot of sceptics that such a victory was possible. This potential was further underlined a few months later when Richard Elvin, another battle-hardened repeat candidate, managed 24 per cent, and another second place, in David Miliband's old seat of South Shields, in the Labour heartlands of the industrial North East.[38]

The by-elections that UKIP contested between 2011 and 2013 were the first ever organised, resourced and sustained effort by the party to compete at parliamentary by-elections. The results demonstrate that, like the other minor insurgents before them, UKIP could be potent local competitors when properly organised. A party who had never managed third place in a fully contested seat before 2010 had finished at least third in half of the fourteen by-elections fought since the coalition government took office, with five second places and two third places. During this period UKIP also broke their record constituency vote share four times, raising it from 11 per cent to nearly 28 per cent. The mainstream parties, and the national media, who previously regarded UKIP by-election candidates as an amusing sideshow, now began to see the party as a genuine threat. On top of this, UKIP now had half a dozen seats where, at the 2015 general election, they can use by-election results to convince sceptical voters that they were a genuine local contender. Rotherham, Eastleigh and South Shields may not have fallen to UKIP candidates, but they convinced many that someone, somewhere, could soon win the first UKIP seat.

Alongside by-elections, the second prong of UKIP's Westminster strategy was a determined effort to compete and win in local elections, enabling them to establish the kind of local government strongholds used by the Liberal Democrats as a springboard to Westminster success. Prior to 2010, UKIP's record in local elections was dismal: in eleven sets of council elections between 2000 and 2010, they managed just eleven wins, and less than 200 second places. The party devoted few resources to local elections and made little effort to develop a coordinated local campaign strategy, so candidates, resources and votes were scattered randomly across the map, as one of their former leaders, Jeffrey Titford, admitted: 'We were too widely spread [in previous domestic elections]. This is something that we've learned now, and which we are trying to change. The reason that we are running with the councils now is to form little pockets. It's following the Liberal line. We hadn't got that strength together. We hadn't got local councillors.' This general lack of interest in local politics owed much to the party's general outlook, which saw local elections as parochial distractions from the bigger issue of Europe. But UKIP had also faced another problem in local elections, which was strong competition from another right-wing party with a much more effective local campaigns operation.

Between 2001 and 2010, UKIP and the BNP attracted similar voters with similar concerns, particularly in domestic elections where Euroscepticism was less relevant (see Chapters 4 and 5). But the BNP had also developed a local strategy much earlier, since 2001, seeing local legitimacy as an essential step to winning Westminster seats and bypassing their ostracism from national politics. The BNP had effectively shut UKIP out of much of the most promising territory: economically struggling areas in Northern England, where there were large populations of ageing, white, and less educated working-class voters, and significant local tensions over immigration, crime and ethnic change. As we saw in Chapter 2, UKIP's leadership were well aware of this challenge, which had led some to even voice the idea of an electoral pact between the two parties. While these voices were quickly silenced, at least until 2010 UKIP knew they could not compete with the BNP in areas where the extreme right were locally entrenched, as one senior Ukipper recalled: 'The BNP have always been far better at working the ground in certain very limited locations, because they come out of a street movement. They come out of the council estates. "Why is it that somebody from Somalia gets a house but my daughter doesn't? I'm going to fucking do something about it. I'm going to shove poo through their door." When we were founded we were a bunch of academics. That's where UKIP came from.'

During their peak years from 2003 to 2010, the BNP stood hundreds of candidates in each round of local elections, taking an average of 15 per cent or more of the vote in the seats they fought, and winning dozens of seats. In their best ever election cycle in 2006 their 364 candidates won nearly 230,000 votes, an average of 19.4 per cent each, and 33 seats, including 12 on Barking and Dagenham council, enough to make them the official opposition. This proved to be the BNP's peak, and they have declined continuously since, a slump that accelerated as they disintegrated and flirted with bankruptcy after failure in the 2010 general election. By 2013, the BNP were only able to field 100 candidates, winning only 13,000 votes, while the next year their leader Nick Griffin was actually declared bankrupt. They were a pale shadow of their former selves.[39] The muscular and tightly organised campaigns that had intimidated UKIP in the 2000s were no more, and the disaffected voters that the BNP brought into local polling booths were up for grabs, as Nuttall and Farage were keenly aware (see Chapter 2).

UKIP did not only focus on BNP heartlands, however. After 2010, their ambitious local strategy aimed to field as many candidates as possible, which partly reflected the goal of replacing the Liberal Democrats as the third force in British politics, but was also an experiment to find potential local breakthrough areas. While Ukippers talked a great deal about strategy, outside of by-elections few had a clearly defined picture of the kinds of local areas they should be targeting. As we saw in Chapter 2, the party's new plan was inspired by Farage's close study of the growth of the Liberal Democrats under the leadership of Paddy Ashdown. Elaborating on this influence, Farage explained: '[O]nce you hold a number of council seats that you've won under first-past-the-post at local level, the perception that you are a wasted vote and you can't win at Westminster level disappears.'[40]

Some activists in UKIP had long been applying this method. Between 2004 and 2007 Paul Nuttall had quickly built up a UKIP branch in Bootle, one of the safest Labour seats in the country. 'We really began to take local elections quite seriously. I was always of the belief that if you *are* going to make a success in domestic politics in this country then it's got to be done in the Liberal Democrat model and it's got to come via local elections.' In 2008, this heavy focus on local elections was reflected in a 38 per cent share of the vote for Nuttall, who only narrowly missed out on winning a local seat. 'It was unheard of really in UKIP, I mean someone taking it seriously in the inner cities and in the North of England. Back then UKIP was primarily a Southern party, which relied on disgruntled Tory votes. There was just a gap in the market.'

These early local exceptions aside, the debut of UKIP's new local election strategy did not arrive until 2011, and the impact was immediately clear. Table 6.5 compares the party's performance in local elections since 2010 with their results in the same sets of seats four years earlier. This shows how, in 2011, UKIP stood over 1,100 candidates, well over double the number they stood when the same seats were up for election in 2007. They won nearly 300,000 votes, almost tripling their total in 2007. Although in 2011 UKIP managed only seven local victories, they chalked up over a hundred second place showings and established themselves as the main opposition in clusters of wards on councils up and down the country, from the gritty North-East port of Hartlepool (where UKIP won six second places) to the leafy shire suburbs of Aylesbury Vale (where they scored one victory and five second places). The message from these local elections in 2011 was clear: UKIP could compete in local politics, had learned how to campaign, and where to find their strongest support.

UKIP refined their approach in 2012, standing fewer candidates in an effort to target their resources more effectively and achieve a larger set of breakthrough results. Victories once again proved elusive as UKIP added only five new councillors, but the party did manage some impressive local vote shares. Twelve UKIP candidates won an average of 25 per cent in Rotherham – ten finished in second place – while in Great Yarmouth thirteen candidates managed an average of 22 per cent each and four finished in second place. In authorities as diverse as Thurrock, Tunbridge and Sunderland, UKIP stood large slates of candidates who won an average of 15 per cent or more each. The party won more than twice as many votes as in the equivalent elections in 2008, and secured a large swathe of second place finishes, further expanding the territory where UKIP were the de facto local opposition. These local campaigns in 2011 and 2012 laid the groundwork, but it was the 2013 campaign that delivered the first major local breakthrough.

According to one of the activists who oversaw the 2013 campaign, Rob Burberry, this was driven by a broad four-point plan: defend existing seats; gain new councillors; impact on the balance of power in county councils; and increase the total UKIP vote. UKIP dramatically increased their number of candidates, standing in 75 per cent of the available contests, more than the struggling Liberal Democrats. For the first time, the party also subsidised leaflets for candidates that led with the issue of immigration, while before the

TABLE 6.5 UKIP's local election progress since 2010

	Candidates		Total votes		Mean % vote		Seats won		Second places	
	This	Previous	This	Previous	This	Previous	This	Previous	This	Previous
2010	620	323	226,569	72,167	7.9	9.1	1	1	13	18
2011	1112	442	297,662	102,119	11.6	11.0	7	1	122	24
2012	694	454	218,671	96,933	13.6	9.3	5	4	139	32
2013	1,742	550	1,141,487	314,148	24.3	16.0	147	7	827	119

Source: Plymouth University Elections Centre.

contest Farage also made full use of his high profile by visiting at least thirty towns as part of a 'common sense tour'.[41] UKIP's election broadcast barely mentioned Europe, instead presenting people from different walks of life explaining what their ideal Britain was like: 'My Britain', explained one, 'would understand why ordinary hard-working people are really finding it a struggle to make ends meet'.

A local campaign effort making full use of old and new techniques, and the experience built up over the previous two campaigns, culminated in an extraordinary wave of success for the party. UKIP won over 1.1 million votes, triple their total in the equivalent 2009 elections, and the most the party had ever won in a set of first-past-the-post elections. UKIP's average share of the vote surged to over 24 per cent, an increase of 8 percentage points on 2009, when a far smaller slate of candidates stood on the same day as European elections were held. The surge to nearly a quarter of the total vote took UKIP past the 'tipping point' where their vote became sufficient to deliver local victories in serious numbers. The party won a total of 147 council seats, and became the largest opposition party on six county councils: Cambridgeshire, Essex, Kent, Lincolnshire, Norfolk and West Sussex. On top of this, UKIP notched up an extraordinary 827 second places, meaning that UKIP placed in the top two in nearly half of the May 2013 races they contested.

UKIP's overall progress in local elections mirrors that seen in the by-elections – the new strategy yielded uncertain gains at first but after a few years of consistent application began to produce dramatic improvements in results. Indeed, UKIP has advanced even further in local contests than it has in by-elections – while a break-through to Westminster still eludes the party, they now have a large cohort of local councillors returned in the elections of 2013. The 2014 local elections will provide the party with a good chance to add a second wave of victories, as they are held on the same day as European elections, and UKIP will make a much stronger effort to coordinate support across both contests, as Nigel Farage is more than aware: 'Bring it on', he stated. 'As UKIP strengthens and our ability to put up candidates in all elections increases, having both these polls in the same day will lead to the prospect of a major breakthrough both in Europe, where we have the chance of topping the poll, and more importantly in the District, Borough and Metropolitan elections across the country.'[42] If Farage's predictions are correct, and the party manage a second wave of local election successes, then UKIP will go into the 2015 general election with the resource they sought: a set of local stronghold areas where they have a track record of electoral success, and the credibility and experienced local campaigners which come with such success. All the pieces will be in place for a UKIP Westminster breakthrough in 2015 – but is this possible?

The challenge ahead: what would it take?

As we have seen, the electoral barrier to entry in domestic British politics is formidable. It has thwarted UKIP repeatedly in the past, as it did with the larger and more popular SDP. With first-past-the-post, where you get your votes is as important as how many votes you get. UKIP's past failure reflected a reluctance to recognise and respond to this challenge, a product both of the party's ideological bias towards the issue of Europe and their organisational weakness, which made UKIP reluctant to compete in elections they felt were unwinnable. Since 2010, however, this picture has changed dramatically. A committed and intensive domestic focus, combined with a more coherent and credible message, has been rewarded with achievements in local elections and parliamentary by-elections beyond what the party believed possible even a few years earlier. But despite these impressive gains, UKIP still face a daunting challenge. The social and geographical distribution of their support, and its relation to the other parties' support, continue to throw large hurdles on the path to Westminster.

UKIP have made impressive progress in local elections but their support remains very evenly spread. Even in the 2013 local elections, UKIP support varied much less than support for any of the mainstream parties, suggesting the rebels had still not managed to sufficiently concentrate their support in strongholds.[43] This poses the party two problems – the even spread in votes makes it difficult to convert votes efficiently into seats but also makes it harder for the party to identify target areas, as they lack clear electoral signals of local strength. The parliamentary by-elections have provided some useful hints – UKIP have done much better in older, poorer, whiter seats in England than in other kinds of seats – but they still seem to perform similarly in very different contexts. UKIP managed 22 per cent in Rotherham, 25 per cent in South Shields and 28 per cent in Eastleigh – three very different seats. Which of these seats should UKIP prioritise in the 2015 general election, and on what basis? UKIP still have little to go on in judging which seats offer the best prospects.

Credibility also remains a problem. Although they now have a large cohort of local councillors, many of these won their seats in areas where UKIP may have little chance of winning in a general election. As we saw in Chapter 4, UKIP's strength is with older, less educated, white working-class men, yet many in UKIP's 'class of 2013' won their seats in prosperous Southern shires, without many such voters. It will be much harder for UKIP to build a winning general election coalition in such seats than in seats where demographics give them a good starting position. Yet this leads us to another problem for UKIP: many of the seats where their demographic starting position *is* strongest are poor prospects for a breakthrough due to the local dominance of a single mainstream party.

Table 6.6 outlines the 'Top 10' seats in terms of proportions of pensioners, working-class and low education voters, three of UKIP's strongest demographics. This highlights two problems for UKIP. First, UKIP's core demographic groups cluster in very different seats. Low education and blue-collar voters concentrate in urban seats in the North and Midlands, while pensioners are more strongly concentrated in southern coastal towns. Second, most of the seats where UKIP's core groups concentrate are very safe seats with huge majorities for one of the established parties, typically Labour in seats that have large proportions of working-class and poorly educated voters, and the Conservatives in seats that are dominated by pensioners. There are only four seats in the list that UKIP could win with a swing of less than 20 points: Wolverhampton North East; Scunthorpe; Walsall North; and Great Grimsby.

Table 6.7, which shows the results from the Eastleigh and South Shields by-elections, illustrates why this is a problem. In South Shields, despite UKIP's surge, the local Labour candidate still won half of the vote. As a result, UKIP's 24 per cent still leaves them with a mountain to climb in 2015 – the party would need a 13.1 point swing away from Labour to take the seat. In Eastleigh, however, UKIP are in a far better strategic position despite winning only a slightly higher vote share, because the rest of the vote is more fragmented. A swing of just over two points from the Liberal Democrats to UKIP would hand them the seat. Local fragmentation thus lowers the bar for victory. The problem for UKIP is that their core voting groups, when they cluster at all, tend to do so in seats where one party is dominant.

The last, and perhaps biggest, problem for UKIP in their quest for seats in Westminster is this: gathering enough voters to win will usually require the party to recruit significant support from groups who do not traditionally back them and, in this book, we have found very little evidence that Ukippers are capable of this. In Chapters 4 and 5 we saw how UKIP's rise in national polls has come by 'deepening' their support, not 'broadening' their reach to new groups. The party have become very competitive among their core groups, but they have made little headway elsewhere. UKIP barely registers with younger voters, graduates, ethnic minorities or voters who do not share their opposition to the EU. UKIP also struggles with women, even those who share the social background and political concerns of male UKIP supporters. Yet there are few seats where a coalition of older, white, working-class Eurosceptic men can get UKIP anywhere near winning the local vote. UKIP's by-election and local election performances may be misleading on this front, as such elections have much lower turnout than general elections, and the groups UKIP already prosper with – particularly the old, men, and white voters – tend to be over-represented among the voters who *do* show up at such elections. Finding a way to bring in the groups who, to date, have shunned UKIP is therefore

TABLE 6.6 Top ten seats in England and Wales on three key UKIP demographics

Seat	Incumbent	2010 share	UKIP 2010 share	Swing needed
Pensioners				
Christchurch (32.2%)	Conservative	56.4%	8.5%	24.0
Clacton (30.3%)	Conservative	53.0%	n/a	26.5
New Forest West (29.5%)	Conservative	58.8%	5.9%	26.5
North Norfolk (29.4%)	Lib Dem	55.5%	5.4%	25.1
Bexhill and Battle (26.9%)	Conservative	51.6%	n/a	25.8
East Devon (26.7%)	Conservative	48.3%	8.2%	20.1
West Dorset (26.6%)	Conservative	47.6%	3.8%	22.4
Worthing West (26.4%)	Conservative	51.7%	6.0%	22.9
Louth and Horncastle (26.4%)	Conservative	49.6%	4.3%	22.7
Totnes (26.3%)	Conservative	45.9%	6.0%	20.0
Working-class voters				
Wolverhampton South East (62.3%)	Labour	47.7%	7.7%	20.0
Blaenau Gwent (61.1%)	Labour	52.4%	1.5%	25.6
Nottingham North (60.8%)	Labour	48.6%	3.9%	22.4
Hull East (60.5%)	Labour	47.9%	8.0%	20.0
West Bromwich West (60.5%)	Labour	45.0%	4.3%	20.4
Walsall North (60.3%)	Labour	37.0%	4.8%	16.1
Great Grimsby (60.0%)	Labour	32.7%	6.2%	13.3
Wolverhampton North East (59.1%)	Labour	41.4%	3.3%	19.1
Scunthorpe (58.1%)	Labour	39.5%	4.6%	17.6

TABLE 6.6 (*cont.*)

Seat	Incumbent	2010 share	UKIP 2010 share	Swing needed
Birmingham Hodge Hill (58.0%)	Labour	52.0%	1.7	25.2
Low education voters				
Birmingham Hodge Hill	Labour	52.0%	1.7	25.2
Walsall North	Labour	37.0%	4.8%	16.1
Clacton	Conservative	53.0%	n/a	26.5
Rhondda	Labour	55.3%	1.2%	27.2
Wolverhampton South East	Labour	47.7%	7.7%	20.0
West Bromwich West	Labour	45.0%	4.3%	20.4
Liverpool Walton	Labour	72.0%	2.6%	34.7
Knowsley	Labour	70.9%	2.6%	34.2
Blaenau Gwent	Labour	52.4%	1.5%	25.6
Nottingham North	Labour	48.6%	3.9%	22.4

essential to securing Westminster representation. This explains why the party have repeatedly stood female candidates in high-profile by-elections, and why their leadership's reaction to veteran MEP Godfrey Bloom's outburst at their 2013 conference – when he appeared to call a room full of women 'sluts' – was so furious. Winning over a larger female vote has to be at the centre of UKIP's general election strategy, not only because there are so many women voters who share UKIP's political concerns but shy away from the party, but also because strong female support would greatly improve the credibility of UKIP's claims to be an inclusive and tolerant party, helping its prospects with other groups, too.

What would it take for UKIP to win a seat in the 2015 general election? A strong candidate and a well-resourced local organisation will be essential, while previous election success and a presence in local government would be highly desirable. The seat would ideally have a large concentration of voters from core UKIP groups, to give the party a good platform to build from, and relatively low numbers

TABLE 6.7 South Shields and Eastleigh by-election results

Seat	Vote share	Swing needed to win
South Shields by-election 2013		
Labour	50.4	n/a
UKIP	24.2	13.1
Conservatives	11.5	19.5
Liberal Democrats	1.4	24.5
Others (5 candidates)	12.5	n/a
Eastleigh by-election 2013		
Liberal Democrats	32.1	n/a
UKIP	27.8	2.2
Conservatives	25.4	3.4
Labour	9.8	11.2
Others (10 candidates)	4.9	n/a

of voters from groups who shun the rebels: young, university graduates, middle-class professionals and ethnic minorities. In addition, the best prospects for the party will be in politically fragmented seats, with significant support for as many other parties as possible. Given the number of local conditions that UKIP would need, identifying the best prospects is difficult, but in Table 6.8 we attempt to estimate where the strongest UKIP territory might be.

To do this, we rank all the English constituencies on a measure of 'UKIP attraction' using data on the relative size of different social groups from the 2011 census. In areas with a higher attraction score, the core UKIP groups such as pensioners and working-class voters are larger, and the UKIP avoiding groups such as graduates and ethnic minorities are smaller (full details of this measure's construction are provided in the appendix). We then filter out all of the seats where the incumbent party has more than 45 per cent of the vote, thereby removing constituencies where UKIP would need to achieve an extreme and unlikely swing in support to win. The seats that are left, and which emerge as the 'Top 10' would-be targets for UKIP, are then ranked in order of the two-party swing from 2010 vote levels that UKIP would need to win. Below these, and in italics,

TABLE 6.8 Strongest UKIP prospects based on census data and two-party swing

Seat	Incumbent	Majority	Incumbent share	UKIP 2010 share	UKIP attraction	UKIP local election results (year)	Two-party swing needed
Great Grimsby	Labour	2.2	32.7	6.2	36.5	10 stood, 21.4%, 1 win, 4 second (2012)	13.3
Plymouth, Moor View	Labour	3.9	37.2	7.7	33.9	19 stood, 20.6%, 7 second (2012)	14.8
Ashfield	Labour	0.4	33.7	1.9	36.4	4 stood, 22.3%, 2 second (2013)	15.9
Walsall North	Labour	2.7	37.0	4.8	35.1	8 stood, 13.2%, no wins or seconds (2012)	16.1
Waveney	Conservative	1.5	40.2	5.2	34.4	6 stood, 28.5%, 2 wins, 2 second (2013)	17.5
Hartlepool	Labour	14.4	42.5	7.0	34.5	8 stood, 14.0%, 5 second (2012)	17.8
Bishop Auckland	Labour	12.7	39.0	2.7	34.0	22 stood, 19.0%, 12 second (2013)	18.2

Blackpool South	Labour	5.2	41.1	3.8	34.3	5 stood, 10.3%, no wins or seconds (2011)	18.7
Stoke-on-Trent North	Labour	20.6	44.3	6.2	34.7	9 stood, 10.5%, no wins or seconds (2011)	19.1
Great Yarmouth	Conservative	9.8	43.1	4.8	35.6	9 stood, 36.4%, 5 wins, 4 seconds (2013)	19.2
Eastleigh	Liberal Democrat	4.3*	32.1*	27.8*	18.9	7 stood, 33.4%, 3 firsts, 3 seconds (2013)	2.2
Rotherham	Labour	24.5*	46.3*	21.8*	31.1	12 stood, 25.0%, 10 seconds (2012)	12.3
South Shields	Labour	25.8*	50.4*	24.2*	32.7	No candidates stood (2012)	13.1
Barnsley Central	Labour	48.0*	60.2*	12.2*	34.1	3 stood, 14.0%, 1 second (2012)	24.0
Middlesbrough	Labour	48.7*	60.5*	11.8*	28.2	1 stood, 12.2%, no firsts or seconds	24.4

* By-election share.

we show the five seats where UKIP have moved into second place in by-elections since 2010.

These are the seats where UKIP's path to power will be easiest: they have the largest concentrations of sympathetic groups, the lowest concentrations of opposed groups and a relatively low electoral bar to clear.

Only one seat in our top ten is in the South-West, traditionally UKIP's favoured area, but there are five in a large cluster along the east coast from Durham to Norfolk: Grimsby, Yarmouth, Waveney, Hartlepool and Bishop Auckland. Here, UKIP find their ideal combination of an ageing population, a large, low skilled and traditionally blue-collar workforce and a small population of graduates, ethnic minorities and middle-class professionals. This cluster of declining and blue-collar seats on the east coast may represent the best bet for a UKIP breakthrough – a local concentration of good prospects will make it easier for UKIP to apply their resources effectively, and the party also has a strong presence in local government, having won some of their biggest 2013 victories in this part of the country. Seats in this region have also experienced some of the largest inflows of Eastern European migrants, making local voters particularly receptive to UKIP's campaigns against EU migration. We have focused on seats where the local bar to a UKIP victory is currently lower based on 2010 results, but this picture may change if, as current polling suggests, the national swing is away from the coalition and towards Labour. More rural and heavily Conservative seats in the same region such as Boston and Skegness, Gainsborough, and North-East Cambridgeshire, all areas that now have a strong UKIP presence in local government, may become attractive prospects if the Conservative vote falls back sharply. For most of their first decade, UKIP were strongest, and campaigned hardest, in the prosperous South-West coastal towns and villages of the 'English Riviera'. It is therefore no small irony that the party's best chances of a Westminster breakthrough in fact lie at the opposite end of the country, both geographically and socially.

Notes

1 'Barroso says UKIP could win European elections in UK', *BBC News*, 11 September 2013.
2 'Nigel Farage: We will fight every seat in 2015', *The Daily Telegraph*, 19 September 2013.
3 Lord Ashcroft (2012) 'UKIP: They're thinking what we're thinking: Understanding the UKIP temptation'. Published by Lord Ashcroft. Available online: http://lordashcroftpolls.com (accessed 20 August 2013).
4 The SDP were in first place in eight of nine polls conducted between November 1981 and January 1982.
5 In the same year they achieved a stunning by-election result in the previously safe Conservative seat of Crosby. The SDP candidate, Shirley Williams, gained the seat after polling 49 per cent of the vote, ahead of the Conservative Party on 39.8 per cent.
6 Ron Johnston (1985) *The Geography of English Politics: The 1983 General Election*, London: Croom Helm; also David Butler and Dennis Kavanagh (1984) *The British General Election of 1983*, London: Macmillan.
7 Ivor Crewe and Anthony King (1995) *SDP: The Birth, Life and Death of the Social Democratic Party*, Oxford: Oxford University Press, p. 287.
8 Crewe and King, *SDP*, p. 288.
9 The other political insurgency of the period, by the Scottish and Welsh nationalists, was relatively more successful, because nationalist sentiment was geographically concentrated, making it easier to convert votes into constituency victories. The Celtic nationalists' four seats in 1983 cost an average of 113,000 votes each, one-third of the figure for the Alliance.
10 Crewe and King, *SDP*, p. 455.
11 Sara B. Hobolt, Jae-Jae Spoon and James Tilley (2009) 'A vote against Europe? Explaining defection at the 1999 and 2004 European Parliament elections', *British Journal of Political Science*, 39(1): 93–115; Karlheinz Reif and Hermann Schmitt (1980) 'Nine second-order national elections: A conceptual framework for the analysis of European election results', *European Journal for Political Research*, 8: 3–44; Cees van der Eijk and Mark Franklin (1996) *Choosing Europe? The European Electorate and National Politics in the Face of Union*, Ann Arbor: University of Michigan Press; Michael Marsh (1998) 'Testing the second order election model after four European elections', *British Journal of Political Science*, 28: 591–607.
12 Anthony Heath, Iain McLean, Bridget Taylor and John Curtice (1999) 'Between first and second order: A comparison of voting behaviour

in European and local elections in Britain', *European Journal of Political Research*, 35(3): 389–414.

13 Ascroft, 'UKIP: They're thinking what we're thinking'.

14 This was the European Parliamentary Elections Act 1999, which received royal assent in January 1999.

15 In 1999 the Conservatives, Labour and Liberal Democrats won 89 per cent of seats; in 2004 they won 66 per cent of seats and in 2009 they recovered only slightly to win 71 per cent of seats.

16 For a more detailed analysis of these data see Robert Ford, Matthew J. Goodwin and David Cutts (2012) 'Strategic Eurosceptics and polite xenophobes: Support for the United Kingdom Independence Party (UKIP) in the 2009 European Parliament elections', *European Journal of Political Research*, 51(2): 204–34.

17 Edward Fieldhouse and Andrew Russell (2006) *Neither Left Nor Right: The Liberal Democrats and the Electorate*, Manchester: Manchester University Press; David Cutts, Edward Fieldhouse and Andrew Russell (2010) 'The campaign that changed everything and still did not matter? The Liberal Democrat campaign and performance', *Parliamentary Affairs*, 63(4): 689–707; David Cutts (2013) 'Local elections as a "stepping stone": Does winning council seats boost the Liberal Democrats' performance in general elections?', *Political Studies*. Available online: http://onlinelibrary.wiley.com/doi/10.1111/1467-9248.12029/abstract?deniedAccessCustomisedMessage=&userIsAuthenticated=false

18 UKIP finished third place in Boston and Skegness in 2005, and then in Buckingham (the Speaker's seat), Devon North, Devon West and Torridge and Cornwall North in 2010.

19 Sarah Birch (2009) 'Real progress: Prospects for Green Party support in Britain', *Parliamentary Affairs*, 62(1): 53–71.

20 As Spoon notes: 'Recognizing that setting its sights on Westminster was unrealistic at first, the party decided to concentrate on building up its base of support and credibility as an electable party in local elections through the 1993 "Basis for Renewal" plan.' Jae-Jae Spoon (2009) 'Holding their own: Explaining the persistence of Green parties in France and the UK', *Party Politics*, 15(5): 615–34. For a detailed history of the Greens see also Jon Burchell (2000) 'Here come the Greens (again): The Green Party in Britain during the 1990s', *Environmental Politics*, 9: 145–50; and (2002) *The Evolution of Green Politics: Development and Change within European Green Parties*, London: Earthscan.

21 The Greens annually elected two 'principal speakers' – one man, one woman – to act as their national representatives from 1992 until 2008.

22 The Greens switched to having a single elected leader with a four-year term following a referendum in 2007. Lucas, who had served four one-year terms as the female principal speaker, won the first leadership election with 92% of the vote in 2008.

23 The Greens' other double-digit showings, in Lewisham and Norwich, also came from candidates with long-established local electoral presences and a high profile in the national party. Darren Johnson, who managed 11.4 per cent in Lewisham was an incumbent local councillor and London Assembly member, a former co-leader of the party and the Greens' candidate for London Mayor in 2000 and 2004. Adrian Ramsay, who managed 14.9 per cent in Norwich South in 2010, had been a local councillor for seven years (after first winning election at the age of 21) and was the party's deputy leader at the time of the election.

24 Tim Peace (2013) 'Muslims and electoral politics in Britain: The case of the Respect Party', in Jorgen S. Nielson (ed.) *Muslim Political Participation in Europe*, Edinburgh: Edinburgh University Press, pp. 299–321.

25 Over half of the British Muslim population live in just fifty constituencies, and in ten of these seats the local Muslim population is over 20 per cent. In Bradford West and Bethnal Green and Bow the population approaches 40 per cent. See Peace, 'Muslims and electoral politics in Britain'.

26 On Labour and Muslim communities see K. Purdham, 'Settler political participation: Muslim local councillors' in W. A. R. Shadid and P. S. van Koningsveld (eds.) *Political Participation and Identities of Muslims in Non-Muslim States*, Kampen: Kok Pharos, pp. 129–43.

27 In 2005, Salma Yaqoob contested the Birmingham, Sparkbrook and Small Heath seat, finishing second with 27.5 per cent. In 2010 she contested Birmingham Hall Green, and finished second with 25.1 per cent.

28 Peace, 'Muslims and electoral politics in Britain', p. 317 See also L. Baston (2012) *The Bradford Earthquake*, Liverpool: Democratic Audit.

29 For more on Respect's electoral record, see T. Peace (2013) '"All I'm asking for is a little respect": Assessing the performance of Britain's most successful radical left party', *Parliamentary Affairs* 66: 405–24.

30 On types of areas where the BNP polled strongest see Robert Ford and Matthew J. Goodwin (2010) 'Angry white men: Individual and contextual predictors of support for the British National Party', *Political Studies*, 58(1): 1–25. On the BNP's strategy of local activism see also Matthew J. Goodwin (2011) *New British Fascism: Rise of the*

British National Party, Abingdon: Routledge. On BNP local support see Benjamin Bowyer (2008) 'Local context and extreme right support in England: The British National Party in the 2002 and 2003 local elections', *Electoral Studies*, 27(4): 611–20.

31 David Cutts and Matthew J. Goodwin (2013) 'Getting out the right-wing extremist vote: Extreme right party support and campaign effects at a recent British general election', *European Political Science Review*, forthcoming; see also Matthew J. Goodwin and David Cutts (2012) 'Mobilizing the workers? Extreme right party support and campaign effects at the 2010 British general election', in Jens Rydgren (ed.) *Class Politics and the Radical Right*, Abingdon: Routledge, pp. 190–205.

32 Nigel Farage, interview with Andrew Gimson, ConservativeHome. com, 17 July 2013. Available online: http://conservativehome.blogs. com/interviews/2013/07/somewhat-to-my-surprise-i-found-nigel-farage-leader-of-ukip-sitting-in-the-same-small-cheerless-office-on-the-fifth-fl.html (accessed 22 August 2013).

33 Norwich North by-election leaflet. Available online: http://by-elections.co.uk/norwich09/nnukip06b.jpg (accessed 12 August 2013).

34 In Oldham East and Saddleworth, in 2001 the BNP polled 11.2 per cent compared to UKIP's 1.5 per cent, in 2005 the BNP polled 4.9 per cent compared to UKIP's 2 per cent, and in 2010 the BNP polled 5.7 per cent compared to UKIP's 3.9 per cent. In Oldham West and Royton, the BNP polled a then-record 16.4 per cent when Griffin stood in 2001 while UKIP did not stand. In 2005, the BNP polled 6.9 per cent and UKIP 2.6 per cent and in 2010 the BNP secured 7.2 per cent and UKIP won 3.2 per cent.

35 In Barnsley Central, as in Oldham East, UKIP had finished a weak fifth place in 2010, with 4.7 per cent behind all the main parties and the BNP (8.9 per cent).

36 The two larger by-election swings were also both famous minor party breakthroughs – Simon Hughes' victory for the Liberals in Bermondsey in 1983 (44.2 point swing from Labour) and Winifred Ewing's win for the Scottish National Party in Hamilton in 1967 (37.9 point swing from Labour).

37 Incumbent Labour MP Denis MacShane was forced to resign after the House of Commons Standards and Privileges Committee found that he had submitted nineteen false invoices to the expenses authorities in 2004–8.

38 Elvin also stood in Middlesbrough in November 2012, finishing second.

39 On the decline and internal problems of the BNP see Matthew J. Goodwin (2013) 'Forever a false dawn? Explaining the electoral collapse of the British National Party BNP', *Parliamentary Affairs* (in print). Available online: http://pa.oxfordjournals.org/content/early/2013/01/16/pa.gss062.abstract (accessed 21 September 2013).

40 Jonathan Walker, 'Nigel Farage plans to bring UKIP into the mainstream', *Birmingham Post*, 6 July 2013.

41 Nigel Farage visited a diverse range of areas during the tour: Callington; Taunton; Tiverton; Lydney; Worcester; Newcastle under Lyme; Stone; Marston; Oswaldtwistle; Carlisle; Gravesend; Durham; Prudhoe; Hexham; Morpeth; North Tyneside; Newport; Harrogate; Gainsborough; Lincoln; Peterborough; Corby; Kettering; Huntingdon; St Ives; Hertford; Aylesbury; Wendover; and Tunbridge Wells.

42 Christopher Hope, 'UKIP chances of 2014 Euro Election win "strengthened by polling date change"', *The Daily Telegraph*, 26 June 2013.

43 The standard deviation in UKIP support, a measure of how much it varied from seat to seat, was 7.8 per cent, about half the level seen for Labour (17.0), the Conservatives (15.4) and the Liberal Democrats (15.8). The distributions of all three mainstream parties' support show a long 'tail' of locally dominant performances – UKIP's does not.

7
THE PARADOXES AND POTENTIAL OF UKIP'S REVOLT

When UKIP's activists gathered to celebrate their twentieth birthday in September 2013, they had much to feel good about. As some of the founding members took to the stage, people who had first met in Alan Sked's LSE office twenty years earlier, they looked out at a party that must have seemed barely recognisable: a large audience of motivated activists; a growing membership that now stood at over 30,000; rows of interested journalists; and their leader, Nigel Farage, who had just been voted the second most influential right-winger in Britain, behind Prime Minister David Cameron.[1] The anti-EU pressure group had grown into a fully fledged political party, that now appeared at ease talking about a full range of issues on the British political agenda. As the celebrations got underway, a flurry of UKIP press releases attacked the main parties' policies on the environment, responded to terror attacks in Kenya, opposed the privatisation of Royal Mail and demanded migrants have evidence of health insurance. Somehow, UKIP's long-serving true believers had overcome the odds, surviving one crisis after another, to establish their party as a household name, with enough popular support to prompt talk of a realignment of British party politics.

Typically for UKIP, however, the conference did not go entirely to plan. Much of the media focused on one of their MEPs, Godfrey Bloom, who had hit a journalist with a magazine and described women in a fringe meeting as 'sluts'. The incident fuelled speculation of a popular backlash, but the opinion polls told a different story: four polls released after the conference put UKIP on an average of 11 per cent, the same as before Bloom's outbursts, and far above their level of support just a year or two earlier.[2]

As the conference got underway, the influential pollster and Conservative peer Lord Ashcroft published a new study of marginal constituencies, which highlighted the potential power of the party's growing revolt. Ashcroft's study suggested that public support for UKIP in the thirty most marginal Conservative seats had risen from 3 per cent in 2010 to 11 per cent. Farage's party, argued Ashcroft, was now squeezing support for the Conservatives and could split the right, helping the Labour Party return to power in 2015. Drawing on the study, one journalist looked ahead to the general election and claimed that 'a geographically concentrated UKIP effort and a push in the marginals will do major damage to the Tory campaign even if Farage does not win a single seat'.[3] UKIP's radical right revolt had truly arrived and looked set to dominate headlines throughout the European Parliament and local elections in 2014, the general election in 2015, and – with talk of a national referendum on Britain's EU membership – possibly beyond.

We wrote this book because we wanted to make sense of this revolt, the most significant change in Britain's party system for a generation. We have drawn on a wealth of survey data and interviews with key insiders to examine the party's evolution, from their beginnings as a single-issue pressure group into a serious contender for votes, influence and power. Along the way, we have looked at how wider social and political trends came together to create room for the radical right, identified which voters have switched to UKIP and why they have done so, and outlined how the party's future depends heavily on their ability to overcome the barrier of a formidable electoral system. In this final chapter, we bring all of these elements together to summarise our findings, discuss the paradoxes of UKIP's support and the challenges they now present to the established parties. We will also address one final question: how can can the revolt on the right go?

Explaining the radical right revolt

The conventional wisdom about UKIP is that they draw mainly on disgruntled, middle-class and southern Conservatives, who are hostile towards the EU but also to David Cameron's more socially liberal brand of Conservatism. UKIP's support is typically explained in terms of the day-to-day conflicts of British party politics, highlighting an entrenched resistance to the EU among the electorate and Cameron's current unpopularity among traditional social conservatives. Our study has shown this conventional wisdom to be mistaken. The true drivers of UKIP's support are more complex, and the roots of their revolt lie far deeper, in social divisions that have been growing for decades.

UKIP's revolt is a working-class phenomenon. Its support is heavily concentrated among older, blue-collar workers, with little education and few skills; groups who have been 'left behind' by the economic and social transformation of Britain in recent decades, and pushed to the margins as the main parties have converged in the centre ground. UKIP are not a second home for disgruntled Tories in the shires; they are a first home for angry and disaffected working-class Britons of all political backgrounds, who have lost faith in a political system that ceased to represent them long ago.

Support for UKIP does not line up in a straightforward way with traditional notions of 'left' and 'right', but reflects a divide between a political mainstream dominated by a more financially secure and highly educated middle class, and a more insecure and precarious working class, which feels its concerns have been written out of political debate. In a sense, UKIP's rise represents the re-emergence of class conflicts that Tony Blair's New Labour and David Cameron's compassionate Conservatism submerged but never resolved – conflicts that reflect basic differences in the position and prospects of citizens in different walks of life. Before the arrival of UKIP, the marginalisation of these conflicts had already produced historic changes in political behaviour. Blue-collar voters turned their backs on politics en masse, causing a collapse in electoral turn-out to record lows,[4] and fuelling a surge in support for the extreme right BNP, making it briefly the most successful extreme right party in the history of British elections.[5] Since 2004, Farage and his foot soldiers have channelled these same social divisions into a far more impressive electoral rebellion.

In some other European democracies, this revolt happened decades ago, and has since become an established part of the political landscape, a standing challenge to the political status quo. The fact that Britain did not see a similar radical right breakthrough led some to conclude that, perhaps, Britain might be different. In Chapter 3, however, we showed this is not true; the potential for a political insurgency of this kind has existed for a long time. Its seeds lay among groups of voters who struggled with the destabilising and threatening changes brought by de-industrialisation, globalisation and, later, European integration and mass immigration. These groups always occupied a precarious position on Britain's economic ladder, and now, as their incomes stagnated and their prospects for social mobility receded, they found themselves being left behind.

Many within this left behind army also grew up before Britain experienced the recent waves of immigration and before the country joined the EU, and their political and social values reflect this. This is a group of voters who are more inclined to believe in an ethnic conception of British national identity, defined by birth and ancestry, and who have vivid memories of a country that once stood independent and proudly apart from Europe. They also came of age in an era where political parties offered competing and sharply contrasting visions of British society, and had strong incentives to listen to, and respect, their traditional supporters. Shaped by these experiences, today these voters look out at a fundamentally different Britain: ethnically and culturally diverse; cosmopolitan; integrated into a transnational, European political network; and dominated by a university-educated and more prosperous middle class that holds a radically different set of values, all of which is embraced and celebrated by those who rule over them. This is not a country that the rebels recognise, nor one they like.

Those who have flocked to the revolt are not driven only by specific grievances about David Cameron's leadership, reform of the EU or the balance of immigration policy, and they are not likely to be satisfied with piecemeal changes on these, and other, concerns. Their motivations are far broader and intense: they see a world and a way of life slipping away, feel powerless to stop it happening, and are angry at the established political class for not seeming to understand their concern, or care about what is being lost. These feelings are not likely to be resolved by a new party leader, a referendum promise or a net migration target. UKIP's revolt was a long time coming, and it may have a long way to run.

Victor Hugo once remarked how an invasion of armies can be resisted but not an idea whose time has come. For the left behind in modern Britain, UKIP has come to represent and articulate their deeply held concerns about the direction of Britain. The most prominent of these is strong hostility towards the EU, which is a necessary condition for backing UKIP, though seldom a sufficient one (see Chapter 4). Those who support UKIP are deeply Eurosceptic, but they are not single-issue, anti-EU voters. Their motives are 'Brussels plus': voters who combine hostility to Europe with opposition to immigration, anger with established politicians, or deep feelings of dissatisfaction with how the main parties and their leaders have performed on key issues. We used the analogy of a salesman; Farage and his party have got their foot in the door with the large chunk of the British electorate who oppose their country's EU membership, but to close the sale they need to also tap into other concerns. UKIP's ability to mobilise these broad concerns is testament to their successful change of strategy, as they now merge their traditional hard Euroscepticism with opposition to immigration and to the political establishment. Farage's party now encourages voters to say 'no' three times: no to the Eurocrats in Brussels and Strasbourg; no to the politicians in Westminster; and no to immigration. This is not a grand ideological vision – there is no 'Farage-ism' – but it is a coherent and highly effective message. In an era in which parties rarely offer 'the big idea', and weary voters have little appetite for ideological battles, UKIP do not need a clear ideological basis. Their narrative is simple but effective: enough is enough. No more immigration. No more EU. No more cosmopolitan condescension from liberal and London-focused elites.

Ukippers were not responsible for this anti-politics outlook, but since 2010 they have learned how to express and exploit it. Some saw the potential for a cross-party coalition of disaffected working-class voters from early on; looking to the right, they saw socially conservative voters who were mocked by the Conservative elite as 'swivel eyed loons'; looking to the left, they saw a disadvantaged Old Labour base who were similarly being written off by their representatives as 'bigots', a view reiterated in 2013 when a senior Labour strategist described his party's traditional base as a 'lumpen mass with … half formed thoughts and fully formed prejudices'.[6] UKIP saw these social divisions and found a way to articulate them, giving voters an outlet for concerns that had been festering for years, and one that did not force them to compromise on their democratic principles. For activists such as Paul Nuttall, these are the groups who they expect to fuel the revolt over the longer-term: 'If we're going to win those European elections next year [2014], that Conservative vote is going to come back to us like night follows day. The key is to hold on to the Old Labour vote. If you get those two together, we're walking.'

The profile of UKIP's support has strong parallels with support for the radical right in Europe and, in earlier years, the BNP. As we have stressed throughout this book, UKIP and the BNP are different types of parties, with different histories, ideas and goals, but the overlaps in their support are clear. Some analysts, like Catherine Fieschi, dismiss the idea that the two movements draw on the same well of support as 'mainly nonsense'.[7] Our evidence is conclusive: the two parties have mobilised the same social and political divisions. Nor are UKIP unaware of this. As we saw in Chapter 2, their senior activists now openly concede that after the fall of Nick Griffin's BNP, and internal support for a pact with the extreme right had been squashed, they actively targeted voters who had previously 'held their nose' while supporting extremists. That they were able to forge ties with these voters owed much to their origins in the British Eurosceptic tradition, which contrasts sharply with the BNP's discredited neo-Nazi past. This provided UKIP with a 'reputational shield', which they have used to rebut charges that they are agents of intolerance and ensured they are accepted as legitimate by other mainstream actors in a way that other parties that mobilise anti-immigration sentiment are not. This reputational shield has been carefully cultivated by the party in other ways, as in the summer of 2013 when Farage criticised a government pilot scheme designed to encourage illegal migrants to leave Britain as 'nasty' and 'not the British way'.[8] Politicians might laugh at UKIP, but few see them as lying beyond the pale of normal, democratic politics, as they see the BNP.[9] Indeed, we have seen how the collapse of the BNP has been an important part of the UKIP story, as it cleared the way for the party to unite the radical right electorate in economically and socially deprived communities where these voters congregate, but where for many years UKIP could not compete with the intensive street campaigning of BNP activists.

The paradoxes of UKIP support

Our analysis of UKIP's support has thrown a great deal of light on the nature of their appeal, which we can use to resolve three paradoxes about the party. The first is this: why did a Eurosceptic party broken into politics at a time when, for most voters, Europe was not a pressing concern? Euroscepticism is a core part of UKIP's message, and a critical precondition for supporting the party. Yet UKIP's breakthrough has occurred during a period when Europe is well down the list of voters' political priorities. The share of voters naming Europe as one of the top issues facing the country peaked in 2003, and in the period since 2010 when UKIP support has surged it has remained firmly in single digits. Europe is seldom the main priority even for UKIP voters – they are much more likely to name immigration or the economy as their most pressing concerns.

The resolution to this paradox comes from the way in which Europe has become associated in voters' minds with other, more powerful concerns. UKIP's voters are motivated by concerns about immigration, the protection of traditional British identity and values, and a remote and unresponsive political elite. For these voters, the European Union has become a symbol of all of these concerns: EU institutions undermine British sovereignty and independence; EU legislation has enabled unlimited migration into Britain, threatening British identity and undercutting British workers; the British political elite favours the EU over their own voters; and the EU itself is an elitist, out of touch institution with no interest in the values and everyday concerns of ordinary Britons. The EU, in short, has come to represent all of the ills in modern society that radical right voters resent.

The second paradox is that opposition to immigration and Euroscepticism are core pillars of UKIP's support, yet their greatest breakthrough has come under the most Eurosceptic, immigration-focused government in living memory. Cameron's Conservatives pledged to reduce net immigration to the 'tens of thousands', introduced restrictive reforms to student migration, labour migration and family reunion migration and wasted no opportunity to make their opposition to immigration clear. They have resisted calls for a one-off amnesty for illegal immigrants, endorsed suggestions that immigrants are a burden on public services, pushed to curb migrants' access to welfare benefits and the NHS and sent vans that encourage illegal migrants to 'go home or face arrest' through some of the most diverse neighbourhoods in Britain.[10] Cameron's Conservatives have also been relentless in emphasising their Euroscepticism: withdrawing from the main centre-right group in the EU, vetoing a new EU treaty to deal with the Eurozone crisis and promising an 'in or out' referendum on Britain's EU member-ship – all powerful, substantive expressions of Euroscepticism that go beyond anything the famously Eurosceptic Margaret Thatcher did as Prime Minister. In short, the current government is seem-ingly offering UKIP supporters most of what they want on their two core issues of Europe and immigration; yet the rebels continue to angrily reject them. Why?

One explanation is the broader outlook of radical right voters in Britain, which makes them very hard to satisfy. Our evidence sug-gests UKIP voters are so disaffected, and so distrusting of politicians, they cannot easily be 'bought off' by policy offers. There are also more limits than there used to be on the capacity of mainstream parties to respond to these concerns over Europe and immigration. The radical actions demanded by these voters come with large risks and large costs, and are opposed by many other voters as well as significant organised interests, like the business community. Policy-makers face the difficult task of having to balance these demands, but the compromises that result do not satisfy the radical right elec-torate. Meanwhile, politicians are generally unwilling to explain to voters that they cannot have the policies they want. Few people in politics want to admit to being powerless, particularly on issues like immigration and Europe, where many of their constituents have very strong opinions. Therefore, they often make incremental pol-icy shifts and try to sell them as radical reforms. This, however, can backfire dramatically: if already sceptical voters feel they are being hoodwinked, such reforms can reinforce the dissatisfaction and dis-trust they are designed to address. UKIP feeds off this dynamic as it can, and regularly does, promise the kind of dramatic policy shifts voters say they want. As an insurgent party with little prospect of governing, UKIP do not have to give much thought to the con-sequences of their promises. Many voters find the voice of radical change seductive and much more attractive than the tepid compro-mise options put forward by mainstream parties conscious that they will be held to account for their pledges.

Attempts to appease UKIP voters may instead increase the rebels' appeal by adding to their legitimacy. As we saw in Chapter 6, one of the greatest obstacles facing insurgent parties is the barrier to entry posed by the electoral system; voters are reluctant to waste their votes on a fringe party with little prospect of success. When surges in UKIP's support in the opinion polls are met with immediate pol-icy concessions from the mainstream parties, it demonstrates to vot-ers that the revolt can force real change even without Westminster representation, undermining the argument that UKIP are a 'wasted vote'. Second, such support may be a *more* effective way to bring policy changes on the issues that UKIP voters care about, given that these are often a low priority for the mainstream parties, or issues on which they are internally divided and hence reluctant to act decisively. Switching en masse to UKIP, or threatening to do so, can achieve more than staying loyal ever could. 'Why accept a copy when you can have the original?' as the leader of the Front National in France, Jean-Marie Le Pen, once said.

The final paradox of UKIP support is this: at a time of falling real incomes and unprecedented economic uncertainty, voters from poorer and more insecure social groups should rally behind the party who can offer them the best prospect for economic support and assistance. Instead, as we have seen, struggling blue-collar voters from the 'left behind' social groups have moved behind a party with a barely coherent or credible economic policy, no track record of helping the disadvantaged and a libertarian activist base who openly favour free markets over support for the disadvantaged. The explanation for this paradox is that politics, for the voters who back UKIP, has ceased to be defined primarily as a battle for economic resources. UKIP voters, who are by some margin the most politically disaffected group in the electorate, have lost faith in the ability of traditional politics to solve their everyday problems and have instead turned their anger towards groups they feel are responsible for the decline in their standards of living and their loss of control over their lives. They do not consider mainstream politicians to be people who can protect them from the effects of the financial crisis, but rather as part of the corrupt and distant class who inflicted this crisis upon them. This presents a serious problem for Labour going forward, as groups of voters who should be naturally sympathetic to the economic policies of the left no longer trust politicians to help them.

UKIP's potential: have attitudes shifted in their favour?

Our analysis has clarified the motives driving UKIP voters, but also raises new and intriguing questions. How widespread are these motives within the British electorate? How much potential is there for the radical right revolt to expand further, just by mobilising those who already hold sympathetic views towards UKIP's agenda? And has the climate shifted in UKIP's favour over time, with more voters adopting the views we know encourage UKIP support?

The revolt on the right stands on the three pillars of hard Euroscepticism, anti-immigration and a populist backlash against

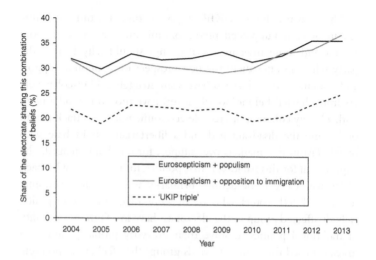

FIGURE 7.1 Prevalence of UKIP motives, 2004–2013
Source: Continuous Monitoring Study.

the established political class – all views that have been held
by a large section of the British electorate for some time (see
Chapter 3).[11] Moreover, and as Figure 7.1 demonstrates, there is
also still plenty of potential for further growth. Around 30 per cent
of voters are both Eurosceptic *and* opposed to immigration, or
Eurosceptic *and* politically dissatisfied, while around 20 per cent
hold all three of these attitudes. This means that 20–30 per cent of
the electorate hold the combination of beliefs we have identified
as motivating UKIP support, which is roughly twice the level of
support they received in polls during 2013, their best ever year.
The pool of potential UKIP recruits is also growing: the share of
voters holding Euroscepticism and at least one other radical right
belief is up by around 5–7 points since 2008, while the share holding all three is up by around 5 per cent, revealing that the army of
potential supporters for UKIP is growing in size. This is mirrored
in other measures, such as the importance of immigration to voters, which after a brief pause during the economic crisis has begun
to rise again, and support for a British exit from the EU, which

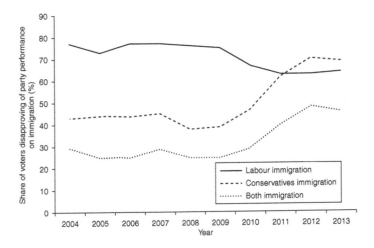

FIGURE 7.2 Share of voters disapproving of the main parties' performance on immigration

Source: Continuous Monitoring Study.

has risen sharply since the onset of the Eurozone crisis (see also Figures 3.3–3.5 in Chapter 3).

As we saw in Chapter 5, UKIP also draws support from voters who feel that both traditional governing parties have failed on the issues that matter to them. On this front, too, the climate for UKIP has been steadily improving, as we show Figures 7.2 and 7.3, which chart public perceptions of mainstream party performance on the two big issues of the late 2000s: immigration, and the financial crisis. On both of these issues, a common dynamic has played out since 2010 which is very helpful to UKIP: voters have remained angry about Labour's poor performance in government, but after an initial willingness to give Cameron's Conservatives a try, they have swiftly turned against his party as well. As a result, the proportion of voters dissatisfied with both parties has risen sharply since 2010 to an all time high in 2013. On immigration nearly half of the respondents polled in 2013 were dissatisfied with both Labour and Conservatives performance, double the level seen in 2009. On the

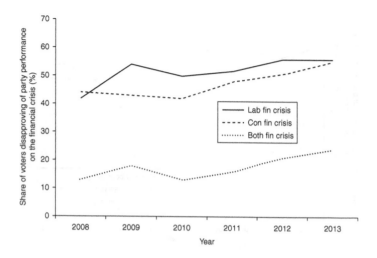

FIGURE 7.3 Share of voters disapproving of the main parties' performance on the financial crisis

Source: Continuous Monitoring Study.

financial crisis, the share of voters who believe that both Labour and the Conservatives are failing on the defining political issue of the age is approaching one in four, again double the level seen around the 2010 general election. In terms of issue performance, therefore, the environment has firmly shifted in UKIP's favour. On the two issues that topped the political agenda in 2013, both issues that UKIP are campaigning heavily on, the share of voters who think the mainstream parties have failed is rising rapidly.

UKIP also stand to profit from the sharp decline in the popularity of David Cameron among their core voting groups, as shown in Figure 7.4. When the Conservatives were in opposition Cameron had relatively high mean ratings, particularly among voters sharing core UKIP motivations. Since the coalition began, however, Cameron's ratings have fallen, and the fall has been much larger among Eurosceptics, anti-immigration voters and, particularly, populist voters. As a result, there is a growing electorate who UKIP can woo on two counts – they agree with the rebels on the issues, and they share Nigel Farage's disdain for David Cameron.

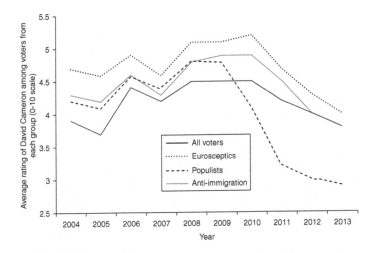

FIGURE 7.4 Ratings of the Conservative leader, 2004–2013

Source: Continuous Monitoring Study.

There are also problems ahead for UKIP, however. The first concerns their foundations. Euroscepticism is both a strength and weakness for the party. It is the strongest motive for activists, and many supporters, and the large population of voters with intensely negative views of the EU are providing the party with a crucial source of support. Euroscepticism is a powerful motive for elites in British politics too, including influential Conservatives and journalists, enabling UKIP to recruit activists, funders and journalists, such as Roger Knapman, Stuart Wheeler and journalist Patrick O'Flynn, who bring money, experience and elite connections. Yet UKIP's image as the authentic voice of Euroscepticism, which is so appealing to anti-EU elites, also complicates their efforts to appeal to the mass electorate. UKIP currently have little or no appeal for the half of the British electorate who do *not* share their hostility towards the EU, even when these voters share other concerns that UKIP target. The party might talk about immigration, grammar schools and high-speed rail, but our evidence has shown that they have yet to connect with voters worried about issues such as these but are not Eurosceptic. This situation has not changed even as UKIP has expanded rapidly, suggesting that their identification with the Eurosceptic cause is so strong that pro-EU voters will rarely even consider the party, regardless of their other views.

UKIP's second problem is its persistent failure to appeal to three large groups of voters: the young, women and ethnic minorities. In all three cases, UKIP faces a difficult strategic dilemma: their core messages, and the views held by many of their voters and activists, severely limit their appeal to these groups. Women are the largest of the three groups, and the group where there is the greatest potential for further growth. Indeed, our analysis revealed that many women share the concerns mobilised by UKIP, but do not currently back them. Yet UKIP's efforts to appeal to women, by standing female candidates in prominent elections, have been repeatedly undermined by the chauvinistic and anti-feminist views aired by some outspoken UKIP members and politicians, and shared by many of its older, male, blue-collar supporters. Such outbursts reinforce female distrust of UKIP, and as UKIP recruits voters with low levels of trust in the first place, this can be hard to repair.

The story with ethnic minorities is a similar one – UKIP's efforts to appeal to this group are undermined by the attitudes of their existing voters, and widely reported outbursts by politicians and activists. UKIP has made considerable efforts to reach out to ethnic minority communities, for example sending activists to speak in mosques and temples in 2013 and standing ethnic minority candidates in high-profile election races. Members of ethnic minority groups who do support the party have also been wheeled out to counter claims that UKIP are racist, or to front their election broadcasts. Yet such efforts are continually hampered by the less than welcoming views held by many UKIP members and voters. For example, a YouGov poll in September 2013 showed that 60 per cent of UKIP voters were uncomfortable with the idea of an ethnic minority Prime Minister. Stories about intolerant statements by UKIP activists have appeared frequently in the media, which reinforces the party's image as one that is not welcoming to ethnic minorities, as does its strident and often emotive language about the social effects of immigration.

For young Britons the problem is less distrust and more disinterest. Younger voters are less concerned about immigration, social change or Europe, more likely to have gone to university, to work in middle-class jobs, and are more comfortable with the identity and values of twenty-first century Britain. UKIP's core messages simply fall flat with such voters, who also find the worldview of many of the party's politicians and activists almost comically out of touch with their own. As we saw in Chapter 4, UKIP's leadership is keenly aware of the party's failure to connect with younger generations of Britons who have been hit by the post-2008 financial crisis, have not benefited from higher education and are now struggling to find a place in the labour market. While the party have attracted some young people into their ranks, connecting with younger Britons more widely and sustaining their revolt over the longer term remains one of their major challenges.

Responding to UKIP: dilemmas for the main parties

The emergence of the first new political force with national reach in a generation has forced all of Britain's mainstream parties to reconsider their political strategies. How, if at all, should they respond to the UKIP revolt? This is not an easy question for any of them, as this revolt exposes latent internal divisions and sharpens strategic dilemmas, and there is little precedent for dealing with the new rebel movement, making past experience an imperfect guide.

For the Conservatives, the key strategic dilemma is how far to take their efforts to win back support lost to the rebels. As we saw in Chapter 5, since 2010 UKIP's rebellion has taken more votes from citizens who backed Cameron's party at that general election than from any other party. Winning an electoral majority, or even emerging as the largest party in a hung Parliament, will be very difficult for the Conservatives unless they can win at least some of these rebels back. Yet the other attributes of UKIP voters – their blue collar social backgrounds, economic struggles, negative view of British politics and politicians, the low marks they give the Conservatives on their key issues of immigration and the financial crisis, and their strongly negative views of David Cameron – will make this a very tough task. The Conservatives would have to offer a truly radical policy shift to overcome these obstacles and win back significant UKIP support. Yet a radical shift on Europe and immigration, or the replacement of Cameron with a new, more UKIP-friendly leader, would also risk alienating the more moderate voters the Conservatives have worked so hard to win over and who are also essential to an electoral victory. The Conservatives cannot afford to lose voters to UKIP, but they may not be able to afford winning them back, either.

The dilemma Labour face is between short-term and long-term strategy. In the short term, the strong temptation for Labour will be to sit back and let UKIP divide the Conservative vote at the next general election, thereby lowering the bar for their own victory and a return to power. Some Labour commentators have taken pleasure in the irony of an electoral split undoing the right in the same way as the left has been undone many times in the past.[12] Yet such a 'laissez faire' approach to UKIP comes with serious longer-term risks. As we saw in Chapters 3 and 4, the UKIP vote comes primarily from 'left behind' social groups who were once solidly Labour. UKIP have driven a wedge between the struggling, blue-collar 'Old Left', who once supported Labour on economic grounds, and the educated, white-collar 'New Left' who often back them on the basis of social values. If they allow UKIP to become established as part of the mainstream political conversation, either with MPs at Westminster or a strong presence in Labour heartlands, the centre-left risks making that divide permanent. It will be much harder for Ed Miliband and his party to win back working-class voters with Ukippers running continuous and high profile campaigns on Europe, immigration and traditional British values. Labour also need to remember that UKIP's rise has been driven as much by populist hostility to the political establishment as by ideology or policy. This does not hurt them much at present, as they are in opposition and therefore not the main focus of anti-system feeling. If they were to win the next election, they would find UKIP's populist barbs directed at them. A failure to combat UKIP before 2015 will result in a stronger populist opponent to future Labour governments.

For the Liberal Democrats, the key problem is how to respond to a party that has stolen their political clothes. Much of the Liberal Democrats' success over the past twenty years has come from being a permanent opposition party, able to mobilise voters discontented with the government of the day but unwilling to consider the main opposition party. In the 1990s, they could pick up long-time Conservative voters who were disheartened by the corruption and weak leadership of the Major administration, but still unwilling to vote Labour, as well as Labour voters looking for the best local means for dislodging Conservative incumbent MPs. In the 2000s, the Liberal Democrats could win over Labour left wingers alienated by the centrism of Tony Blair, as well as voters of all political persuasions who opposed Blair's war in Iraq (which they were the only major party to oppose). The Liberal Democrats harnessed discontent with the government of the day through intensive, locally focused campaigns, building a presence in local government and seeking to pick seats off in anti-incumbent by-elections.

After entering government for the first time in seventy years after the 2010 general election, the Liberal Democrats now find themselves victims of their own success, as UKIP turn their old strategy against them. They can no longer market themselves as the choice for voters 'sick of the old politics' when they are now clearly part of the 'old politics' they once railed against. UKIP have appropriated the anti-incumbent mantle, and adopted the Liberal Democrats' campaigning strategy. It is now purple rosettes, not gold ones, which flood into the nation's boroughs and shires as local elections approach, and UKIP candidates whom incumbent parties fear as the lightning rod for anti-government sentiment at Westminster by-elections. By becoming a party of government, the Liberal Democrats have thus rendered ineffective the principal strategy they have used to get there. The question posed by UKIP's insurgency is this: how can a small party, without a clearly defined social base, survive when the permanent opposition political strategy it relied upon is no longer available? Can the Liberal Democrats ever hope to credibly campaign again as a party of opposition to 'politics as usual' after their five-year spell in coalition? And if they cannot, how can they hope to compete for the kind of discontented voters who once backed them and are now considering a vote for Nigel Farage's rebels instead?

UKIP and the EU referendum: if we stay there will be trouble, but if we go it will be double[13]

UKIP's remarkable rise means that, for the first time, their paramount goal of EU exit is on the political agenda, with the Conservatives pledging to offer a referendum on Britain's EU membership if they win an electoral mandate in 2015. Yet practically every possible outcome of the referendum debate poses significant strategic problems for the rebels. The likeliest no-referendum scenario, a Labour election victory, will lead many on the right to blame UKIP for splitting the vote and preventing a Conservative government from delivering on its referendum commitment. This will reopen the dormant, but never resolved, internal debate about the party's strategic priorities. UKIP activists who regard exit from the EU as their party's political purpose, and favour close relations with mainstream Eurosceptics to achieve this goal, will be angered that their party played a key role in preventing that outcome. Those who favour building UKIP as a broad-based political movement will counter that the Conservatives could not be trusted to deliver on this commitment, and that close relations with them would have fatally tarnished the UKIP brand.

While this would be a difficult debate for the party to resolve, UKIP will face even sharper dilemmas if Britain does decide to hold a referendum on EU membership, regardless of the result. If the British public voted to remain in the European Union, it would reduce the potency of Euroscepticism, settling the debate over the EU, for the short term, at least. If UKIP politicians continued to agitate for exit, they would risk looking like out-of-touch obsessives, undoing years of hard work to shed this image. Yet for many senior UKIP members, the EU is such a fundamental problem that it would be hard for them to leave it alone, even if the public voted clearly against departure. The bitter infighting which has crippled the party in the past might re-emerge, as advocates of a long-term, party-building approach face off against those who would regard a 'no' vote as proof that the case against Europe needed to be made more robustly.

On the other hand, if the British public did vote to leave the EU, which at the time of writing appears unlikely, UKIP would enjoy its great policy triumph – and the next day would find itself deprived of its reason for being. As we have seen, Europe is far from the only factor driving UKIP's support; it may not even be the main one. There would still be an opening in the electoral market for a populist radical right party in a Britain outside of Europe, but it would be extremely difficult for UKIP to fill that opening. A large majority of the party's senior politicians, activists and funders joined the revolt in order to pull Britain out of the EU. It would be hard for UKIP to sustain their interest with that goal achieved. No doubt some would remain, to try and rebuild the movement around domestically focused radical right issues such as immigration, traditional values and the defence of national identity, but it would be a hard slog. Journalists and voters alike would ask what the point of UKIP now was, when they had already achieved their stated goal. These are the dilemmas that come with success, and it is a sign of how far UKIP have come that debating what would become of them if they achieved their defining goal is no longer an implausible academic exercise. However the next election and the debate over Europe play out, UKIP's revolt remains a remarkable political achievement.

In the summer of 1994, a young man from Kent put himself forward for Parliament in Eastleigh, fighting his first election for a party that had been founded less than six months earlier. It was a lonely campaign for Nigel Farage. He had no money, no organisational support, no media attention and virtually no interest from the voters. He finished in fourth place, an obscure footnote to a famous Liberal Democrat by-election triumph, his sole achievement beating perennial novelty candidate 'Screaming' Lord Sutch. Less than twenty years later, and not yet fifty, Farage returned to the scene of his youthful political humiliation at the head of the most successful grassroots political insurgency in modern British political history. Though his candidate did not win the second Eastleigh by-election, it was his turn to inflict humiliation on his right-wing rivals, as the Conservatives were forced into third place in a seat they had hoped to win. UKIP were once the laughing stock of the British right; now Farage was having the last laugh. His party have recruited more activists, raised more funds and won more votes than any grassroots political insurgent in living memory. UKIP's future remains unclear, their capacity to win domestic elections remains unproven, but one thing is certain: the revolt on the right has already changed the face of British politics.

Notes

1 Paul Nuttall was placed 64th on the list. 'Top 100 most influential right-wingers', *The Daily Telegraph*, 2 October 2013. Available online: http://www.telegraph.co.uk/news/politics/conservative/10350283/Top-100-most-influential-Right-wingers-50-1.html (accessed 3 October 2013).

2 A poll by Populus days after the conference had UKIP on 9 per cent and three polls by YouGov had the party on 10 per cent, 11 per cent and 12 per cent. See http://ukpollingreport.co.uk/voting-intention-2 (accessed 4 October 2013). UKIP also continued to turn in strong local election performances, averaging 16.9 per cent in local by-elections held in the third quarter of 2013. http://averypublicsociologist.blogspot.co.uk/2013/09/quarter-three-local-by-election-results.html (accessed 5 October 2013).

3 Iain Martin, 'What the hell can the Tories do about UKIP?' *The Daily Telegraph Blog*, 19 September 2013. Available online: http://blogs.telegraph.co.uk/news/iainmartin1/100236803/what-the-hell-can-the-tories-do-about-ukip/ (accessed 3 October 2013). Lord Ashcroft, 'Labour still on course in the marginals – but it's not over yet', 15 September 2013. Available online: http://lordashcroftpolls.com/2013/09/labour-still-on-course-in-the-marginals-but-its-not-over-yet/ (accessed 3 October 2013).

4 Geoffrey Evans and James Tilley (2012) 'How parties shape class politics: Explaining the decline of the class basis of party support', *British Journal of Political Science*, 42(1): 137–61.

5 Robert Ford and Matthew J. Goodwin (2010) 'Angry white men: Individual and contextual predictors of support for the British National Party', *Political Studies*, 58(1): 1–25; Matthew J. Goodwin (2011) *New British Fascism: Rise of the British National Party*, Abingdon: Routledge.

6 John McTernan (2013) 'The left has to get politically tough on Labour migration'. Available online: http://www.policy-network.net/pno_detail.aspx?ID=4474&title=The+left+has+to+get+politically+tough+on+labour+migration (accessed 4 October 2013).

7 Catherine Fieschi (2005) 'Far right alarmism', *Prospect Magazine*, 108 (March).

8 'Nasty tactics will hardly bring illegal immigrants out of their nail bars, says Bishop', *The Daily Telegraph*, 4 August 2013.

9 On this point, it is worth noting evidence that suggests that the strategy of exclusion is actually not as effective as many assume, and can have the opposite effect in strengthening a sense of solidarity among activists and resulting in further ideological radicalisation. Joost Van Spanje and Wouter van der Brug (2007) 'The party as pariah: The exclusion of anti-immigration parties and its effect on their ideological positions', *West European Politics*, 30(5): 1022–40; see also J. Van Spanje and W. Van der Brug (2009) 'Being intolerant of the intolerant: The exclusion of Western European anti-immigration parties and its consequences for party choice', *Acta Politica*, 44: 353–84.

10 'David Cameron: Immigration is constant drain on public services', *The Daily Telegraph*, 23 July 2013; 'Downing Street says "go home" van ads are working', *BBC News*, 29 July 2013.

11 Robert Ford (2010) 'Who might vote for the BNP? Survey evidence on the electoral potential of the extreme right in Britain', in Roger Eatwell and Matthew Goodwin (eds.) *The New Extremism in 21st Century Britain*, Abingdon: Routledge, pp. 145–68; Peter John and Helen Margetts (2009) 'The latent support for the extreme right in British politics', *West European Politics*, 32(3): 496–513.

12 See, for example, N. Thomas-Symonds (2013) 'An historic split?', *Progress Online*. Available online: http://www.progressonline.org.uk/2013/03/06/a-historic-split/ (accessed 6 October 2013); P. Wintour (2013) 'Tories fear UKIP could cause as much harm as SDP did to Labour', *The Guardian*. Available online: http://www.theguardian.com/politics/2013/mar/01/tories-ukip-harm-sdp-labour (accessed 6 October 2013).

13 With apologies to The Clash.

APPENDIX: DATA AND METHODS

Analysing UKIP's voters

1. The Continuous Monitoring Survey

Our main data source for the analysis of UKIP's voters in Chapters 4 and 5 was the British Election Study Continuous Monitoring Survey (BES–CMS), a monthly sample of around 1,000 British citizens drawn from the YouGov Internet panel every month since April 2004. We chose this dataset because of its exceptionally large sample size, long time frame and large number of core questions, which enabled us to carry out a level of analysis of UKIP's evolving support that would not have been possible with any other available dataset. The representativeness of Internet panel samples remains, however, a subject of considerable academic discussion. Such samples are not a random selection of the electorate, as is normally the case in survey research, but are drawn instead from large pools of citizens who volunteered to receive regular survey requests from an Internet panel company. Such companies make great efforts to ensure that their panels are broadly representative of the general population, in particular by actively recruiting new panel members from under-represented groups. YouGov are the longest running and largest Internet panel company in Britain, and have regularly been employed by leading academics such as the BES team, so we are confident that the data are as good as can reasonably be expected from an Internet panel. Analysis of earlier datasets drawn from the YouGov panel have found that they deliver similar results about the patterns and drivers of electoral choice as survey samples gathered using traditional survey sampling techniques and face-to-face interviewing.[1]

Nonetheless, there are issues with Internet panel data that we must bear in mind. Internet panels will tend to under-represent certain groups, in particular groups with lower levels of Internet access such as older voters and those on very low incomes. They also tend to under-represent groups with lower education levels or English language proficiency, who are more likely to struggle with the survey interface. Finally, they will tend to under-represent voters with lower levels of interest in the subjects they survey, in this case politics. Conversely, groups with higher than average Internet access, high education levels and the politically interested, will tend to be over-represented among survey respondents. YouGov produces survey weights that are designed to correct for these biases, but they cannot be eliminated. In our case, there is some cause for concern as many of the factors which predict UKIP support – age, education level, social class, ethnicity, and views of the political system – are also likely to predict Internet survey participation. As such, there is a risk that some of the estimates in our analysis are biased. To guard against this risk, we acquired a second dataset from Ipsos MORI – a cumulative file of all their monthly public opinion surveys from 2002 to 2013. Ipsos MORI conduct their surveys using traditional survey methods: from 2002–8 they conducted face-to-face interviews with clusters of people collected in a randomly drawn set of sampling points; from 2008 onwards they conducted telephone interviews with respondents sampled by dialling random telephone numbers. To check that the results of our analysis were not being influenced by the quirks of our sample, we replicated our analysis using the Ipsos MORI data wherever similar measures were available. We found that the pattern of effects was largely identical to those seen in our YouGov sample.[2]

2. Data and measures used in analysis

Chapter 3: Origins: a long time coming

Most of the analyses in this chapter made use of the British Election Studies (1964–2010) and the British Social Attitudes surveys (1983–2012). Both surveys conduct face-to-face interviews on stratified random samples of the British population. The survey datasets and technical reports detailing sampling strategy, response rates and weighting are freely available at the UK Data Archive. All analyses are conducted with appropriate population weights applied.

The measures we used in the analysis were as follows:

Social class: Where available, we have used the Goldthorpe–Heath class schema, which is the most robust and theoretically well-grounded way to measure social class. Where this is not available, we have used the National Statistics Socio-Economic Classification (NS–SEC). Checks in datasets where both are available suggests their categorisations of working class and professional middle class are generally very similar.

Education: In most cases, this is straightforwardly measured using the highest qualification reported by the respondent. In a few cases this is not available and we then use school leaving age as a proxy. Respondents who report leaving school at 16 or earlier are classified as 'no qualifications'; those leaving school at 19 or later are classified as 'university educated'.

Age and housing status: Measured using survey self-reports.

The data for Figure 3.7 come from the 'Euro Mega Poll' conducted by YouGov immediately after the 2009 European Parliament election, which sampled 32,268 members of the YouGov panel. YouGov measures social class using a lengthy set of questions designed to record a respondent's precise work role. These include questions on who the chief income earner is in the household; the working status of the chief income earner, whether they are self-employed or not; their current or more recent occupation type; the sector they work in; their level of qualification; their position within their work and their level of management responsibility. These questions, along with others, are used to classify people in accordance with the National Readership Survey social grade schema, which is as follows:

A: Higher managerial, administrative and professional
B: Intermediate managerial, administrative and professional
C1: Supervisory, or clerical and junior managerial, administrative or professional
C2: Skilled manual workers
D: Semi- and unskilled manual workers
E: Casual or lowest grade workers, pensioner and others dependent on the welfare state for their income, including students

We define 'professional middle class' as classes A and B from this schema, and 'working class' as classes C2, D and E (excluding students).

Chapter 4: The social roots of the revolt

Data and measures

All analysis in this chapter is conducted using the BES–CMS data. Age, ethnicity and gender are self-reported. Education is measured using the age respondents report leaving school. Social class is measured using the YouGov measures detailed above. Vote choice in the previous election is measured using self-reported recall.

Additional regression models

We report the detailed results from additional statistical analysis for this chapter below. Table A.1 presents details of the social predictors of support for each party, along with two measures of non-voting. These are presented using logistic regression coefficients, rather than the odds ratios used in the main text. Positive coefficients indicate an increased likelihood of supporting a party relative to the reference group, and negative coefficients indicate a reduced likelihood. Table A.2 presents separate logistic regression models of UKIP support for each of the four time periods we consider in the main text, once again using standard logistic regression coefficients to indicate the strength and direction of relationships.

TABLE A.1 Social predictors of party support, detailed logistic regression models

	UKIP	BNP support (2007–13)	Cons	Labour	Lib Dems	Greens	Non-voters 1	Non-voters 2
Social class (ref: professionals/ higher managers)								
Lower managers	0.10	0.19	0.25*	-0.07*	-0.23*	-0.29*	0.10	-0.03
Routine non-manual	0.21*	0.36*	-0.11*	0.07*	-0.11*	-0.10	0.50*	0.31*
Skilled manual	0.42*	0.85*	-0.25*	0.08*	-0.21*	-0.25*	0.61*	0.43*
Unskilled manual	0.30*	0.76*	-0.45*	0.20*	-0.25*	-0.03	0.81*	0.54*
Other/never worked	0.28*	0.56*	-0.23*	0.003	-0.21*	0.11	0.72*	0.64*
Education: age left school (ref: 19 or older)								
15 or younger	0.50*	1.36*	-0.31*	0.31*	-0.53*	-1.10*	0.67*	0.50*
16	0.47*	0.95*	-0.05*	0.08*	-0.49*	-0.76*	0.57*	0.47*
17 or 18	0.34*	0.54*	0.15*	-0.06*	-0.36*	-0.51*	0.35*	0.27*
Gender (ref: female)								
Male	0.37*	0.58*	0.06*	-0.08*	-0.06*	-0.06	-0.40*	-0.63*
Age (ref: 18–24)								
25–34	-0.02	-0.08	-0.00	0.12*	-0.12*	0.06	-0.10	-0.09*
35–44	0.43*	0.05	0.06	0.18*	-0.19*	-0.01	-0.55*	-0.39*

45–54	0.73★	0.04	0.14★	0.14★	−0.12★	−0.02	−0.97★	−0.71★
55–64	1.01★	−0.20	0.33★	−0.09★	−0.08★	−0.06	−1.23★	−0.90★
65 plus	1.21★	−0.79★	0.68★	−0.28★	−0.19★	−0.67★	−1.75★	−1.27★
Ethnicity (ref: non-white)								
White	1.24★	1.34★	0.81★	−0.79★	0.47★	0.54★	−0.29★	−0.45★
Pseudo- R square	0.043	0.058	0.020	0.008	0.011	0.024	0.047	0.044
N	122,946	78,486	122,946	122,946	122,946	122,946	122,946	122,946

Notes: Figures show results from logistic regression models predicting support for each party vs all other options. Figures are standard coefficients rather than the odds ratios used in the main text tables.

★ = $p < 0.05$; ★★ = $p < 0.01$

TABLE A.2 Evolving social predictors of UKIP support, detailed logistic regression models

	Blair	Brown	Cameron I	Cameron II
Social class (ref: professionals/higher managers)				
Lower managers	−0.06	0.15	0.14	0.18
Routine non-manual	0.02	0.45★	0.28★	0.18
Skilled manual	0.48★	0.51★	0.33★	0.31★
Unskilled manual	0.08	0.53★	0.29★	0.35★
Other/never worked	0.17★	0.38★	0.36★	0.29★
Education: age left school (ref: 19 or older)				
15 or younger	0.65★	0.36★	0.38★	0.52★
16	0.50★	0.56★	0.21★	0.54★
17 or 18	0.34★	0.41★	0.27★	0.34★
Gender (ref: female)				
Male	0.29★	0.44★	0.24★	0.46★
Age (ref: 18–24)				
25–34	−0.11	0.05	−0.48	0.36
35–44	0.25	0.55★	0.04	0.80★
45–54	0.57★	0.84★	0.41	1.08★
55–64	0.70★	1.16★	0.66★	1.48★
65 plus	0.82★	1.32★	0.80★	1.80★
Ethnicity (ref: non-white)				
White	1.17★	1.75★	1.24★	1.27★
Pseudo-R square	0.036	0.044	0.034	0.070
N	47,959	38,632	19,572	16,783

★ = p < 0.05; ★★ = p < 0.01

Chapter 5: The motive for rebelling

Data and methods

The data used throughout this chapter comes from the BES–CMS. Each of the four motives we examine in the first section of the analysis has several measures available. For the figures which chart the impact of these motives on UKIP support (Figures 5.1–5.3), we employ the measure which has the strongest relationship with UKIP support. The full set of measures used is detailed in Table A.3, with the measure employed in the figures highlighted in bold. The measures of issue performance and views of the parties' leaders are set out in full in Table A.4. Note that, for issue performance, the questions ask about how 'the government' has handled each issue and how the main opposition party (Conservatives until 2010, Labour after this) would handle each issue. In order to have a consistent measure across the full run of data, we code 'the government' as Labour handling of each issue until May 2010; after this point 'the government' is coded as Conservative handling of each issue. Unfortunately, there is no way of separating out perceptions of Liberal Democrat performance within the coalition, as this is not measured.

We also report additional regression models presenting the detailed statistical analysis which informed the arguments in our main text. These are as follows. Table A.5 presents logistic regression models of UKIP support among all voters. Model 1 presents the baseline model of demographic predictors from Chapter 4; model 2 adds in all the measures of the three motives we find significant correlate with UKIP support; model 3 adds in all measures of party performance on the issues; model 4 adds in ratings of the parties' leaders; and model 5 presents a 'reduced' model with all insignificant factors dropped. Table A.6 performs the same set of analyses for Eurosceptic voters only, reflecting UKIP's almost complete lack of appeal to voters who approve of British EU membership.

Table A.7 illustrates the 'sod the lot' phenomenon discussed in the main text, whereby UKIP win their strongest backing from voters who are dissatisfied with the performance of both

TABLE A.3 Measures of the four motives predicting UKIP support

	Measurement scale	Mean	Standard deviation
Euroscepticism			
Views of Britain's EU membership	4 point scale: 1: Strongly Approve – 4: Strongly Disapprove	2.54	0.95
Spontaneous mention of Europe as one of the nation's most important problems	Binary coding – respondents who mentioned coded 1, all others coded zero	0.036	0.19
Populism			
Satisfaction with democracy	4 point scale: 1: Very satisfied – 4: Very dissatisfied	2.70	0.85
Populism Scale 1: Govt not honest/trustworthy	3 binary agree/disagree measures: 1: Government is not honest/trustworthy 2: Government doesn't treat people like you fairly 3: Big gap between what you expect in life and what you get 3 measures are added together to form scale	1.86	1.09
Political influence	On a scale of 0 to 10, how much influence do you have on politics and public affairs? (0 = no influence – 10 = a great deal of influence)	2.1	2.2
Attitudes to immigration			
Importance of asylum (scale)	Using the 0–10 scale, how important a problem is the number of asylum seekers coming to Britain these days?	7.7	2.7

Spontaneous mention of immigration as one of the nation's most important problems	Binary coding – respondents who mentioned coded 1, all others coded zero	0.16	0.37
Views of the asylum situation 'these days'	5 point scale 1= a lot better – 5 = a lot worse	4.10	1.08
Negative emotions about asylum seekers	Which, if any, of the following words describe your feelings about the number of asylum seekers coming to Britain (respondents could pick up to four): angry, happy, disgusted, hopeful, uneasy, confident, afraid, proud. Scale adds together all negative emotions named by respondents	1.57	1.37
Social pessimism			
Economic sentiment index	Scale made by combining four items: personal economic circumstances last 12 months; personal economic circumstances next 12 months; national economic circumstances last 12 months; national economic circumstances next 12 months. Scaled to run from 0 (most positive) to 1 (most negative)	0.64	0.21
Trust in others	Think for a moment about whether people with whom you have contact can be trusted. Use the 0 to 10 scale again, where 10 means definitely can be trusted and 0 means definitely cannot be trusted	6.33	2.18
Life satisfaction	Thinking about your life as a whole, are you very satisfied, fairly satisfied, a little dissatisfied or very dissatisfied with your life as a whole? 4 point scale 1:Very satisfied, 4:Very dissatisfied	2.30	0.79

TABLE A.4 Measures of issue performance and views of party leaders

	Measurement scale	Mean	Standard deviation
Issue performance*			
Labour handling of immigration	How well do you think the present government has handled (before May 2010)/a Labour government would (after May 2010) the number of asylum seekers coming into the country? 5 point scale running from 1 = Very well to 5 = very badly, rescaled to 0 (very well) to 1 (very badly)	0.77	0.26
Conservative handling of immigration	As above, but asks how 'a Conservative government would handle' (before May 2010)/'the present government has handled' (after May 2010)	0.59	0.32
Labour handling of the financial crisis	How well do you think the present government has handled (before May 2010)/a Labour government would handle (after May 2010) the financial crisis	0.65	0.31
Conservative handling of the financial crisis	As above but asks how 'a Conservative government would handle' (before May 2010) and 'the present government has handled' (after May 2010)	0.57	0.29
Labour handling of crime	How well do you think the present government has handled (before May 2010)/a Labour government would handle (after May 2010) the crime situation in Britain?	0.64	0.27
Conservative handling of crime	As above but asks how 'a Conservative government would handle' (before May 2010) and 'the present government has handled' (after May 2010)	0.54	0.28
Labour handling of the NHS	How well do you think the present government has handled (before May 2010)/a Labour government would handle (after May 2010) the National Health Service?	0.59	0.30

Conservative handling of the NHS	As above but asks how 'a Conservative government would handle' (before May 2010) and 'the present government has handled' (after May 2010)	0.63	0.29
Labour handling of education	How well do you think the present government has handled (before May 2010)/a Labour government would handle (after May 2010) Britain's education system?	0.61	0.29
Conservative handling of education	As above but asks how 'a Conservative government would handle' (before May 2010) and 'the present government has handled' (after May 2010)	0.58	0.29
Labour handling of terrorism	How well do you think the present government has handled (before May 2010)/a Labour government would handle (after May 2010) the risk of terrorism to British citizens?	0.56	0.29
Conservative handling of terrorism	As above but asks how 'a Conservative government would handle' (before May 2010) and 'the present government has handled' (after May 2010)	0.51	0.27
Views of party leaders			
Views of Labour leader	Using a scale of 0 to 10, where 10 means strongly like, and 0 means strongly dislike, how do you feel about Tony Blair/Gordon Brown/Ed Miliband	3.8	2.9
Views of Conservative leader	Using a scale of 0 to 10, where 10 means strongly like, and 0 means strongly dislike, how do you feel about Michael Howard/David Cameron?	4.3	2.9
Views of Liberal Democrat leader	Using a scale of 0 to 10, where 10 means strongly like, and 0 means strongly dislike, how do you feel about Charles Kennedy/Menzies Campbell/Nick Clegg?	4.2	2.4

* Please see notes above for details of how these measures were recoded to make them consistent across the change of government in 2010.

TABLE A.5 Models of UKIP support, all voters

	Model 1: Demographics	Model 2: Add core motives	Model 3: Add issues	Model 4: Add leaders	Model 5: Reduced
Demographics					
Class (working class)	0.22**	0.02	−0.05	−0.05	–
Gender (male)	0.36**	0.38**	0.34**	0.30**	0.28**
Age (over 54)	0.70**	0.28**	0.32**	0.34**	0.35**
Education (left before 16)	0.48**	0.06	−0.01	0.01	–
Ethnicity (white)	1.51**	0.99**	0.75*	0.72	0.81**
Euroscepticism					
Views of EU membership		4.36**	3.78**	3.70**	3.95**
Europe most important problem (spontaneous)		0.99**	0.82**	0.78**	0.79**
Populism					
Dissatisfaction with democracy		0.88**	0.64**	0.58**	0.55**
No influence on politics		0.32**	0.30**	0.24**	0.22**
Populist views scale		1.05**	1.24**	1.05**	1.05**
Anti-immigration					
Importance asylum (scale)		0.58**	0.18	0.17	–
Immigration most important problem (spontaneous)		0.38**	0.38**	0.35**	0.38**
Negative views asylum seekers		0.19**	0.11	0.06	–
Dissatisfaction asylum		0.14	−0.08	0.01	–

Issue performance (higher scores = less satisfied)

Labour asylum			2.58**	2.44**	2.49**
Cons asylum			1.16**	1.15**	1.16**
Labour financial crisis			0.78**	0.69**	0.66**
Cons financial crisis			0.82**	0.26	0.30
Labour education			0.66**	0.59**	0.61**
Cons education			-0.41**	-0.55**	-0.62**
Labour NHS			-0.43**	-0.39**	-0.43**
Cons NHS			0.14	-0.05	–
Labour terror			-0.42**	-0.41**	-0.41**
Cons terror			0.12	-0.02	–
Leaders (higher scores = dislike more)					
Labour leader				0.56**	0.66**
Conservative leader				1.29**	1.40**
Liberal Democrat leader				-0.21	–
Chi-squared change	2019**	4510**	470**	85**	–
Model fit (Pseudo-R sq)	0.073	0.255	0.329	0.339	0.339
N	124,110	97,617	37,413	35,013	39,716

Source: British Election Study Continuous Monitory Study 2004–13. Controls also included for survey year.

** = p < 0.01; * = p < 0.05

Pessimistic attitudes, Labour and Conservative performance on crime are not included in the models as they are never significant when other factors controlled.

TABLE A.6 Models of UKIP support, Eurosceptic voters only

	Model 1: Demographics	Model 2: Add core motives	Model 3: Add issues	Model 4: Add leaders	Model 5: Reduced
Demographics					
Class (working class)	0.13**	0.05	-0.03	-0.04	–
Gender (male)	0.47**	0.39**	0.38**	0.35**	0.33**
Age (over 54)	0.53**	0.30**	0.35**	0.36**	0.36**
Education (left before 16)	0.17**	0.03	-0.02	-0.02	–
Ethnicity (white)	1.32**	1.08**	0.90*	0.88*	0.94*
Euroscepticism					
Strongly disapprove EU membership		3.46**	2.73**	2.66**	2.78**
Europe most important problem (spontaneous)		1.02**	0.86**	0.82**	0.83**
Populism					
Dissatisfaction with democracy		0.94**	0.71**	0.64**	0.62**
No influence on politics		0.32**	0.31**	0.25**	0.23**
Populist views scale		1.00**	1.21**	1.02**	0.99**
Anti-immigration					
Importance asylum (scale)		0.39**	0.04	0.01	–
Immigration most important problem (spontaneous)		0.39**	0.39**	0.37**	0.36**
Negative views asylum seekers		0.12	0.05	0.02	–
Dissatisfaction asylum		0.05	-0.21	-0.11	–

Issue performance (higher scores = less satisfied)

Labour immigration			2.38**	2.40**	2.36**
Cons immigration			1.28**	1.26**	1.19**
Labour financial crisis			0.73**	0.64**	0.59**
Cons financial crisis			0.86**	0.37*	0.41*
Labour education			0.77**	0.65**	0.73**
Cons education			-0.45**	-0.35**	-0.64**
Labour NHS			-0.51**	-0.47**	-0.52**
Cons NHS			0.10	-0.09	–
Labour terror			-0.41**	-0.42**	-0.39**
Cons terror			0.12	-0.01	–
Leaders (higher scores = dislike more)					
Labour leader				0.60**	0.67**
Conservative leader				1.20**	1.29**
Liberal Democrat leader				-0.19	–
Chi-squared change	1459**	2041**	453**	78**	
Model fit (Pseudo-R sq)	0.061	0.154	0.236	0.249	0.248
N	53,618	49,505	19,978	18,662	20,312

Source: British Election Study Continuous Monitory Study 2004–13. Controls also included for survey year.

** = p < 0.01; * = p < 0.05

Pessimistic attitudes, Labour and Conservative performance on crime are not included in the models as they are never significant when other factors controlled.

TABLE A.7 'Sod the lot' models – testing the effects of dissatisfaction with both parties

(a) All voters

	Model 1: Separate party and leader effects	Model 2: Add party interactions	Model 3: Add leader interactions
Issue performance (higher scores = less satisfied)			
Labour immigration	2.49**	0.84**	0.98**
Cons immigration	1.16**	–0.71**	–0.49**
Labour financial crisis	0.66**	–1.47**	–1.00**
Cons financial crisis	0.30	–2.61**	–1.94**
Labour AND Cons immigration		1.71**	1.44**
Labour AND Cons financial crisis		3.06**	2.22**
Leaders (higher scores = dislike more)			
Labour leader	0.66**	0.53**	–1.27**
Conservative leader	1.40**	1.38**	–1.80**
Labour AND Cons leader			2.05**
Model fit (Pseudo-R sq)	0.331	0.337	0.338
N	40,397	40,397	40,397

(b) Eurosceptic voters

	Model 1: Separate party and leader effects	Model 2: Add party interactions	Model 3: Add leader interactions
Issue performance (higher scores = less satisfied)			
Labour immigration	2.30**	0.45**	0.59**
Cons immigration	0.98**	–0.93**	–0.72**
Labour financial crisis	0.59**	–1.58**	–1.14**
Cons financial crisis	0.04	–2.64**	–1.99**

TABLE A.7 (*cont.*)

	Model 1: Separate party and leader effects	Model 2: Add party interactions	Model 3: Add leader interactions
Labour AND Cons immigration		2.00★★	1.74★★
Labour AND Cons financial crisis		3.14★★	2.34★★
Leaders (higher scores = dislike more)			
Labour leader	0.66★★	0.56★★	−1.28★★
Conservative leader	1.33★★	1.28★★	−1.67★★
Labour AND Cons leader			1.98★★
Model fit (Pseudo-R sq)	0.236	0.243	0.244
N	20,973	20,973	20,973

★ = $p < 0.05$; ★★ = $p < 0.01$

mainstream parties, or dislike both of their leaders. To do this, we use three interaction terms: two which multiply together both parties' ratings on the two main issues associated with UKIP support (immigration and the financial crisis) and one which multiplies together voters' ratings of the parties' leaders (with higher scores equating to more negative ratings) The strong positive interaction effects and negative main effects indicate that voters with negative views of both parties on each of these dimensions are far more likely to support UKIP, while voters who reject one party, but not the other, are much less likely to do so. In Tables A.8 and A.9 we illustrate the evolution of UKIP predictors by presenting logistic regression models of UKIP support in each of the four time periods discussed in the main text, for all voters and for Eurosceptic voters only. In order to maximise cases and statistical power, and for parsimony, only significant predictors are included in each of these models.

TABLE A.8 Evolution of strongest effects over time: all voters

	Blair	Brown	Cameron 2010–11	Cameron 2012–13
Demographics				
Gender	0.25★★	0.44★★	–	0.37★★
Age	0.27★★	0.38★★	0.25★	0.59★★
Euroscepticism				
Dissatisfaction with EU membership	4.75★★	3.92★★	4.11★★	4.18★★
Europe most important problem	1.31★★	1.26★★	0.96★★	0.59★★
Populism				
Dissatisfaction with democracy	0.44★★	0.61★★	0.83★★	0.45★★
No influence on politics	0.22★	0.33★★	–	–
Populist views scale	0.87★★	0.91★★	0.98★★	1.15★★
Anti-immigration				
Immigration MIP (spontaneous)	0.45★★	0.29★★	0.30★★	0.46★★
Issue performance (higher scores = less satisfied)				
Labour asylum	1.60★★	1.72★★	2.04★★	2.44★★
Cons asylum	0.67★★	1.10★★	1.24★★	0.59★
Labour financial crisis	–	–	1.30★★	0.86★★
Cons financial crisis	–	–	–	–
Labour education	0.50★★	–	–	–
Cons education	–	−0.58★★	−0.73★★	–
Labour NHS	–	–	–	–
Cons NHS	–	–	–	–
Labour terror	−0.55★★	−0.46★★	–	–
Cons terror	–		–	–
Leaders (higher scores = less satisfied)				
Labour leader	–	1.07★★	–	0.69★★
Conservative leader	1.53★★	1.74★★	1.02★★	1.47★★
Liberal Democrat leader	0.70★★	–	0.55★★	–
Chi-squared change	1793★★	1341★★	986★★	1316★★
Model fit (Pseudo-R sq)	0.263	0.256	0.304	0.350
Model fit (BIC)	7,610	5,638	3,910	5,823
N	29,561	27,201	14,564	12,534

★ = p < 0.05; ★★ = p < 0.01

TABLE A.9 Evolution of strongest effects over time: Eurosceptic voters

	Blair	Brown	Cameron 2010–11	Cameron 2012–13
Demographics				
Gender	0.29★★	0.43★★	–	0.40★★
Age	0.27★★	0.39★★	0.23★	0.58★★
Euroscepticism				
Dissatisfaction with EU membership	3.59★★	2.63★★	2.93★★	2.91★★
Europe most important problem	1.32★★	1.30★★	1.00★★	0.61★★
Populism				
Dissatisfaction with democracy	0.45★★	0.60★★	0.84★★	0.62★★
No influence on politics	0.20★	0.29★★	–	–
Populist views scale	0.70★★	0.68★	0.95★★	1.16★★
Anti-immigration				
Immigration MIP (spontaneous)	0.44★★	0.23★	0.28★★	0.45★★
Issue performance (higher scores = less satisfied)				
Labour asylum	1.09★★	1.19★★	1.91★★	2.50★★
Cons asylum	0.71★★	1.24★★	1.26★★	0.57★
Labour financial crisis	–	–	1.25★★	1.05★★
Cons financial crisis	–	–	–	–
Labour education	–	0.81★★	–	–
Cons education	–	−0.62★★	−0.72★★	–
Labour NHS	–	−0.49★★	–	−0.50★★
Cons NHS	–	–	–	–
Labour terror	−0.61★★	−0.42★★	–	–
Cons terror	–	–	–	–
Leaders (higher scores = less satisfied)				
Labour leader	0.38★	0.97★★	–	0.73★★
Conservative leader	1.56★★	1.70★★	1.04★★	1.51★★
Liberal Democrat leader	0.60★★	–	0.56★	–
Chi-squared change	907★★	839★★	627★★	809★★
Model fit (Pseudo-R sq)	0.153	0.164	0.215	0.257
Model fit (BIC)	7,610	4,927	3,702	5,249
N	13,525	12,515	7,965	6,729

★ = p < 0.05; ★★ = p < 0.01

Chapter 6: Overcoming the barriers to entry

The measures in Table A.8 are all questions worded as indicated, with the percentages detailing the proportion of responses in the indicated direction. The measure of class used here is the YouGov measure previously discussed. The figures presented in Table A.8 come from local election results data kindly provided to us by Professor Michael Thrasher of the Plymouth University Elections Centre. The 'UKIP attraction index' employed in Table A.9 is constructed using 2011 census data for the current (2010) parliamentary constituencies. We calculated the mean share of voters belonging to four UKIP-friendly demographics (over 65s, whites, those with no educational qualifications, working class) and the mean share belonging to four UKIP-unfriendly demographics (under 30s, ethnic minorities, degree holders, and middle-class professionals). To calculate the UKIP attraction index, we take the mean share from UKIP-friendly groups and subtract the mean share from UKIP-unfriendly groups. This gives us a crude, but clear, measure of the extent to which the balance of social groups in the constituency favours UKIP or works against them.

Notes

1 David Sanders, Harold Clarke, Marianne Stewart and Paul Whiteley (2006) 'Does mode matter for modelling political choice? Evidence from the 2005 British Election Study', *Political Analysis*, 15(3): 257–85.
2 Details of this analysis are available from the authors on request.

INDEX